W9-ANN-144

The Corporate Firm in a
Changing World Economy

The Corporate Firm in a Changing World Economy

Case Studies in the Geography of Enterprise

Edited by

Marc de Smidt

and

Egbert Wever

London and New York

HC
79
D5
C67
1990

First published 1990
by Routledge
11 New Fetter Lane, London EC4P 4EE

Simultaneously published in the USA and Canada
by Routledge
a division of Routledge, Chapman and Hall, Inc.
29 West 35th Street, New York, NY 10001

© 1990 Marc de Smidt and Egbert Wever

Printed and bound in Great Britain by Mackays of Chatham PLC, Kent

All rights reserved. No part of this book may be reprinted
or reproduced or utilized in any form or by any electronic,
mechanical, or other means, now known or hereafter
invented, including photocopying and recording, or in any
information storage or retrieval system, without permission
in writing from the publishers.

British Library Cataloguing in Publication Data

The corporate form in a changing world economy: case studies
in the geography of enterprise.
1. Economic conditions. role in companies. Multinational
I. Smidt, Marc de, *1941–*   II. Wever, Egbert
338.8′88
ISBN 0-415-03497-3

Library of Congress Cataloging in Publication Data

The Corporate firm in a changing world economy: case studies in the
geography of enterprise/edited by Marc de Smidt and Egbert Wever.
  p. cm.
Includes bibliographical references.
ISBN 0-415-03497-3
1. International business enterprises—Location—Case studies.
I. Smidt, M. de. II. Wever, E.
HC79.D5C67 1990   89-77036
338.8′8—dc20   CIP

Contents

ROBERT MANNING
STROZIER LIBRARY

JAN 9 1991

Tallahassee, Florida

Contents

Figures

Figures

Tables

Tables

Contributors

Claes G. Alvstam, Senior Lecturer and Associate Professor, Department of Economic Geography, School of Economics and Legal Science, Gothenburg University, Sweden

Trevor Barnes, Associate Professor, Department of Geography, University of British Columbia, Canada

Peter Dicken, Senior Lecturer, School of Geography, University of Manchester, United Kingdom

Kajsa Ellegard, Research Associate, Department of Human and Economic Geography, School of Economics and Legal Science, Gothenburg University, Sweden

Martina Fuchs, Research Associate, Department of Economic and Human Geography, Johann Wolfgang Goethe-University, Frankfurt, West Germany

Eric Grass, Ph.D. student, Department of Geography, Simon Fraser University, Burnaby, British Columbia, Canada

Roger Hayter, Professor Economic Geography, Department of Geography, Simon Fraser University, Burnaby, British Columbia, Canada

Richard Le Heron, Senior Lecturer, Department of Geography, Massey University, Palmerston North, New Zealand

David Keeble, Senior Lecturer, Department of Geography, University of Cambridge, United Kingdom

Tim Kelly, Telecommunications Policy Analyst, Organization for Economic Co-operation and Development (OECD), Paris, France

Sam Ock Park, Associate Professor, Department of Geography, Seoul National University, Korea

Eike Schamp, Professor Economic Geography, Department of Economic and Human Geography, Johann Wolfgang Goethe-University, Frankfurt, West Germany

Marc de Smidt, Professor Economic Geography, Faculty of Spatial Sciences, University of Utrecht, the Netherlands

Contributors

Atsuhiko Takeuchi, Professor Economic Geography, Department of Geography, Nippon Institute of Technology, Miyashiro, Japan

Egbert Wever, Professor Economic Geography, Faculty of Policy Sciences, University of Nijmegen, the Netherlands

Preface

Back in 1958 Robert McNee made a plea for a geography of enterprise. Since that time there has been a lot of interest within economic geography in large or 'core' firms. The reason for this interest is the spatially structuring effect of those 'core' firms. These effects are not only expressed regionally, more and more frequently they also cross national borders.

However, even for similar and narrowly defined product–market combinations (PMCs) firms can and do pursue different (spatial) strategies. Furthermore, it has become increasingly clear that many processes within firms, that have a non-spatial character, do in fact have strong spatial effects. This book follows these two lines of thought. Nine companies have been selected as case studies in order to illustrate the (different) strategies pursued. Non-spatial trends, which have spatial impacts, are also dealt with. And of course, the influence of the (geographical) environment is considered.

There is an additional advantage in using case studies. It offers an opportunity to confront theories or concepts, mostly derived from aggregate reasoning, with the reality on the micro-level of the individual firm. It is hoped that in this respect this book will contribute to progress in the geography of enterprise.

Most of the contributions in the leading international journals or readers which deal with individual firms, have a strongly Anglo-Saxon bias. This volume tries to have a wider scope by dealing with enterprises in leading industrial nations all over the globe. However, our choice of the particular firms, justified in Chapter 1, is, in a sense, one-sided in that only manufacturing firms have been considered. Without doubt, a volume comprising case studies from the international service sector could make an additional contribution to the further development of the geography of enterprise.

The editors would like to acknowledge gratefully the co-operation they have had with an exceptional and international group of distinguished scholars who have contributed to this volume, each of them making a unique contribution from his specialized field. Nancy Smyth van Weesep and Angela Needham checked the final texts of the non-English-speaking contributors. Annie van Bergen, from the University of Nijmegen, started typing again patiently every time we discovered irregularities in the lay-out of the various chapters. Finally, the cartographic department of the University of Utrecht provided some of the diagrams and charts.

Marc de Smidt
Egbert Wever

Chapter one

Firms
Strategy and changing environments

Marc de Smidt and Egbert Wever

Introduction

Firms constantly face new challenges. Here are five examples of such new challenges found recently in the newspapers.

- President Van der Klugt would like to have the entire range of Philips products produced on the deck of a supertanker. This tanker should then stop off in different countries according to the advantages of moving exchange rates. Philips could then rid itself of one of its biggest worries, extreme fluctuations in exchange rates, which influence sales and profits in unpredictable ways.

- Two companies, Honda and the American Motor Corporation, which have plants located close to each other, are nevertheless very different in kind. Honda produces high quality cars efficiently, its working conditions are first rate, the company is expanding all the time, and is now even exporting cars to Japan. Sales of the AMC Jeep are not at all bad, but the plant and machinery are out of date, corporate culture has had its day, the motivation of the employees is low and still declining, and the management has threatened to close the plant if the unions are not prepared to make concessions.

- 'What you can sell on the USA market is changing too fast,' president Hahn said as an explanation for VW's decision to close the plant in New Stanton, Pennsylvania. However, Japanese competitors have succeeded in strengthening their position in this turbulent market, using imported as well as locally produced cars. The Golf, which is a great success in Europe, is considered to be a dull car by the Americans. On the other hand, the Chevrolet is not appreciated so much by the Europeans. But the Japanese sell their Corollas in America as well as in Europe.

- In the opinion of Kazuma Tateishi, founder and president of

Omron Tateishi Electronics (international) firms are forced to allow middle management more freedom and responsibility, in order to be able to react quickly to changing market conditions. The best way to realize flexibility would be to decentralize the organization, to promote employees on the basis of merit, and to invest in basic research. To avoid the danger of a growing bureaucracy Tateishi decided to create semi-autonomous divisions within the Omron organization, that could handle their own affairs themselves.

• 'After years of relying on cheap manufacturing bases in distant East Asia – with at least three months between order and delivery – clothing manufacturers are beginning to bring production back home. Even companies from traditionally low-wage countries in the Far East are moving their production to the US to escape rising costs and US import quotas, and to get closer to their customers.' 'Two years ago every item sold by Perry Ellis' ladies wear section was imported from contractors in Hong Kong, Taiwan and other distant locations. Today 40 per cent of the line is made domestically.'

(*International Business Week* 7 November 1988).

There are some common elements in the statements given above. All refer to growing international competition and to (new) strategies which the firms involved are pursuing or would like to pursue in order to face this competition and to perform well financially. In this respect it makes no difference if attempts to strengthen competitiveness are based on utilizing locational advantages (Philips), a more productive corporate culture (Honda), a more open eye for market trends (Japanese car producers), intrapreneurship (Omron) or subcontracting and co-makership. This book deals with the growth strategy of individual firms such as Daewoo, Goodman Fielder Wattie, and ccFriesland.

A differentiation can be made between the five examples given. Some have a strong firm-internal character (Omron), others can primarily be seen as a reaction to external changes in the environment of the firm (Philips). However, often there is an interplay between internal and external changes. Changes in the external environment of the firm, for example a growing international competition, frequently have consequences for the way firms are internally structured.

Back to basics

One of the fascinating tendencies in the world economy today is growing international competition. In Western Europe people involved in business are extremely aware of this tendency as firms, governments, and even universities prepare for a united Europe, planned to arrive in 1992. The growing internationalization of competition is taking place because of the wish to make profit of scale economies, to decrease transport and communications costs, and because of more uniform consumer preferences (motor cars, microwaves, videos, hi-fi installations, etc.). Market power becomes the all-decisive element in this competition. However, positions can easily be lost because of the whimsical behaviour of consumers and the shortening product life cycles. Firms therefore strive for strong positions in a restricted number of markets.

The result is a tendency for firms to withdraw from sectors in which they have not been successful, sectors which they do not consider to be 'basic', and sectors in which they do not see prospects, either because of a lack of well-known brand names, or because of an inferior quality of the product, or the lack of effective selling outlets, etc. This tendency is known as 'back to basics' or even 'stick to the knitting'. Two examples: Mobil Oil decided in 1988 to sell its retail trade company Montgomery Ward, even though this company realized a profit of $US130m. the year before. For the same reason AKZO in 1988 decided to sell its consumer goods division which was doing well. For other examples see the contributions about ccFriesland (Chapter 6) and MacMillan Bloedel (Chapter 7).

Firms withdrawing from certain activities try to sell these activities to other firms or to the existing management (management buy-out). At the same time they try to strengthen their own position by buying specific (for them 'core') activities from other firms, by taking them over, by mergers or by joint ventures. The outcome of this process of buying and selling is a diminished number of product–market combinations (PMCs) in an individual firm. However, the firm will have realized a stronger market position, the efficiency of the organization is improved and, by the reduced number of PMCs, there will also be less uncertainty. It is really a process of the restructuring of individual firms in the struggle for global competition.

'Back to basics' means that the strategy of extreme diversification is 'out' nowadays (Wissema 1987). This strategy was popular in the 1960s, after a long period of economic growth. It was connected with a strong belief in risk-minimizing effects and in synergetic effects leading to real conglomerates (Ansoff 1965, 1968). This was the period of the manager. It was assumed to be possible to manage even big conglomerates with hardly any knowledge of the activities

3

themselves. This turned out to be wrong. The expected synergetic effects hardly existed in reality. Moreover, the transaction costs within the conglomerates turned out to be much higher than expected. In the 'back to basics' era the period of the manager has been replaced by the period of the entrepreneur. The back to basics strategy includes decentralization (the Omron case) as firms have to react flexibly, because of the heavy turbulence in the present economic environment (Chapman and Walker 1987). Divisions and subsidiary companies gain more autonomy in order to react quickly to changes in this environment (see the contribution about IBM in Chapter 2). They are increasingly concentrated on activities which strengthen their market position and on the possibilities of operating in these markets with flexibility. Therefore leasing, even of buildings, has become popular. For the same reason the internal structure of the whole organization gets a 'simple form, lean staff' structure. Mars realizes a $US7 mrd sales with a headquarters of no more than thirty staff. Philips wants to reduce the number of employees at the head office in Eindhoven by one-third. Concepts like intrapreneurship, co-makership, and subcontractors also fit into such a strategy of flexibility.

The hollow corporation

There are other tendencies related to the internationalization or globalization trend. 'Regional' markets are disappearing fast, the world is becoming a 'global village' (Levitt 1983). As a consequence, competition has changed and there is now a difference between the 'multinational', operating in many countries but mostly with national strategies and the new 'global' company, operating with one, world-wide strategy. This strategy is one in which competitors are fought whenever and wherever this is found to be necessary. In such a global strategy the manager of the operations in a specific country can be ordered to oppose a competitor (even when this implies making a loss) only to prevent this competitor using the extra profits in this country for competing with the organization elsewhere (Prahalad and Doz 1988). The change from 'multi-national' to 'global' often coincides with a change from area management to product management, as competition within spatially bounded markets is increasingly replaced by competition for one product all over the world. This, of course, does not imply that a situation cannot exist in which local autonomy and local strategies coincide with global capability and interconnectivity as the contribution by Kelly and Keeble in Chapter 2 illustrates.

The change from area to product management has spatial

consequences. Management in general will look for the best and cheapest components. When organized on an area base it may be oriented more to 'regional' suppliers compared with a product-based organization. In that case management will look for suppliers irrespective of their location. This may have its impact on international trade flows. One example: in 1985 Philips UK had a fairly balanced internal trade with Philips establishments outside the UK. In 1986 sales volumes had nearly doubled compared to stable volumes of production. The input of Philips' components and products had increased much more than had exports. The resulting intra-company imbalance of trade is a sign of a change from a 'local for local' production base to a more 'global' division of labour within product divisions of a major corporate firm (de Smidt and Van der Voorn 1989).

Until recently the globalization of the world economy has been related much more to markets than to production. 'Globalisation was reflected in the much faster growth of trade in manufacturing goods than in production' (Dicken 1986:43). In the battle for markets brand names, patents, corporate images etc. are much more effective instruments than production capacity or production costs (see also the contribution by Barnes et al. in Chapter 7). For many firms 'back to basics' means back to the marketing of those products in which they have firm-specific advantages. They even ask themselves: should we make the products ourselves or should we buy most of the components and maybe even the product itself? It turns out that making the components themselves nowadays is no longer attractive. It is nearly impossible to keep up with techno-logical progress, mostly there are no economies of scale and in the high turbulence of all markets, only specialists can operate efficiently. It has resulted in a withdrawal from vertical integration (Scott 1986). Two examples are: the largest publisher in the Netherlands (Elsevier) which has nearly completely withdrawn from printing and the Berkel company, European market leader in scales, which decided to stop the production of all components. They would even prefer to buy (high-quality) scales and sell them with their own brand name. They realized that their strength was in the brand name and the marketing organization.

The last tendency can lead to the hollow corporation as physical production becomes more and more a matter of secondary import-ance. A hollow corporation is only involved with the final assembly, and sometimes even this is done by a subcontractor. Such a corporation has to be valuated primarily according to its goodwill, its know-how, its organizational qualities, its marketing capacities, its patents, etc. and not according to its assets, stocks, and claims. Two examples of this are: when Nestlé and Cadbury were fighting for Rowntree McIntosh, they were certainly not fighting for the production facilities. They were fighting for Kitkat and other brand names. And when Douwe Egberts, a Dutch coffee firm belonging to the Sara Lee concern, bought the consumer division of AKZO in 1988 (considered by AKZO to be a non-core activity), it paid less than 300m. Dutch guilders for the plants but 960m. guilders for the goodwill, in particular for a number of well-known brand names.

Subcontracting

The tendencies of 'back to basics' and 'hollowization' imply subcontracting. But subcontracting at the same time emphasizes the importance of efficient logistic systems. Profit equals profit margins times sales. When competition is on a world scale, profit margins will be minimal. By penetrating more markets and by going global, sales can be increased and, as a consequence, profits too. Nevertheless profit margins have to be optimized by reducing costs. One of the possibilities is by reducing all kinds of stocks. Two options exist: vertical integration and vertical disintegration. Although the popularity of the vertical integration strategy is diminishing, it has certainly not disappeared. However, reducing stocks within a big organization by using more efficient logistic systems implies risks. This became clear when in 1988 there was a strike in UK Ford plants. A couple of weeks later plants in Belgium (Genk) and West Germany (Saarlois, Cologne) had to be closed temporarily because of a lack of vital components.

Vertical disintegration or subcontracting should reduce costs, but should not conflict with the preferences of the customers. Reduction of stocks is therefore only possible when the firm itself and its suppliers operate efficient logistic systems. If the large firm considers these logistics to be a non-basic activity it can try to find a specialized subcontractor for it. The Japanese company, Fuji, having a large production plant in the Netherlands, has lent out its whole internal logistics to a specialized Dutch company. Apart from this it will be clear that the firm should have suppliers of components who can deliver quickly, who are reliable in their deliveries, who always deliver consistently high-quality products, preferably with zero-defects, and who are financially healthy (to guarantee continuity). Here there are risks. To minimize these risks there is a tendency to reduce the number of subcontractors, concentrating on the best and most reliable ones.

From a national economic point of view there is an element of risk connected with the processes of vertical disintegration and hollowization. In the US especially it is recognized that these processes can lead to de-industrialization, including the loss of investments in human capital embodied in the production process (technical skills) and a decreasing control over vital components as these have to be imported.

Technology

It has already been stated that there is a growing competition on a global scale and in specific markets. Technology made increasing market differentiation possible (flexible production automation, CAD/CAM). It has reduced the influence of economies of scale, making possible the production of a small series of specific products without being confronted with high costs. It may open the way to a new organization of work, with perhaps essential implications for plant location in the future, as the contribution by Alvstam and Ellegard illustrates (Chapter 9). It certainly has consequences for the qualifications needed in future. Fuchs and Schamp deal with this aspect (Chapter 4). Technology plays yet another role. The product life cycle of new products and processes is shortening. In global competition a new product, even when it is introduced in only one country, will find its way immediately all over the world. For the innovator it is therefore attractive to introduce the innovation everywhere simultaneously. This is attractive from another point of view too. The costs of R&D are increasing enormously. To be profitable, this expensive R&D needs large markets as monopolistic profits in time are very restricted nowadays. In order to be the first on the market it may be that in the near future R&D activities will become round-the-clock activities, even though this may raise costs. Because of the expense of R&D, many companies competing with each other in many markets are working together in specific research projects. An example is the Megabite-project of Philips and Siemens, or the lab operated together by Siemens, Bull, and ICL in Munich. Co-operation in the field of R&D can also be noticed in the concept of co-makership.

Another avenue of technological change influencing the scale of operations can be labelled as new information technology, 'a set of latent technological and organisational innovations characterised by more communication-intensive techniques of production and governance of transactions' (Antonelli 1988:1). Telematics may decrease both the (external) transaction costs and the (internal) co-ordination costs. The trade-off can result in either disintegration and deconcentration, or integration and concentration. Antonelli emphasizes the importance of the network firm based on economies of scope with the help of telematics and logistics, and at the same time offering 'electronic quasi-integration'. He sees the network firm as 'a new non-market/non-hierarchy institutional arrangement' offering an alternative for big business, but at the same time giving corporations an opportunity for reorganization along the lines of selective vertical and lateral integration of production phases and intensive subcontraction.

Restructuring

The question the management of a firm has to pose itself again and again is 'On what product–market combinations should we concentrate now and in the (near) future?' To answer this question it is necessary to know both what is possible and what is desirable. What is possible depends upon the competitive position of the firm, what is desirable depends upon the long-term goals of the company.

The competitiveness of a firm depends partly on factors within the firm itself (the Honda case), partly on external developments in the environment of the firm (the Philips case). Economic geographers are by tradition well aware of the influence of external factors on the choice of location and the performance of a firm. Some factors internal to the firm that are relevant for the competitive position of the firm and therefore influence its performance are (Deams and Douma 1984):

- the product mix of the firm;
- the quality of the products offered;
- the possibilities of product differentiation;
- the power to control marketing channels;
- the possession of well-known brand names;
- the efficiency of production (lower costs);
- the finances to cover bad periods;
- the possibilities of attracting capital;
- the degree of independence;
- the quality of the management.

Together it is the weaknesses/strengths internal to the firm and external threats/chances which fix the competitive position of the firm. However, this position is not stable. In order to guarantee its continuity a firm is always in a process of restructuring (De Jong 1988), in order to:

- organize production and distribution in a more efficient way;

- reduce uncertainties in the market;
- introduce innovations of all kinds.

Management is continuously trying to optimize the trade-off between internal weaknesses/strengths and external threats/chances. That means optimizing internal production conditions and being able to anticipate the turbulence in the external environment as well as possible. A number of contributions in this book (IBM, Philips, ccFriesland) deal with restructuring processes, the motives behind them, and the regional impacts. Barnes et al. (Chapter 7) relate the process of restructuring within MacMillan Bloedel to labour market segmentation theories.

Segmentation

The 'back to basics' strategy with its management buy-outs, strategic take-overs, subcontractors, and co-makers indicates the need to differentiate between firms as well as activities. In the back to basics strategy the growing globalization of the big core companies coincides with the development of an intensive network of relationships between companies. A quite simple differentiation between firms is given in Figure 1.1. The types mentioned can be (legally) independent firms or parts of an integrated company. An example is, in the motor car industry, where the 'knowledge' and 'production' segments are mostly integrated within one company. Within the category of 'jobbers', and in a certain sense within the category of 'consultants' too, a differentiation can be made. Firstly, the firms that are hired occasionally by larger firms in order to satisfy a sudden extra demand for their products or to solve an acute problem: i.e. the 'real' jobbers or consultants. Secondly, the subcontractors who have a more permanent relationship with the core firm, and thirdly the co-maker with a position between the jobber and the 'knowledge' segment.

It has to be stressed that the differentiation given above is strongly related to the tendency of vertical disintegration in assembly-like activities (consumer electronics, car production: see the contributions about Nissan and Daewoo). Activities in which it is easy to split up the total number of activities into a large number of separate, individual activities. For many companies such a splitting up of the production process is not possible. Processing industries such as the dairy industry, petrochemicals, oil-refining cannot be disintegrated. Resource-based industries and industries producing perishable consumer goods have hardly any degree of freedom in their location.

9

Marc de Smidt and Egbert Wever

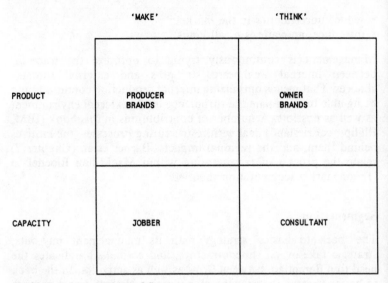

Figure 1.1 A typology of firms
Source: van Gunsteren 1987

Apart from differences amongst large firms, there are differences between large and small firms. It is well known that small firms do not have the same possibilities as large ones. But even within the small-firm segment there are differences between jobbers, consultants, subcontractors, and co-makers. All these categories supply products or services to large firms. The quality of their product and its price are mostly fixed by the large company. Delivery has to follow the just-in-time principles of the large firm, leaving the small firm with the cost of storage. The jobber is the most dependent. In theory at least the co-maker has a more independent position. For another classification see Taylor and Thrift 1983.

Apart from a segmentation between firms a segmentation can also be made in activities within one company (Törnqvist 1970). The dichotomy decision versus production unit and the dependency relations between them (external control) have to do with this internal functioning segmentation. To some extent this can result in a dual regional economy (of an Averitt–Galbraith type). The position of a region depends on the position it has within the corporate hierarchies and on the market position of its firms. Geographically this implies a strong impact on labour market segmentation between and within regions. (See the contribution about MacMillan Bloedel, p. 145.)

PRODUCT-MIX / MARKET SEGMENT	CONTRACTION	EXISTING PRODUCTS	NEW PRODUCT		
			SAME TECHNOLOGY	RELATED TECHNOLOGY	NON-RELATED TECHNOLOGY
CONTRACTION	– LIQUIDATION – SPECIALIZATION – CONCENTRATION	– MARKET CONCENTRATION	PRODUCT DEVELOPMENT (HORIZONTAL DIVERSIFICATION)		
EXISTING MARKETS	– PRODUCT-SPECIALIZATION	– MARKET PENETRATION (INTENSIFYING)			
NEW AND RELATED	MARKET DEVELOPMENT (VERTICAL DIVERSIFICATION)		ADDITIVE DIVERSIFICATION		CONCENTRIC DIVERSIFICATION
NEW AND NON-RELATED					CONGLOMERATE DIVERSIFICATION
FOR OWN USE	SPECIALIZATION	VERTICAL INTEGRATION (FORWARD)	VERTICAL INTEGRATION (BACKWARD OR FORWARD)		

Figure 1.2   Product–market strategies of global companies
Source: Loeve 1989:55

Strategic management

Changes in the environment, be it the appearance of new competitors or changing consumer preferences, force a firm to look for strategies to survive. An illustration: the managing director of Daimler–Benz stated after the acquisition of AEG (and previously of Dornier and MTU): 'In the past we didn't need partners. Today we do. It is not Daimler–Benz but the world we operate in that has changed' (*Fortune*, 15 September 1986). One of the basic concepts in this respect is the product–market combination. As well as the traditional emphasis on production it also encompasses a new emphasis on marketing. Starting from the present-day internal strengths and weaknesses of the firm and chances and threats from the external environment, a strategy can be formulated. The product/market matrix of Ansoff (1965) distinguishes four strategies: market penetration, product development, market development and diversification. Figure 1.2 is based upon the Ansoff classification.

In the beginning of the 1970s diversification was a very popular strategy. When, during the 1970s the economic climate changed drastically, the large diversified firms had to decide for themselves which PMCs would become profitable in the near future. Based on the product life cycle and the learning curve, the portfolio approach was developed. The most simple one was introduced by the Boston Consulting Group (Figure 1.3). In this matrix the two axes consist of the most important external (market growth) and internal (market share or competitive position) factor. Four quadrants can be identified, each with a PMC with differing prospects (Wever and Grit 1984).

The most central element in the relationship between firm and environment is the strategy a firm should pursue in order to prevent competitors, existing or potential, from starting activities into PMCs on which the firm wants to concentrate. Creating entry barriers may be such a strategy. The firm can start product differentiation (structural barrier) or it can invest deliberately in overcapacity as a threat to potential newcomers (strategic barrier). The market behaviour of a firm is primarily a reaction to how its managers think they should react to environmental turbulence. Even in the same sector, firms follow different strategies. Digital concentrates more than IBM on product differentiation and less on cost differentiation. Of the two large Korean companies, Hyundai follows an aggressive marketing policy based on its own brand names. Daewoo is constantly looking for market partners to avoid pressures from the importing countries. As a consequence, the name Daewoo is hardly known in Western Europe.

Strategic management, how to react to turbulence in the environment or the task environment of the firm, is, of course, a non-spatial concept as the difference between Hyundai and Daewoo illustrates. However, the spatial environment influences the financial performance of the firm too. When Van der Klugt dreams about producing Philips products on the deck of a big supertanker, then he is dreaming about spatial differences in production costs. When Japanese firms such as Sanyo, Sony, Hitachi, and Mitsubishi assemble consumer electronic goods near Tijuana in Mexico (near the US border) they want to avoid some of the disadvantages of Japan (the expensive yen) and make a profit out of the advantages of Mexico (low labour costs with good access to the US market – see van den Ende et al. 1984). In this process some countries with abundant, cheap labour have undergone 'bloody Taylorization' ('sweatshops' of a non-mechanized nature with a great deal of female employment). Others have become engaged in 'peripheral Fordism' as for example in the automobile industry (Lipietz 1986). As a contrast to this 'global outlook' for labour on the bottom line

		MARKET SHARE	
		HIGH	LOW
M A R K E T G R O W T H	H I G H	STARS	WILD CATS
	L O W	CASH COWS	DOGS

Figure 1.3 The two-factor portfolio matrix
Source: van der Lee et al. 1987:76

of production, the international recruitment of staff for corporate headquarters and R&D laboratories has increased. IBM and Shell both have 5,000 expatriates on their job lists. Therefore, very large numbers of people are moving in what are undoubtedly global systems under company umbrellas (Salt 1988).

The process of vertical disintegration, implying a strong emphasis on subcontractors, co-makers and just-in-time deliveries, implies spatial pre-conditions too. It is hardly possible to create such pre-conditions when supplier and buyer are not connected by a high-quality infrastructure.

The examples given above relate to that part of strategic management that deals with location. It deals with location factors, a factor that influences the performance (via the location) of a firm. Location factors can be divided according to the scale upon which they are operating. The exchange rate between the US dollar and the main European currencies is an example of a location factor influencing the choice of a location in Europe or the US. Other factors are primarily working on a national scale. In that case they do not discriminate within the country: taxes, political constellation, environmental regulations, labour regulations, etc. On the lowest level, the level where economic geographers mostly work, elements such as labour availability, investment premiums, availability of raw materials, and (international) airports play their role.

Because of the globalization process, the influence of the environment upon the performance of firms is growing. More firms are going international. Even when they do not, their task environment includes more international relations. As a consequence they, and, indirectly, their suppliers as well, are confronted with more turbulent environments, environments in which even the biggest companies have difficulties in reducing uncertainty. On the other hand a growing 'locational tolerance' can be seen on the lowest, local or regional scale. In the Netherlands the local differences in pre-conditions for businesses have been reduced remarkably. Even high-tech firms are now located nearly everywhere and it is hard to distinguish a spatial pattern in their performance. Distance friction, in particular, has diminished, partly because of infrastructural improvements, partly because of the increased value added to the products made, making transport costs less prohibitive. For a growing number of manufacturing activities, the Netherlands can be considered to be one urban field (de Smidt and Wever 1990) with the possible exclusion of its extreme northern part.

Institutional and physical environment

As has been said before, the competitive position of a firm is also dependent on (external) environmental factors. In this environment threats and chances can be identified. Generally, the external environment means uncertainty and risk. Firms are able to reduce this uncertainty only to a certain degree. In their relations with customers, suppliers, and competitors especially, it makes sense to try to reduce uncertainty. It is, however, much more difficult to include other elements of the external environment in the long-term strategy of the firm. It would imply estimates about what will happen in the future in fields such as (van der Lee et al. 1987):

- inflation rates in different countries;
- exchange rates between different currencies;
- environmental regulations of governments;
- working regulations;
- changes in education;
- new international infrastructural networks;
- new materials and biotechnology;
- availability and cost of raw materials;

• disturbances in markets by political troubles.

Especially since the 1950s there has been a growing interest in the relationship between the firm and its environment. According to Ansoff (1968) this has had to do with the growing turbulence in the environment of many firms. 'Environment', a very broad concept, is defined by de Smidt (1975) as 'all conditions, influencing the choice of location and the functioning of a firm, that are external to that firm', or still more simply 'everything outside the focal organization' (McDermott and Taylor 1982). As can be seen from the list given, the business environment does not restrict itself to market relations. In addition, Lambooy (1984) mentions institutional relations (environmental regulations) and physical conditions (infrastructure). A 'task environment' or 'activity space' (Lloyd and Dicken 1977) can be seen as the heart of the environment that is closely watched by the firm. It includes competitors, consumers, suppliers, labour unions, government authorities, etc. Environment in many economic geographical studies coincides with this 'task environment'.

The region in which a firm is located is a part of its 'task environment'. From the firm's point of view this region is a particular configuration of assets. These assets can contribute to the strengthening or deterioration of the firm's competitive position. The different economic performance of firms, therefore, might be the result of differences in these configurations of assets, i.e. by the regionally specific traits of the institutional and physical environment. However, it is very difficult indeed to delineate the influence of environmental factors and factors internal to the firm.

From the point of view of the region, this means that in explaining the differentiation in economic performance of regions, the internal processes of firms cannot be left out of consideration. Reference has already been made to the plants of Honda and Jeep, operating in virtually the same institutional and physical environment but performing quite differently. It is well known that regions strongly oriented to 'traditional' or 'saturated' sectors sometimes perform much better than regions with a higher proportion of 'modern' or 'growing' sectors. Massey and Meegan (1982) have already stressed that the outcome of processes of (internal) restructuring within large firms is crucial for the region, especially when these firms dominate the regional economy, such as Philips in the Eindhoven region, or Toyota in Toyota City.

Although important, it cannot be denied that regional institutional environments in particular are strongly influenced by national policies. On the other hand, globalization and fierce economic restructuring processes have changed the relations between firms and the institutional framework on a national scale. Globalization implies that the 'task environment' of firms will coincide less with regional and national environments. Even nations like France and Sweden, with a long-standing tradition of government steering in the national economy, were confronted with the growing importance of international corporate strategies (the 'meso-planning' indicated by Galbraith (1967) and Holland (1975)). Although in France *l'état patron* is still taken for granted, there is now a clear tendency towards a self-regulation of the economy and to more effective co-operation on a public–private basis (Estrin and Holmes 1983). In France, planning is focused on promoting technology in key sectors; in Sweden, labour market policies have always been at the heart of the planning system. Even these defensive policies have been altered according to the advice of the Boston Consulting Group so that Sweden can move to a more general industrial policy which would be a more promising and appropriate instrument for adapting to economic change (Katzenstein 1985).

In this respect the changing institutional environment in 'Europe 1992' is quite fascinating. A number of factors, which previously differentiated between countries, will disappear (Verkennis et al. 1988). We want to mention only two of them. Restrictions on transport markets (the cabotage system) and on governmental building activities (exclusion of foreign companies) will not be allowed after 1992. The coming free-market zone has already resulted in a wave of mergers and take-overs, clear signs that formerly national firms are now able and willing to operate on the European market. The same wave could be observed when the US was integrating institutionally in the 1920s (De Jong 1988).

From a locational point of view it is even more important that differences in excise duties on oil products will disappear, that measures which distort competition such as subsidized railways, ports or problem regions will no longer be permitted. In general, the institutional environments that were financially attractive for the business sector (taxes, subsidies, excises) will become less attractive. The spatial differences between those factors influencing the financial performance of firms will diminish. As a consequence the degree of freedom to choose a location within Europe will increase and secondary location factors (climate, living conditions, infrastructure, working attitude of employees, availability of employees) will become more important. The same development has already gone on for many years in individual countries, leading to ideas about 'urban fields' in small countries like the Netherlands. Another consequence of this development will be that in 'Europe

1992' there will be less competition between the EC countries and more competition between the regions within the EC. There will be a Europe of regions more than a Europe of nations.

Conclusion

Within the context of a growing locational tolerance and of the existence of urban fields, the exact location where a firm is established becomes of less interest. The competition between the larger agglomerations within Europe will gain in interest. This does not mean that the 'where' question in general is becoming less important, as the example of Japanese firms in Mexico illustrates. Ohmea (1985) argues that because of the swiftly rising cost of R&D, the more uniform consumer preferences, and the threat of protectionist measures taken by importing countries, global companies should be present in the three big markets of today: US, EC, and Japan (Triad Power). Without doubt in future there will be more large markets. The decision to start activities in these three markets is a location decision, as is the decision to locate within the EC in Spain and not in the Netherlands; in the Paris area and not in the Munich region; near an airport at Frankfurt and not in London.

Moreover, every location decision, be it the closure of an old plant, the establishment of a new one or the expansion of an existing one, will consider local or regional factors, even when the relevance of these factors for the financial performance of the firm decreases. Some factors continue to influence location decisions even nowadays. The most important one without doubt is the labour market. Although there is a process of up-grading of jobs and although the more highly educated employees are tending to become yet more mobile, the need for employees is a factor that cannot be overseen by firms, especially not in the ageing European countries.

Nevertheless, against the background given in this chapter it will be clear that trying to explain the variations in economic performance between regions is a difficult and complex task. If we believe that we can explain these regional variations we should also include elements belonging to the internal functioning of firms. Maybe the approach followed in this book in this respect will put forward some new ideas.

A few remarks upon the structure of the book: there are of course several options which could be considered for grouping the nine companies. One option would have been to follow the main theme within the various contributions. It would have resulted in the grouping of MacMillan Bloedel, SEL, and Philips which all deal mainly with labour market aspects. In the same way Daewoo, ccFriesland, and Goodman Fielder Wattie could be grouped on the basis of their emphasis on growth strategies.

However, we decided to divide the firms into groups on the basis of types of PMC. After the general overview given in this chapter, a study of three firms in the high-tech electronics sector will constitute the immediately succeeding three chapters: IBM, Philips, and Standard Elektrik Lorenz. In the next three chapters, firms with much older PMCs will be dealt with: Goodman Fielder Wattie (meat products), ccFriesland (dairy products) and MacMillan Bloedel (forest products). The next three chapters deal with less old, but more traditional PMCs: the motor car industry (Nissan and Volvo) and a large Korean conglomerate, which includes motor cars, car components and shipbuilding (Daewoo). The final chapter attempts to discover some general trends from a geographical point of view. Some suggestions for further research are also made.

References

Ansoff, H. I. (1965) *Corporate Strategy*, New York: McGraw Hill.

Ansoff, H. I. (1968) *Business Strategy*, Harmondsworth: Penguin.

Antonelli, C. (1988) 'A new industrial organization approach', in C. Antonelli (ed.) *New Information Technology and Industrial Change: the Italian Case*, Dordrecht: Kluwer: 1–9.

Averitt, R. T. (1968) *The Dual Economy*, New York: W. W. Norton.

Chapman, K. and Walker, D. (1987) *Industrial Location*, Oxford: Basil Blackwell.

Clarke, I. M. (1985) *The Spatial Organisation of Multinational Corporations*, London: Croom Helm.

Daems, H. and Douma, S. W. (1984) *Concurrentie: Analyse en Strategie*, Deventer: Kluwer.

Dicken, P. (1986) *Global Shift. Industrial Change in a Turbulent World*, New York: Harper & Row.

Ende, A. van den, Haring, H. and de Smidt, M. (1984) 'Corporate organization, linkages and labour market', in M. de Smidt and E. Wever (eds) *A Profile of Dutch Economic Geography*, Assen: Van Gorcum: 85–105.

Estrin, G. and Holmes, P. (1983) *French Planning in Theory and Practice*, London: Allen & Unwin.

Galbraith, J. K. (1967) *The New Industrial State*, Boston: Houghton Mifflin.

Gunsteren, L. A. van (1987) 'Technologische vernieuwingen en innovatie', presentation symposium 'Technologie=Toekomst. Een uitdaging voor het Noorden', Groningen.

Holland, S. (1975) *Capital Versus the Region*, London: Macmillan.

Jong, H. W. De and Shepherd, W. G. (eds) (1986) *Mainstreams in Industrial Organisation*, Dordrecht: Martinus Nijhoff.

Jong, H. W. De (1988) *Fusies en Overnames. Het concentratieproces in de westerse markteconomie van de twintigste eeuw*, The Hague: SMO.

Katzenstein, P. J. (1985) *Small States in World Markets*, Ithaca: Cornell University Press.

Krijnen, H. G. (1983) *Strategie en Management*, Groningen: Wolters-Noordhoff.

Lambooy, J. G. (1984) 'The Regional Ecology of Technological Change', in J. G. Lambooy (ed.) *New Spatial Dynamics and Economic Crisis*, Tampere: Finn publishers: 63–76.

Lee, H. J. van der, Moëd, J. and Dierckxsens, M. J. B. L. (1987) *Strategisch Management*, Alphen aan den Rijn/Brussel: Samson.

Levitt, T. (1983) 'The globalisation of markets', *Harvard Business Review*, May–June: 92–102.

Lipietz, A. (1986) 'New tendencies in the international division of labour; regimes of accumulation and modes of regulation', in A. J. Scott and M. Storper, *Production, Work, Territory. The Geographical Anatomy of Industrial Capitalism*, Boston: Allen & Unwin: 16–40.

Lloyd, P. E. and Dicken, P. (1977) *Location in Space: a Theoretical Approach to Economic Geography*, New York: Harper & Row.

Loeve, A. (1989) 'Buitenlandse ondernemingen in regional perspectief?, Ph.D., Utrecht.

Massey, D. and Meegan, R. (1982) *The Anatomy of Job Loss*, London: Methuen.

McDermott, P. and Taylor, M. (1982) *Industrial Organisation and Location*, Cambridge: Cambridge University Press.

Nods, R. and Wieringa, P. A. (1988) *Nieuwe Sporen: De Alomvattende Herschikking van het Internationale Bedrijfsleven*, Utrecht: Bruna.

Ohmea, K. (1985) *Triad Power: the Coming Shape of Global Competition*, New York: Free Press.

Prahalad, C. K. and Doz, Y. (1988) *The Multinational Mission*, New York: Macmillan.

Porter, M. E. (1985) *Competitive Strategy*, New York: The Free Press.

Salt, G. (1988) 'Highly-skilled international migrants. Careers and internal labour markets', *Geoforum*, 19: 387–400.

Scott, A. J. (1986) 'Industrialization and Urbanization: a geographical agenda', *Annals of the Association of American Geographers* 76: 25–37.

Smidt, M. de (1975) 'Bedrijfsstruktuur en arbeidsmarkt in een ruimtelijk kader', Ph.D. Utrecht.

Smidt, M. de and Wever, E. (1984) *A Profile of Dutch Economic Geography*, Assen: Van Gorcum.

Smidt, M. de and Wever, E. (1990) *An Industrial Geography of The Netherlands*, London: Routledge.

Smidt, M. de and van der Voorn, A. F. G. J. (1989) 'Philips in the UK', *Area* 21: 2, 145–9.

Taylor, M. and Thrift, N. (1982) *The Geography of Multinationals*, London: Croom Helm.

Taylor, M. and Thrift, N. (1983) 'Industrial linkage and the segmented economy: 1. Some theoretical proposals', *Environment and Planning* A: 14, 1601–13.

Törnqvist, G. E. (1970) *Contact Systems and Regional Development*, Lund: Lund University.

Verkennis, A., van Dongen, R. C. and Groot, C. S. (1988) *1992, Pleisterplaats op weg naar 2015*, Rijks Planologische Dienst, Den Haag, Studierapport nr. 46.

Wever, E. and Grit, S. (1984) 'Research Methods and Regional Policy, in M. de Smidt and E. Wever (eds) *A Profile of Dutch Economic Geography*, Assen: Van Gorcum: 39–63.

Wissema, J. G. (1987) *De Kunst van Strategisch Management*, Kluwer: Deventer.

Chapter two

IBM
The corporate chameleon

Tim Kelly and David Keeble

Introduction

The International Business Machines Corporation (IBM) domi-
nates the information technology (IT) industry in a way which few
companies in other markets can claim to match (Kelly 1987). It is a
market leader, a trend-setter, a model employer, and an innovator,
but above all, a superb marketeer. Its 1987 turnover of $US54.2bn
made it the largest IT operator world-wide. Indeed, its global sales
exceed the gross domestic product of several smaller European
countries such as Greece or Portugal and its global employment of
385,000 workers is larger than the work-force employed in Iceland
or Luxemburg. Among IBM's rivals in the IT field (Figure 2.1), the
closest in terms of size are the newly-privatized or liberalized PTOs
(public telecommunications operators) of Europe and Japan, or the
vertically integrated Japanese multinationals such as Matsushita,
NEC, Toshiba or Fujitsu. That its nearest US rival, the telecommunications giant AT&T, has generally failed in its recent drive
to become a major computer company, is a tribute to IBM's
successful resistance and market power.

IBM's dominant position gives it a strong claim to the title of a
'global company', selling the same products in Seoul, Suhl or
Solihull. IBM is often cited as an example of the trend towards the
'internationalization' of markets. Certainly by using culturally
homogenized images such as the Charlie Chaplin character and a
red rose to market its personal computers, it fits well in the mould
of the stateless transnational beloved of business school theorists.
Yet this is only part of the story. If its product marketing is blandly
international, its corporate advertising is the opposite; often
crudely nationalistic in its attempt to appear British in Britain or
French in France. In the same way that the chameleon changes
colour to suit its natural environment, so IBM changes its corporate identity to blend in with its geographical environment.

21

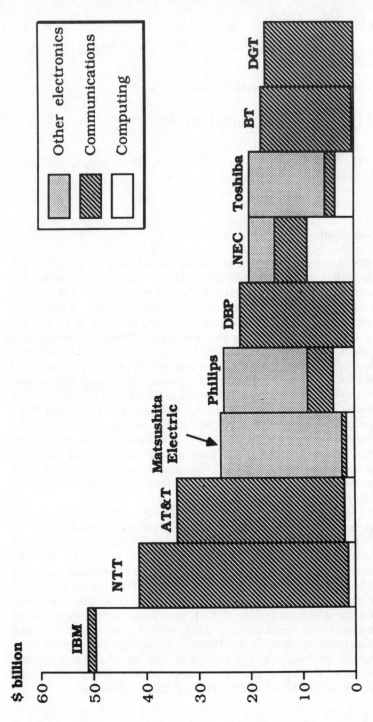

Figure 2.1 Global informatics operators; international sales, 1987

This study examines how a global multinational such as IBM structures its activities over space, and particularly the politically fragmented but increasingly economically integrated space that is Western Europe. It begins with a brief review of alternative theoretical perspectives relevant to the study of locational behaviour and restructuring in multinational companies, before examining the period of growth and expansion of IBM up to 1984. In this period the formerly independent European national subsidiaries coalesced into IBM Europe, with its continental-scale division of production functions. Sustained growth was combined with a considerably higher level of profitability than the industry average. The third section looks at IBM in the period since 1984, which has been one of slower growth, reduced profits, and restructuring of production functions and labour-force composition; above all, a period of technological uncertainty. The response since 1984 has been a radically new approach of growing through alliances, joint ventures, and partnerships. The final section looks at the winners and losers in this recent restructuring phase, and argues that market trends are forcing IBM increasingly to adopt locally-differentiated development strategies notwithstanding the process of European integration towards 1992.

The IT industry is experiencing rapid technological change which demands flexibility in product and management organization. At the same time, technological change can be seen as a liberating force spatially in which advanced telecommunications services and miniaturization of electronics components have progressively eroded the constraints of distance, freeing the company to align its activities more closely with new marketing imperatives. It is the interplay of these two determinants, changing technology and market demands, which lies at the heart of the locational issue, and the broader geographical question of who does what, where.

Enterprise location and restructuring: some theoretical issues

Recent vigorous theoretical debate in industrial geography has generated at least two types of theoretical framework of apparent relevance to IBM's locational evolution. The first is the notion of intra-national, and inter-national, spatial divisions of labour and functional specialization within multiplant corporations. Intra-nationally, workers such as Massey (1984) have argued persuasively that since the 1960s, intensified competition and profitability crises have forced large firms to locate mass-production assembly operations in low labour cost regions characterized by supplies of docile, non-unionized workers. Head office and R&D functions have, however, remained in core regions which afford the accessibility to information and customer networks, and to highly qualified staff, which they need. The result is systematic regional functional differentiation and inequality as a direct result of the activities of multiplant firms. Internationally, similar processes have been claimed by Fröbel et al. (1979) to be resulting in disinvestment from high-cost developed countries and a flight of multinational production in sectors such as electronics to low labour cost third-world countries. The result is the development of a New International Division of Labour.

These theoretical frameworks have been criticized empirically and as generating stereotypes which may well be invalid in particular cases (Sayer 1985; Morgan and Sayer 1988; Morris 1988). Seneschall (1984) for example shows how the vast majority of new European multinational manufacturing investment since 1971 has been directed at Europe and North America, not third-world countries, for market and technological reasons. And a wide range of empirical evidence (Keeble 1978) identifies regional policy pressures and incentives, coupled with greater labour availability, as the key determinants of branch plant investment in peripheral UK regions, not low labour costs. IBM provides an interesting further case study for assessing these radical perspectives.

Even more significant theoretically, however, is the current debate over the notion of a contemporary radical shift from a Fordist to a flexible regime of accumulation in Western Europe, and its spatial implications (Lipietz 1986; Scott 1988; Gertler 1988; Martin 1989; Milne 1989; Schoenberger 1989). From an enterprise perspective, this set of theoretical ideas argues that market saturation and falling profitability have brought about a crisis of post-war Fordist production methods. 'Fordism' is usually defined as a system of assembly-line mass production of standardized articles by relatively large firms characterized by a pronounced technical division of labour. In the 1980s, however, intensified global competition and increasing demand for 'customized' products of greater variety and quality are enforcing a rapid shift towards new, more flexible methods of production. These involve new work practices and organizational structures, such as 'just-in-time' (JIT) supply systems, and are being enabled by radical new process technologies, based on micro-electronics and computers. Labour inputs have been significantly reduced, while the work-force required is increasingly skilled and qualified. In many sectors, these changes seem to be benefiting small and new firms even more than large ones, with their greater rigidity and inherited investment in older production methods (Keeble and Kelly 1986).

The rapid burgeoning of geographical literature on the theory of an 'emerging flexible regime' of industrial production cannot possibly be reviewed more than very crudely in the space available here. It can, however, be criticized for often failing to stress enough the fundamental importance of rising consumer incomes and dramatic changes in process technology as influences on the nature of market demand and capitalist production in the 1980s. Moreover, the most frequently hypothesized spatial impact, of 'reconcentration' or spatial clustering of new investment in already developed core regions, to the detriment of peripheral regions (Camagni 1988), is not necessarily supported by empirical evidence (Milne 1989). The emphasis by several authors (Martin 1989) on the importance of associated political changes is, however, well illustrated by the information technology sector, via the impact of telecommunications deregulation and liberalization (see pp. 44–7). So too is the role of inter-firm strategic alliances as a means of reducing market uncertainty and sharing R&D costs in a highly turbulent competitive environment (Cooke 1988). A flexible production theoretical framework would thus seem potentially very relevant to an understanding of the restructuring of the computer industry generally (Kelly and Keeble 1988), and of IBM in particular, in the 1980s.

Dynamic growth and European development: 1910 to 1984

Origins

IBM was formed in the USA as the Computing-Tabulating-Recording Company by the merger in 1911 of the International Time Recording Company, the Computing Scale Company, and Hollerith's Tabulating Machine Company. The name was changed to International Business Machines in 1924 and the company joined the commercial market for electronic stored memory computers in 1953 with the 700 series. IBM did not 'invent' the computer; that distinction is disputed by a number of European and US research centres, though the Manchester University Mark I, which ran a stored programme successfully on 21 June 1948, is generally acknowledged to have been the first. IBM did not even market the first commercial computer; companies such as Univac (now part of Unisys) in the USA or Leo in the UK recognized that opportunity before IBM. Curiously, computer industry folk history records that senior IBM executives saw little potential for the computer apart from a handful of sales to the defence sector. IBM was not the first to introduce transistorized computers, minicomputers or microcomputers and, despite its formidable technical resources, it is not primarily regarded within the industry as an innovative company. In the field of technological change, IBM is a settler rather than a pioneer.

IBM's reputation rests on its marketing skills. While it was slow to forecast the growth of demand for computer power, nevertheless its second computer range, the IBM 650, eventually sold some 1,800 machines. IBM already had a substantial user base of customers for its conventional calculating and tabulating machines: and it was careful to 'wean' these customers onto the new technology by retaining familiar working practices such as the use of punched cards to store data and programmes rather than electronic memories. This cul-de-sac in the history of the computer industry was followed by manufacturers well into the 1970s.

IBM's great success in the new industry came ten years after selling its first computer when the 360/370 series was introduced in 1964. This was the first true 'range' of machines stretching across the spectrum from small business machines to large-scale scientific mainframes. Furthermore IBM promised its user base operating systems and applications software which would be 'upwards compatible' throughout the range and 'forwards compatible' with future models. At the mainframe end of the range, at least, IBM has largely kept this promise through successive generations of 30XX machines of which the most recent is the 3090 'sierra' range.

By the mid-1960s the market structure of the computer industry in America was already tending towards monopoly. The familiar 'Snow White and the Seven Dwarfs' structure had emerged in which the dominant IBM was challenged by a number of smaller companies collectively referred to as the BUNCH (Burroughs, Univac, NCR, Control Data, Honeywell). This structure persisted into the 1980s, but in recent years there has been some rationalization (Burroughs, Univac, and Sperry now trade as Unisys; Honeywell has joined forces with Bull of France and NEC of Japan). IBM's main competition comes now from specialists in specific product fields and market niches (e.g. IBM compatible mainframes – Amdahl, Fujitsu; minicomputers – Digital Equipment Corporation, Wang; microcomputers – Apple, Far Eastern clone manufacturers) as much as from across-the-range suppliers. IBM's pattern of market leadership is now more blurred and fragmented than in the 1960s, in line both with increasing computer market technological fragmentation (see Figure 2.2, based on 1987 data) and with the 'emerging flexible regime' thesis argued on pp. 24–5.

	Mainframe	Minicomputer	Microcomputer	Applications software
USA	IBM IBM plug-compatible manufacturers Unisys 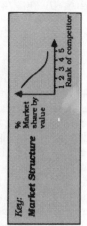	Digital IBM Hewlett-Packard	IBM IBM clones Apple	IBM EDS CSC
EUROPE	IBM Siemens ICL Unisys	Digital IBM Olivetti Bull	IBM IBM clones Apple	CGS SD–Scicon Software AG
JAPAN	NEC Fujitsu Hitachi IBM Japan	NEC Fujitsu IBM Japan	NEC Toshiba Epson	NTT CSK Intec

Key:
Market Structure

% Market share by value
1 2 3 4 5
Rank of competitor

Figure 2.2 Market share matrix by product and area for the computer industry

Tim Kelly and David Keeble

IBM in Europe: 1910 to 1984

West Germany

West Germany currently accounts for the largest national total of IBM employees in Western Europe, with 28,512 workers in 1986. This partly reflects the fact that West Germany was the location of its earliest European facility, in the form of the Dehomag company which was established in Germany in 1910 to market Hollerith machines from the Tabulating Machine Company throughout continental Europe. In 1923 90 per cent of the stock of the company was acquired by the Computing-Tabulating-Recording (CTR) company, shortly before the name changed to IBM. Until recently there were four manufacturing plants in Germany involved mainly in the manufacture of peripherals, including disc file units (Berlin), disc file accessories (Mainz), and power supplies and memory units (Hanover). The main German site is at Sindelfingen near Stuttgart. It was opened by Dehomag in 1924 and is chiefly involved in the manufacture of memory components. It was the first site in Europe to manufacture the 1Mbit microchip.

Sindelfingen also has a number of software product development responsibilities including text and data editing, financial systems and open systems interconnection (OSI) for the transport and session layers of the OSI reference model. The nearby R&D centre at Boeblingen has development responsibilities for mid-range computer systems. This has long been a problem area for IBM in which poorly co-ordinated sector specific strategies has left it with an incompatible series of ranges which have provided poor competition to Digital Equipment Corporation's range of VAX minicomputers. The Boeblingen site has European development responsibility for the 43XX series and, latterly, the 9370 'Vaxkiller' range which is IBM's latest response to the mid-range problem. Boeblingen also looks after very large scale integration (VLSI) component developments and consumer systems, especially for the finance market. In addition to the four manufacturing plants and two R&D facilities in Germany, there are seven designated 'international centres' including the European networking centre at Heidelberg, which conducts joint research with major European vendors into developing open systems networks, and the computer integrated manufacturing (CIM) centre in Munich.

The concentration of IBM employment in southern Germany has contributed to the development of this area as one of the major clusters of high-technology employment in Europe. As well as IBM, there is Siemens in Munich and a number of aerospace manufacturers including MBB. It is undoubtedly the case that these major employers have fed off each other in fostering a mutually beneficial labour market, characterized by a concentration of highly skilled scientists, engineers, and technically qualified staff. This has also been greatly aided by the area's residential attractiveness, in terms of climate, access to the Alps for skiing, and historic towns. The latter, and the presence of an historic university, explains the choice of Heidelberg for IBM's European networking centre. The critical factor underlying IBM's continuing presence in southern Germany is thus the availability of highly skilled labour, though the actual balance of skills required differs between the separate functions of manufacturing and research.

France

France is second only to West Germany in terms of the national volume of IBM employment, with 22,225 employees in IBM France in 1986 plus a further 2,281 in the headquarters of IBM Europe. Offices of the CTR company were established in Paris in 1914 and the first manufacturing plant in France began operating eleven years later in Vincennes. IBM now has four manufacturing plants and two research centres in France with a total surface area of over 400,000 square metres. Manufacturing and R&D now provide 10,000 jobs directly through IBM's operations, while it estimates that a further 3,000 jobs are sustained in a network of around 200 small and medium-sized sub-contracting firms. The largest of the French plants is the component manufacturing operation at Corbeil-Essonnes just south of Paris. This was opened in 1941, during the war, as a plant specializing in electro-mechanical office and accounting machines. In 1956 it had the distinction of manufacturing one of the first IBM valve computers, the IBM 650, and later, in 1960, the first generation of transistorized computers. The speciality mission of Corbeil-Essonnes developed after 1964 when silicon was first used in the manufacture of integrated circuits. It now manufactures both BIPOLAR high performance semiconductor chips and FET/CMOS chips for high density applications among a full range of over 22,000 designs. It accounts for around one-third of IBM's annual world-wide silicon chip production and exports some 85 per cent of its annual output to other IBM production plants in the Europe/Middle East/Africa (EMEA) complex. IBM does not sell chips directly, unlike rivals such as Fujitsu or Siemens, but is nevertheless one of the world's major manufacturers for use entirely in its own products. The Corbeil-Essonnes plant was extended by the addition of a development laboratory for components in 1971. This now employs 130 people while the plant as a whole employs 4,300 workers within a site spread over 77 hectares. A new 45,000 square metres facility for manufacturing bipolar semiconductors, completed in 1987, represented at the time the largest-ever single private sector investment in France.

The two plants located in the previously less-developed south ('Le Midi') of France, at Montpellier and La Gaude (near Nice), were both established in the 1960s in accordance with French regional development policy aimed at decentralizing industry away from the Paris region. Indeed, in its promotional literature, IBM Europe specifically acknowledges the aim 'to locate plants where they will help achieve regional development plans, wherever possible'. The choice of the south coast was a happy one for IBM for it was the attractiveness of the residential and physical environment to highly qualified staff as much as the dictates of French government regional policy which brought IBM to the area. This was particularly true of the location of the Centre d'Etudes et Recherches (CER) at La Gaude in 1962. This also benefited from the proximity of an international airport and the university at Nice, particularly the Laboratoire d'Analyse des Signaux et des Systèmes. The La Gaude facility now functions as a telecommunications development centre within EMEA with product development responsibilities for 37XX communications controllers and 58XX series modems. More significantly, La Gaude has world-wide responsibility for development of open systems interconnection (OSI) communications products including X.25 (packet switching), X.21 (teletex) and X.400 (message-handling systems). Again, location is significant, for La Gaude is within easy reach of Geneva where many of the important standards-making bodies are located including the International Standards Organization (ISO) and the Consultative Committee for International Telegraph and Telephone (CCITT) which is the chief standards-making arm of the International Telecommunications Union (ITU). The recent decision by the Directorate General XIII of the Commission of the European Communities to locate the European Telecommunications Standards Institute (ETSI) at Sophia Antipolis near Nice is fortuitous for IBM but was undoubtedly influenced by the body of local expertise in the labour force which has developed since IBM's move there. Ironically, the hidden agenda of ETSI is to free the European data communications industry from the hegemony of proprietary IBM systems network architecture (SNA) standards in favour of open systems. For IBM, OSI is an ideal to which it pays lip service, but which represents only a fallback position if its user-base demands migration from SNA.

The Montpellier facility was opened shortly after La Gaude in 1965. Decentralizing the production of computers to an 'assisted region' such as Languedoc-Roussillon was a direct response to French government regional policy pressure and incentives, while for IBM it also achieved a simple division of functions between component manufacture, which remained at the core of the French operations in Paris, and computer assembly in the southern periphery.

The Montpellier plant has the EMEA mission to produce IBM's largest mainframe computers; initially the 360/370, progressing through the 303X, the 308X ranges, and latterly the IBM 3090 or 'sierra' range, introduced in 1986. Like most well-established product ranges, there are two other parallel production units serving the Americas (at Ploughkeepsie, USA) and the Far East (at Yasu, in Japan). Mainframe computers remain the most profitable part of IBM's range, but have been the most affected by technological change. The market for mainframe computer use has been undercut in the 1980s by minicomputers and networked microcomputers that offer a much more attractive price/performance ratio. Mainframe computing is the slowest growing segment of the computer market and strategy has concentrated on speeding up the cycle of replacements in what is essentially a stagnant market. IBM's revenues from processor sales have been declining in the USA since 1984 and have been growing in the world as a whole only by the modest rate of 5 per cent per year. The Montpellier plant has been one of the worst affected by technological change, the miniaturization of components, and the automation of routine assembly functions. Its current employment level is around 2,800, but it is doubtful whether this can be sustained without the acquisition of new production functions such as the responsibility for manufacturing thermal conduction modules (TCMs) gained in 1980.

IBM's other facilities in France include a plant at Boigny near Orleans which manufactures data processing and office supplies, including magnetic heads, and at Bordeaux which manufactures electronic cards and circuit packaging assemblies, and handles European component procurement for IBM. IBM's European headquarters was moved to Paris from Switzerland in 1946. It is located at La Défense in a futuristic office complex in the western suburbs of Paris.

United Kingdom

For many years, IBM products were marketed, then produced under licence, for UK customers by the British Tabulating Machine Company, under an agreement signed in 1908. IBM (UK) Ltd was not established until 1951, following termination of this agreement in 1949. Its first small London office grew substantially until eventually transferring in 1976 out of London altogether to a new purpose-built office complex in the north-east corner of Portsmouth harbour. In addition to being close to its manufacturing facility at Havant and R&D unit at Hursley, the Portsmouth site also has excellent motorway, train and port facilities, and good access to London's international airports at Heathrow and Gatwick. Costs are much lower than in central London, and south Hampshire is very attractive environmentally to managerial and professional staff.

IBM's manufacturing operations in the UK are carried out at two locations though the division of products is structured on a European basis. The first site to be opened was at Battery Park in Greenock, Scotland, in 1951. This plant transferred locally to the current site in Spango Valley in 1954. Greenock has been a designated 'assisted area' under UK government regional policy since 1934, and still has a level of unemployment well above the national average. Choosing Greenock thus directly reflected IBM's stated policy of assisting national regional policy objectives, at a time of strong pressure from a Labour government. Availability of industrial labour was also a factor.

The Greenock plant originally employed just over 100 people to make typewriters and mechanical accounting machines. Later the plant specialized in assembling and testing optical character recognition (OCR) and other peripheral equipment, before gearing up in the 1970s for high-volume assembly and testing of visual display units, keyboards, power supplies and logic cards. In 1982 Greenock was chosen to become the European base for the manufacture of the highly successful IBM Personal Computer. Since its launch in the USA in 1981 the IBM PC has effectively set an industry standard in this emerging market. Greenock also has responsibility for the rather less successful successor to the IBM PC, the IBM Personal System/2. Marketing of the IBM PC and the PS/2 in the UK is, however, carried out from a special unit set up at Basingstoke, Hampshire, in 1983.

Some 150 engineers are employed in process technology R&D at Greenock where robots are now used extensively on the automated assembly line. Since the introduction of the PS/2, a new process using surface mounted technology (SMT) has been employed in printed circuit board (PCB) assembly. Despite the fact that Greenock has no product R&D or marketing functions, only a third of its work-force is taken up directly in manufacturing. The rest are in managerial and administrative support roles, with between one-quarter and one-third being graduates. This highlights the way in which rapid technological change is eroding many of the formerly labour-intensive functions in the production process. The plant formerly had an extensive machine shop for instance, but latterly has moved towards final assembly and test facilities only.

Greenock enjoys an excellent productivity record (it is claimed by the Scottish Development Agency to be the most productive IBM plant in Europe) and good working relations (no working days lost over thirty-five years). The plant is closely integrated in backward linkages with the regional economy such that around 40 per cent by value of its inputs come from Scotland. One major gap in the supply chain, that of colour display tubes which until recently were imported from the Far East, was filled in 1987 following a £15m. investment by Mullard Ltd in its Durham factory. The facility would not be economic without major contracts from IBM. With forward linkages, however, 85 per cent of IBM's production from its two UK manufacturing plants is exported or transferred internally within IBM's European operations. IBM's heavy investment at Greenock has attracted considerable government financial aid over the years. Between 1975 and 1980 for instance, IBM received nearly 30 per cent of total regional development grants paid to US electronics companies in Scotland.

Greenock is also the site of a recently-completed major automated materials distribution centre. Altogether, IBM's Greenock premises now cover nearly 100,000 square metres of floorspace. With the displacement of labour by new technology in the production process, however, employment has fallen slightly since 1985, from 2,700 to 2,500. IBM none the less remains the major employer in the area.

IBM's other manufacturing plant in the UK began production at Havant near Portsmouth in 1967. The Havant plant has assembled and tested some of IBM's largest computers for EMEA including the System/370 Model 168, but in the later 1970s the large systems 'Mission' was transferred to Montpellier. More recently the Havant plant has concentrated on intermediate range systems, principally the 8100 Information System which is designed for distributed data processing, the 4300 series and communication controllers. Havant now also manufactures all IBM's European banking products except printers and has moved towards high volume manufacture with disc files for the 8100 and AS/400 series, and for the IBM PC and PS/2 ranges. It works in close co-operation with the R&D laboratories at Hursley. In 1982, IBM announced a £20m. investment programme at Havant to produce semiconductor substrates which were previously made at Corbeil-Essonnes and Sindelfingen. Production was expected to reach £40m. per annum, for shipment to Corbeil-Essonnes where memory and logic microchips are manufactured to be mounted on the substrates.

In 1987, Havant also gained from the transfer of Rolm Europe's digital private branch exchange (PBX) operations from Swindon. Theoretically, the integrated services digital networks (ISDN) compatible products manufactured by Rolm, which had been acquired by IBM in 1984, should have had great market potential as Europe's PTTs build up their ISDN infrastructure. In practice, however, customers have so far shown little interest in integrating voice and data. ISDN remains a technology in search of an application, and IBM has now (December 1988) sold Rolm to Siemens. Havant's other new functions, however, have enabled employment to be maintained at around 2,000 despite employment loss because of new production technology.

IBM UK's Development Laboratory at Hursley near Winchester was opened in 1958 after planning permission to locate near Cambridge had been refused. It is now one of the biggest of IBM's European R&D laboratories, with 1,700 employees. The complex is set in parkland and is based around the eighteenth-century Hursley House. Development work there covers a broad spectrum but with a special 'mission' for graphics hardware and software. Developments originating from Hursley include the 3279 Colour Display System, the 8775 Display Terminal, the customer information control system (CICS) package programme, and graphics workstations for the PC and PS/2 ranges. A recent software product, developed jointly with Microsoft Corporation's UK centre at nearby Reading, is Presentation Manager. This employs a user-friendly interface using the windows, icons, mouse, and pull-down menus (WIMPS) format popularized by the Apple Macintosh. A further thirty people work in IBM UK's science centre at Winchester which seeks to develop more general computer applications which benefit society particularly in medical research. This science centre had originally been located in the science park at Peterlee in County Durham in 1969 for regional policy reasons, but was moved to Winchester around 1978 both because of the need for proximity to the Hursley R&D laboratory and because of difficulties in recruiting high-calibre personnel in Peterlee. The much greater availability of highly qualified research staff in southern Britain outside London, partly because of the undoubted attractiveness of the area's residential environment to such workers (Keeble 1988a), has thus been a key determinant of the location and successful development of IBM's research facilities in the UK, as it has also been in France and West Germany.

European-wide functional integration

IBM's largest European operations are those in West Germany, France, and the United Kingdom, described above, which together account for 77 per cent of European employment and 50 per cent of European sales, though because of inter-area transfers, the percentage of European revenue is much higher. IBM has operations in all the other countries of Europe and has important manufacturing facilities in Italy (2), Spain, and Sweden, and R&D facilities in Austria, Italy, Sweden, and Switzerland.

The Santa Palomba and Valencia plants were both opened in the mid-1970s in low-income, high-unemployment assisted regions of southern Europe. IBM argues that their location was strongly influenced by its deliberate strategy of assisting government regional policy objectives, with labour considerations (cost, industrial relations) playing little or no part. Since 1988, Santa Palomba has been assembling the initially very successful AS/400 mid-range computer series, the first developed under IBM's new *glasnost* policy of close customer involvement.

On the research side, the Ruschlikon centre near Zurich is one of three world-wide laboratories in IBM's research division. It has special responsibility for research into physics, device technology, communications, and computer science. It has an outstanding reputation for science and engineering. Notable recent successes include the award of Nobel prizes for basic research on the scanning tunnelling microscope and room temperature superconductivity as well as direct product developments such as the Token Ring Local Area Network (LAN).

The basic logic underlying the division of functions within IBM is intriguingly simple:

- Research and product development functions are undertaken on a global scale. There are three basic research laboratories (including Ruschlikon) and twenty-six R&D laboratories world-wide of which nine are in Europe.
- Manufacturing is carried out on a continental scale with most products being manufactured in at least three different plants world-wide, one each in the Americas, the Far East, and EMEA.
- Marketing, at the bottom level of the functional hierarchy, is carried out at the national level. This includes both product marketing and corporate promotion programmes which incorporate charitable work, secondments, educational projects, and involvement in national initiatives.

There is therefore a three-level functional hierarchy of scale. The

IBM image which the customer sees is a national one in which the international scale of IBM's operations is barely evident. Local advertisements emphasize IBM's exports, investment, employment, and long associations with a particular area. 'Corporate responsibility' advertising features local initiatives and worthy schemes. A good example is the campaign which IBM ran in the UK in the mid-1980s which featured the slogan 'How British do you have to be to contribute to Britain?' underneath various immigrant success stories such as Marks & Spencer, Isambard Kingdom Brunel, Selfridges, and Cunard. A second campaign, playing on concerns about unemployment, utilized the slogan 'Just the job for Britain'.

This national advertising belies the fact that IBM's operations are highly integrated at an international level. Indeed, the promotional literature itself is likely to have been printed centrally at the marketing and publications centre in Copenhagen, Denmark. Figures 2.3 and 2.4 show the European distribution of manufacturing and R&D/software activities respectively. The division of the manufacturing functions may be summarized as follows in approximately descending order of value/volume:

Large, mainframes:	Montpellier, France
Mid-range systems:	Havant, UK
	Vimercate and Santa Palomba, Italy
Communications systems	Havant, UK
	Bordeaux, France
Microcomputers, PCs:	Greenock, UK
	Vimercate, Italy
Memory peripherals:	Berlin and Mainz, West Germany
	Valencia, Spain
Printers:	Stockholm, Sweden
Supplies and accessories:	Boigny, France
Components:	Corbeil-Essonnes, France
	Sindelfingen, Germany

Few of these products can be used alone and none can be used without the accompanying software which is produced elsewhere in Europe. Because the R&D and software activities follow a different, global, scale of integration, there is surprisingly little spatial correspondence in their location pattern with manufacturing. Thus it is that IBM plants typically boast that a very high percentage (80–95 per cent) of their output is exported and that IBM's national

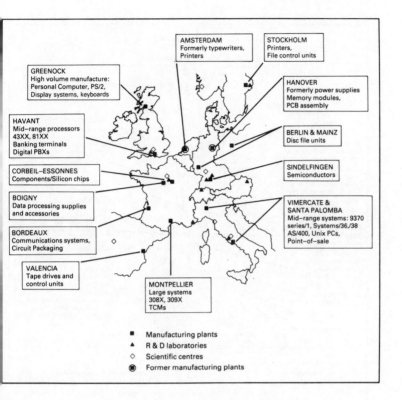

Figure 2.3 IBM manufacturing facilities in Europe

subsidiaries are among the top exporters in each country. This is only part of the story, however, because the corollary is that the national subsidiaries are also among the largest importers. Overall, IBM aims to keep the internal balance of payments for each national subsidiary at about break-even. This equation can be illustrated with reference to the 1987 results of IBM UK which, due to its production of popular IBM PCs and PS/2s, maintains a marginally positive balance (Table 2.1).

IBM UK's overseas sales actually exceed its home sales, but because of the volume of imports from other European branches, net exports are probably closer to 10 per cent rather than 53 per cent of turnover. The actual value-added by IBM UK's 18,026 employees (sales minus costs and overheads) is just £1,053m. or 30 per cent of total sales. The same logic of internationally 'open'

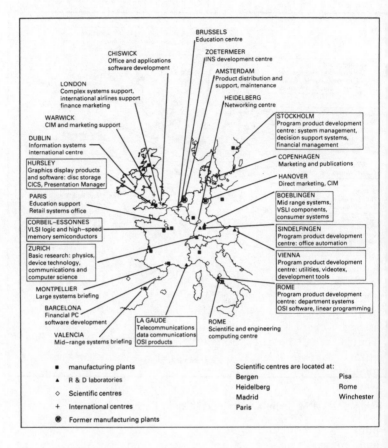

Figure 2.4 IBM research and development laboratories and international centres in Europe

accounting and intra-corporate flows of goods and services is repeated in all the other European subsidiaries with positive balances in the 'producer' subsidiaries such as the UK, West Germany, France, and Italy, and negative balances in the 'marketing' subsidiaries such as Ireland, Greece, and Portugal.

IBM's software and R&D functions are also distributed fairly widely throughout Europe (Figure 2.4). Some are engaged in activities which are related to specific IBM hardware ranges (e.g. graphics workstations at Hursley, UK, departmental systems in Rome); others are related to specific market sectors (e.g. retail

Table 2.1   IBM UK turnover and sales, 1987

1987 turnover	£3,483m.	
of which pre-tax profit	£ 465m.	(13.3%)
Home sales	£1,646m.	(47.2%)
Exported goods	£1,596m.	(45.8%)
Exported services	£ 241m.	(6.9%)
Costs and overheads	£2,430m.	(69.8%)
Supplied by UK firms	£ 941m.	(27.0%)
Supplied by non-UK firms	£1,489m.	(42.6%)
National balance of payments	£ 348m.	(10.0%)

Source: IBM Europe

systems at Paris, financial PC software at Barcelona). Ruschlikon (Switzerland) and the seven European science centres are dedicated to basic research. Though widely distributed, these 'knowledge-based' activities are almost all found in one or other of two types of location, namely in or close to major European capital and cultural cities (Rome, Paris, Vienna, Stockholm, Madrid, London, Zurich), or in physically very attractive residential areas sometimes associated with historic universities (Heidelberg, Pisa, La Gaude). The choice of these locations thus almost certainly reflects their attractiveness as living and working environments to the highly-qualified research scientists, engineers, and professionals, upon whose recruitment, brainpower, and expertise the success of IBM's R&D and related activities crucially depend.

IBM's European division of functions enables the company to pursue a goal of continental scale self-sufficiency in both in-house and brought-in production. Its locational philosophy is founded on the comparative advantage to be gained through local economies of scale and the large-scale shipping of parts and sub-assemblies between disparate locations. The hierarchical specialization of functions works on the principle of 'shipping boxes': the final product sold to the customer is effectively a black box of which less than 10 per cent by value will have been assembled in the country in which it is sold. This principle breaks down when the customer demands something more: a system.

In terms of the theoretical issues raised on pp. 23–5, the preceding sections reveal that assertions of 'capital flight' and the development of a New International Division of Labour (Fröbel *et al.* 1979) are inappropriate and invalid in the IBM case. Developed country market orientation has been and remains the dominant influence on the global geography of IBM's investment activity, coupled with a growing need for access to highly qualified staff. The latter consideration, along with access to clients, information, and communication networks, also explains the development of IBM R&D and headquarter functions in many European core regions, in line with 'spatial division of labour' arguments. But the latter's contention that branch plant establishment in peripheral regions has been motivated by a need to exploit cheaper, less-unionized labour seems much less valid. IBM's peripheral region branch plants – Greenock, Montpellier, Santa Palomba – appear more readily explicable by the corporate chameleon's sensitivity to government regional policy pressures and incentives, as part of a longstanding philosophy of fostering a corporate image of social responsibility and national identification. The end result is, however, certainly one of differing functional regional specialization and quality of job opportunities, in line with spatial division of labour ideas.

The new IBM: 1984 to 1988

Elements of a slowdown

In many ways the mid-1980s represented a peak period for IBM. Profitability stood close to 15 per cent, while a 14 per cent compound growth rate in 1980–5 was slightly ahead of the industry average. IBM executives confidently expected continuing growth and achievement of a target of $US100bn turnover by 1990. Competition from IBM's closest rivals, such as Amdahl in mainframes, DEC in minis, and Apple Computer in micros, had apparently been successfully repulsed. With the deregulation of telecommunications markets, opportunities seemed ripe for IBM to diversify into new fields. In product terms, the IBM PC had been established as a *de facto* industry standard for entry level systems and the 3090 mainframe range had been launched. The famous industry dictum, that no one had ever been sacked for buying IBM, had never seemed more true, as other famous computer companies struggled to survive a period of unparalleled technological change.

In fact, recent years have not lived up to IBM's original expectations. Since 1985, the company's rate of growth has slowed to just 4 per cent per year and profitability has declined (Figure 2.5). US turnover in particular has fallen by 12 per cent, with hardware sales being especially hard hit. Apparent sales buoyancy elsewhere becomes less apparent if converted from dollars into local currency. These changes cannot be conceptualized as a 'crisis', since by industry norms IBM is still highly profitable. None the less, by its own standards and targets, there has definitely been a slowdown.

Employment world-wide has fallen by 15,000, and 'strategic' product decisions have been quietly reversed. This section looks at the causes of this slowdown and the corporate response to it in Europe.

Technological change, flexible production, and competitive advantage

In the late 1980s, the computer industry is undergoing rapid change and it is those companies which exhibit flexibility and foresight which are benefiting. From both a technological and marketing perspective, the notion of an 'emerging flexible regime' of industrial production in Western Europe does seem relevant to IBM's recent experience.

It is conventional to describe the industry's technical evolution since 1950 in terms of successive 'generations' of computers (mainframes, minicomputers, microcomputers) and electronic components (thermionic valves, transistors, integrated circuits, semiconductors, VLSI (very large scale integration) semiconductors). As a rule of thumb, the memory capacity of semiconductor chips has doubled approximately every two years since the late 1960s, when the space race launched the drive for electronics miniaturization. IBM has stayed abreast of this race by maintaining its own semiconductor design and manufacturing capability. The 1 Mbit chip is now commonplace, and the 4 Mbit chip is being incorporated into tomorrow's products.

Figure 2.6, taken from a recent IBM annual report, shows the dramatic impact of technological change in the form of electronics miniaturization on the price/performance ratios of the two key variables of memory storage (£40 to £5 for 1 Mbit in only ten years) and data transmission (£5,000 to £10 for 1 Mbit/second in twenty-five years). This pace of technological dynamism means that firms must sell customers extra capacity at an ever faster rate if turnover is to grow. Moreover, IBM's traditional philosophy, epitomized in its system network architecture (SNA), is that computing is expensive and must be centralized, via a master-slave system of mainframe and terminals. This logic has been progressively eroded by technological developments such that networked workstations now offer a much better proposition than centralized intelligence. The rise of personal computing and distributed processing has also helped shift power away from white-coated professionals to consumers and junior executives. IBM has had to start marketing itself as a 'consumer' company and, at the bottom end of the market, to compete as a commodity producer.

The dramatic improvement in price/performance ratios and the

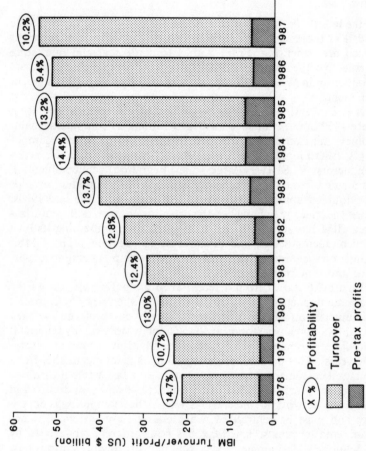

Disc storage

Tape storage trends and directions

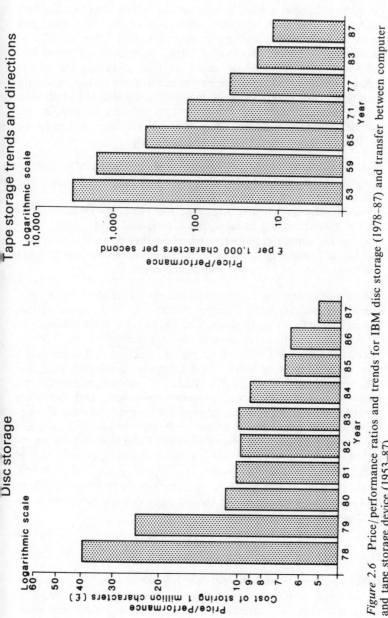

Figure 2.6 Price/performance ratios and trends for IBM disc storage (1978–87) and transfer between computer and tape storage device (1953–87)

demystification of the computer has had an entirely predictable effect on the business economics of computer manufacturing. Profit margins on hardware have been squeezed; the number of units that need to be sold to achieve the same turnover has increased; and there is little scope and no profit in selling 'after sales' and maintenance services. Several of IBM's competitors have shifted volume production to low-cost locations, including the newly industrializing countries of the Far East. IBM can no longer rely on making a profit purely from the manufacturing side of its business.

The profitable side of the computer industry is now in the 'people' business – added value through software and network services. This shift is occurring at three levels:

- in individual systems, the software element embodied in operating systems and applications software now outweighs the hardware element in terms of added value;
- within individual firms, there has been a redeployment of staff from manufacturing to sales, marketing, and R&D roles;
- within the computer industry as a whole the software and services sector is expanding much more rapidly than the hardware sector in terms both of turnover and employment.

A final component in the technical change equation is the convergence of computing, telecommunications, and broadcasting, especially the first two of these. The use of fibre optic cabling and cabling optimization techniques has revolutionized the relative merits of centralizing versus distributing intelligence. The result is a new generation of network-based computer products; local and wide area networks (LANs/WANs), modems, multiplexors, network management units, protocol converters, and the other paraphernalia of data communications. Computer network services based on the provision of remote information and transactional processing services have grown parallel. Examples of such value-added network services (VANS) include computerized information databases, travel agent networks, credit verification, and electronic funds transfer at the point of sale (EFTPOS) in retailing. These trends further emphasize the shift in the computer industry from hardware to service revenues.

IBM's response to technological change

IBM's response to the above trends has varied from active opposition, as with computer downsizing and commodification, to positive promotion, as with computing/telecommunications convergence. Its strategy has been to defend its own territory while attempting to extend its activities into the domains of other firms. For IBM, the microcomputer revolution has threatened to under-cut its existing profitable mainframe production. The dramatic speeding up of semiconductor-based product cycles since the 1960s has made R&D investment increasingly risky. IBM has been slow to participate in the technical developments which have transformed modern computing such as personal computers, local area networks, and microcomputer software. When it has entered these new markets, its product positioning has been far from sure-footed, as illustrated by the IBM PC Junior (home computer), the PC portable and, latterly, the IBM PS/2.

With regard to technical convergence, IBM has done much more to reposition itself. In the field of telecommunications, the mid-1980s witnessed a series of IBM acquisitions, including Rolm Corporation, a US digital PBX manufacturer with production facilities in Europe, and a minority 16 per cent in MCI, a major US long-distance and international carrier. It also briefly held shares in Satellite Business Systems, a US satellite telecommunications ser-vice company. These acquisitions were all made between 1984 and 1986 in the immediate aftermath of the break-up of AT&T which created new opportunities in US telecommunications. However, like AT&T's move into computing, none of these early forays into telecommunications have proved profitable for IBM, as epitomized by the announcement of the sale of Rolm to Siemens in December 1988.

IBM's more recent telecommunications strategy has been based on the different approach of alliances and joint ventures. This is partly a recognition of its lack of expertise in this new field, but it is also a deliberate attempt to appear more acceptable to nationalistic regulators. In trying to break into the formerly protected realm of national telecommunications services, IBM has exploited its chameleon characteristics. This is particularly evident within Eur-ope.

• In Britain, IBM's initial VANS joint venture (JOVE) with British Telecom was vetoed by government on grounds of potentially excessive dominance. Its subsequent more flexible, lower-profile, approach includes offering a managed data network service (MDNS) through a subsidiary, IBM Business Network Services. This involves creating partnerships with closed user groups (CUGs), as with the LIMNET network in the London insurance market. IBM's new systems integration group also works in partnership with other suppliers, consultancies, software houses, and customers to provide project management and turnkey solutions.

- In France, IBM has chosen to create longer-term established partnerships rather than one-off alliances on particular projects. Thus Axone SNC was created as a joint venture between IBM France (45 per cent), Crédit-Agricole (20 per cent), Paribas (26 per cent), Sema-Metra (5 per cent), and Crédit-du-Nord (4 per cent) to offer value-added services, primarily aimed at the financial sector. Another attempt is IB2 Technologies, which was founded as a 50:50 joint venture between IBM France and the construction company Bouygues to offer intelligent building services and perhaps, at a later date, local interactive cable services.

  France has taken a more restrictive attitude towards telecommunications liberalization than Britain, and even the few moves which have been made have slowed down since the election of a Socialist coalition administration in 1988. In November 1988, in a thinly-veiled anti-IBM move, the French regulatory mission decreed that all VANS providers must, within a year, offer X.400 and X.25 open systems access in addition to any proprietary protocols.

- In Italy, IBM has allied with Fiat, parent company of the telecommunications manufacturer Telettra, to establish a VAN service aimed initially at the motor industry but with the possibility of expanding into other business sectors later.

- In Denmark, IBM has set up a joint venture with the Copenhagen Telephone Company (KTAS), one of four regional PTOs.

In parallel with these country-specific alliances, IBM has also entered into a number of transnational alliances with intelligent network suppliers. In Europe, this is illustrated by its technology-sharing alliance with Siemens of West Germany and Ericsson of Sweden to develop IBM's database and network management capabilities in conjunction with the telecom manufacturers' switching technology to produce a virtual private network based around Centrex. Again the final objective is to offer software and services rather than hardware products.

It should be emphasized that between 1964 and 1984, IBM made no acquisitions and formed no alliances, relying instead on organic internal growth. The flurry of external activity since 1984, which has included acquisitions, minority shareholdings, joint ventures, strategic alliances, technology sharing, and product–marketing agreements, therefore represents a radically new strategy. Certainly the fall in profitability in IBM's traditional business has been a powerful push factor: but equally, the new opportunities created in liberalizing telecommunications markets have exerted a strong pull. Either way, IBM's pre-1984 policy of self-sufficiency and internalized structures has been abandoned, and the company is now much more outward-looking. In the language of the day, IBM executives refer to a new phase of *glasnost*. As in any period of radical change, the process has not been without its winners and losers, and the national and regional impact of this changing IBM strategy in Europe will now be considered.

'I've Been Moved': IBM's European restructuring

'I've Been Moved' is a popular internal depiction of the IBM acronym. IBM is well known for moving its employees between jobs and between locations as a method of adapting to changing technological and market demand while maintaining its proud boast that in the seventy years of European operations it has never made any workers redundant. However, the period of slower growth during the mid 1980s has stretched this image of a benevolent employer to the limit. Since 1986 IBM has been undertaking a massive restructuring programme which, it is estimated, will directly affect some 35,000 of IBM's 108,000-strong European workforce between 1986 and 1989.

These changes are occurring at three levels.

- Within IBM's manufacturing operations, employees are being moved out of direct assembly into quality assurance and supervisory functions as routine production functions are increasingly and rapidly automated and 'just-in-time' (JIT) inventory techniques are implemented.
- Within the business as a whole, emphasis is shifting from manufacturing to sales and marketing, software, and product development; and from manual to non-manual occupations, involving an overall upgrading of the skills balance of the workforce.
- In IBM's commercial operations, employees are being moved from mainstream activities to engagement in joint ventures and system integration projects with other firms; a shift from self-sufficiency to interdependency; from products to services.

In 1987 alone IBM spent some $US30m. in retraining reallocated employees in Europe. Most affected have been the manufacturing operations which have shed some 4,500 jobs (a decline of 15 per cent) since mid-1986. Some of these employees have accepted

47

special early retirement packages, but the majority have moved to new positions outside manufacturing. IBM now employs only 27,000 workers directly in the manufacturing process, a quarter of the total European work-force.

The most striking effect of this restructuring has been the assignment of new 'missions' to two of IBM's original fifteen manufacturing plants, at Amsterdam and Hanover, which have taken them out of manufacturing altogether. In January 1987, the Amsterdam plant, which traditionally manufactured typewriters, keyboards, and printers, was re-designated as the European distribution and support centre for high-volume products and maintenance parts. Thus Greenock-produced PCs are now all shipped to Amsterdam by air, for subsequent European distribution. Amsterdam is also acquiring responsibility for the central ordering point (COP) function previously at Orly in France. Amsterdam's central location within Europe, and the plant's proximity and good transport links to Schiphol Airport, undoubtedly played a major part in this decision, as also did the low air freight fares available from Dutch deregulated airlines.

In February 1987, IBM Germany announced that the Hanover plant, which had previously manufactured power supplies, memory modules, and printed circuit board assemblies, would in future become a software and service centre. It will also take over responsibility for direct marketing of IBM's high volume products, such as personal computers. While IBM has moved many of its telecommunications and network-based functions out of West Germany because of the highly regulated and highly priced telecommunications environment there, the country's postal system still retains a reputation for efficiency. Furthermore, Hanover is close to Denmark where IBM prints and publishes all its promotional and product literature for Western Europe.

Several similarities exist between these two major restructuring decisions by IBM. Both units are relatively well-established older plants located in high wage areas of Northern Europe. Both traditionally manufactured relatively 'low technology' products characterized by a low degree of software added value. These products are facing fierce price competition from low-cost Far Eastern suppliers. Finally, both have new missions which take them out of manufacturing and closer to the final customer through the sales, marketing, distribution, and support of high-volume products.

IBM's decision not to close these plants but to bear the cost of conversion and retraining the employees is a credit to its reputation as a socially responsible employer. This is one reason why IBM's

Table 2.2   IBM's European subsidiaries, 1985-7

Country	1987 sales $USm.	% European total	% change 1985-7 (AAC)*
West Germany	3,870.8	21.1	-14.7
France	3,068.7	16.7	- 5.8
United Kingdom	2,691.3	14.7	+34.4
Italy	2,636.1	14.3	+28.9
Spain	9.216	5.0	+ 5.5
Netherlands	833.8	4.5	-15.3
Sweden	688.0	3.7	- 2.1
Rest of Europe	3,62	19.7	
Total Europe	18,332.5	100.0	

Source: IBM Europe
Note: *Per cent change expressed in actual (national) accounting currency

staff turnover is typically only 3–5 per cent, compared with the industry average of 15 per cent.

It is not really possible to identify a direct link between the performance of national subsidiaries and the industrial restructuring reviewed above. A multinational such as IBM is adept at using transfer pricing and artificial currency exchange rates to juggle apparent sales between countries. Furthermore, differences in the performance of subsidiaries do reflect variations in market demand as well as changes in output and added value. Nevertheless the changes recorded in the performance of IBM's subsidiaries since 1985 are consistent with the restructuring process (Table 2.2).

Sales from the Netherlands and West Germany have both declined by around 15 per cent between December 1985 and 1987. This is where IBM's restructuring programme has had most effect. By contrast, sales from the United Kingdom and Italy have grown by around 30 per cent. Significantly, these are the two countries where IBM has invested in production lines for its high volume PC-based products at Greenock and Vimercate, Milan. Sales from France and Sweden have also declined over the last two years, in national accounting currency (though not in US dollars). IBM España has grown to overtake the Netherlands as IBM's fifth largest subsidiary in Europe.

The effect of recent restructuring upon aggregate national employment levels is harder to detect (Table 2.3). Most of IBM's national subsidiaries increased employment slowly to 1986 but have subsequently lost jobs as IBM has encouraged early retirement programmes. The most significant employment changes which have taken place are in the occupational composition of the work-force,

Table 2.3 Employment and sales per employee of IBM's European subsidiaries, 1986

	Employment Dec. 1986 ('000s)	Sales per employee ($US)
West Germany	28,512	13,576
France	24,506	12,522
United Kingdom	18,252	14,745
Italy	13,007	20,267
Spain	3,907	23,588
Netherlands	5,231	15,939
Sweden	4,296	16,015
Rest of Europe	10,289	35,204
Total Europe	108,000	16,965

Source: IBM Europe

with a decline in manual jobs in manufacturing and an increase in non-manual jobs in sales, software, and product development. Figures for sales per employee are somewhat misleading in this respect in that the highest values are recorded in the countries without manufacturing operations.

IBM's position in Europe remains dominant but, as Table 2.4 shows, its market share has declined during the troubled years of the 1980s. Since 1981, IBM's European sales have grown by 13 per cent per year, but this is slower than the market as a whole which has grown by 16 per cent per year. Consequently IBM's share of the sales of the top twenty-five data processing companies in Europe has slipped from 38 per cent to 32 per cent. The list of top ten firms has remained relatively stable, with only two newcomers. Nixdorf and Hewlett-Packard. One firm, Control Data, has been displaced from the top twenty-five and two other firms, Sperry-Univac and Burroughs, have merged to form Unisys.

The most striking change in the top twenty-five is the fact that European-owned firms now account for almost half of sales compared with just a third in 1981. This change has occurred because European firms have taken a larger share of growth markets such as microcomputers, software, and computer leasing to compensate for the shares they lost long ago in mainframe and minicomputer markets. In addition, several US companies, including Digital, Apple, and Hewlett-Packard now manufacture more of their European product range locally.

Table 2.4 The top ten data-processing firms in Europe, by sales, 1981–7

European sales (in $USm.)

		1981		*1987*
1	IBM	8,846	IBM	18,332.5
2	Cii-Honeywell Bull	1,311	Siemens	4,961.6
3	Siemens	1,296	Olivetti	3,802.5
4	DEC	1,162	DEC	3,533.5
5	ICL	1,067	Nixdorf	2,652.2
6	Olivetti	1,006	Groupe Bull	2,345.8
7	Sperry Univac	850	Unisys	2,272.9
8	Control Data	765	Philips	2,055.2
9	Philips	750	Hewlett-Packard	1,800.0
10	Burroughs	742	STC Plc	1,720.4
11	Nixdorf	678		
12	Hewlett-Packard	604		
Top	25	23,126		56,300

Source: *Datamation* magazine

Conclusions

Several general conclusions can be drawn from the above analysis of IBM's recent restructuring in Europe, not least in terms of the theoretical ideas presented before. First, the contentions of new international division of labour theorists are inappropriate and irrelevant to understanding IBM's recent investment behaviour and locational evolution. IBM has not shifted any production to third-world countries, but has instead invested heavily in its European operations. In this advanced IT industry, dynamic technological and demand changes increasingly necessitate European production for European markets.

Secondly, the post-war establishment by IBM of manufacturing plants in some peripheral European regions, coupled with R&D and headquarters investment in core areas, has contributed to a spatial division of labour and regional functional differentiation within the computer industry in several countries, notably Britain, Italy, and perhaps France. However, the empirical evidence strongly suggests that choice of peripheral branch plant locations primarily reflects government regional policy pressures and incentives, rather than a desire to exploit cheap labour. And peripheral operations such as Greenock (PCs) and Santa Palomba (AS/400 computers) have in the 1980s been selected to manufacture IBM's latest and most successful hardware products, with resultant positive regional impacts.

However, perhaps the most interesting theoretical conclusion of this case study is that IBM's current European restructuring, and the impact upon the company of radical technological and market demand changes, does seem in many ways to accord with the notion of an 'emerging flexible production regime' in Western Europe. IBM is indeed investing heavily in new computer-controlled flexible production technology, is reorganizing work practices, and has implemented JIT supply systems in all its remaining manufacturing plants since 1986. Intensified R&D and market sensitivity are necessitating considerable upgrading of the quality of its workforce. Rapidly-changing demand and new technologies are enforcing a new more flexible strategy of inter-firm alliances, the provision of local network services, and closer interaction with clients. Locationally, these changes have been felt most keenly and negatively by older north European plants, traditionally specialized on 'low technology' products. Service employment in major metropolitan regions, and in R&D units in environmentally attractive locations, has been maintained if not increased.

For IBM, therefore, flexible production involves a variety of locational responses, including both computer-controlled mass production of high-volume hardware products with rapidly shortening life cycles in peripheral locations, and an increasing emphasis upon market-oriented and located computer service provision. The crucial and growing importance of R&D in a period of turbulent technological change is also stimulating investment in 'prestige' European locations (Keeble 1988b, 1989) where climatic, scenic, and quality of life advantages maximize ease of recruitment of highly qualified scientists and engineers. Older factories associated with outdated products in northern urban Europe are in contrast undergoing painful manufacturing closure and restructuring.

The European computer industry in general, and IBM in particular, is thus being forced to respond more flexibly to rapid changes in technology and market demand. Of particular importance is the fact that data processing purchasers in Europe are no longer content just to buy standard-issue US-produced models, but demand products which are customized to accommodate the nuances of national market differences. This is a trend which IBM has helped to set, through choosing to manufacture its entire product range in Europe: but it is also one which IBM must follow. To meet this new challenge, IBM has been devolving more responsibility to local subsidiaries, allowing them to develop their own marketing strategies, forge their own alliances, and retain more of their own profits. In particular, the choice over whether to embrace open standards products or to maintain proprietary products is being left to local managers. The shift towards a more flexible production regime is clearly evident in these developments.

Thus the nature of the IT industry has changed since the early 1980s, and IBM can no longer count on sales of 'black box' products to guarantee future revenue growth. Geographically, its new commitment to increasing sales of software, computer services, and value-added network-based services demands a more local and less global approach. Instead of selling the same product in all locations, IBM is increasingly selling highly targeted products and services which are able to communicate between all locations. The economy of scale is realized not through the substitutability of products but through their inter-communication. IBM is able to present itself to its multinational customers as able to handle their international communication and processing requirements while still retaining the ability to provide local solutions. It is no longer sufficient for the corporate chameleon simply to change its colour to fit in with the local environment; rather it must now participate actively to change its local environment through direct involvement. This means local autonomy, local alliances, local strategies but global capability and inter-connectivity. IBM has now realigned itself to follow this new strategy and its competitors must surely follow.

Note

The views expressed in this chapter are those of the authors and do not necessarily reflect those of the OECD or its member countries.

References

Camagni, R. (1988) 'Functional integration and locational shifts in new technology industry', in P. Aydalot and D. Keeble (eds) *High Technology Industry and Innovative Environments: the European Experience*, London: Routledge: 48–64.

Cooke, P. (1988) 'Flexible integration, scope economies, and strategic alliances: social and spatial mediations', *Environment and Planning D, Society and Space*, 6: 281–300.

Fröbel, F., Heinrichs, J. and Kreye, O. (1979) *The New International Division of Labour*, Cambridge: Cambridge University Press.

Gertler, M. S. (1988) 'The limits to flexibility: comments on a post-Fordist vision of production and its geography', *Transactions of the Institute of British Geographers*, new series 13: 419–32.

Keeble, D. (1978) 'Spatial policy in Britain: regional or urban?' *Area* 10: 123–5, 363–5.

Keeble, D. (1988a) 'High-technology industry and local environments in the United Kingdom', in P. Aydalot and D. Keeble (eds) *High Technology Industry and Innovative Environments: the European Experience*, London: Routledge: 65–98.

Keeble, D. (1988b) 'High-tech in pastures new', *The Geographical Magazine: Analysis*, 5, January, 4–7.

Keeble, D. (1989) 'Core-periphery disparities, recession and new regional dynamisms in the European Community', *Geography*, 74: 1, 1–11.

Keeble, D. and Kelly, T. (1986) 'New firms and high-technology industry: the case of computer electronics', in D. Keeble and E. Wever (eds) *New Firms and Regional Development in Europe*, London: Croom Helm: 75–104.

Kelly, T. (1987) *The British Computer Industry: Crisis and Development*, London: Croom Helm.

Kelly, T. and Keeble, D. (1988) 'Locational change and corporate organisation in high-technology industry: computer electronics in Great Britain', *Tijdschrift voor Economische en Sociale Geografie*, 79: 2–15.

Lipietz, L. (1986) 'New tendencies in the international division of labor: regimes of accumulation and modes of regulation', in A. J. Scott and M. Storper (eds) *Production, Work, Territory: the Geographical Anatomy of Industrial Capitalism*, Boston: Allen & Unwin: 16–40.

Martin, R. (1989) 'The new economics and politics of regional restructuring: the British experience', in L. Albrechts, F. Moulaert, P. Roberts, and E. Swyngedouw (eds) *Regional Policy at the Crossroads: European Perspectives*, London: Jessica Kingsley: 27–51.

Massey, D. (1984) *Spatial Divisions of Labour: Social Structures and the Geography of Production*, London: Macmillan.

Milne, S. (1989) 'New forms of manufacturing and their spatial implications: the UK electronic consumer goods industry', *Environment and Planning A*, forthcoming.

Morgan, E. and Sayer, A. (1988) *Microcircuits of Capital*, Cambridge: Polity Press.

Morris, J. (1988) 'Research in industrial geography: a theoretical critique', *Transactions of the Institute of British Geographers*, new series 13: 337–44.

Sayer, A. (1985) 'Industry and space: a sympathetic critique of radical research', *Environment and Planning D, Society and Space*, 3: 3–29.

Schoenberger, E. (1989) 'Thinking about flexibility: a response to Gertler', *Transactions of the Institute of British Geographers*, new series 14: 98–108.

Scott, A. J. (1988) 'Flexible production systems and regional development: the rise of new industrial spaces in North America and Western Europe', *International Journal of Urban and Regional Research*, 42: 171–86.

Seneschall, M. (1984) 'The spatial evolution of the giant EEC-based manufacturing firm, 1970 to 1981', unpublished Ph.D. thesis, University of Cambridge.

Chapter three

Philips
A global electronics firm
restructures its home base

Marc de Smidt

Introduction

Philips will celebrate its centennial in 1991. This Dutch company
started out producing electric light bulbs and has transformed itself
into a global electronics corporation. The company is an outgrowth
of a risky 'joint venture' integrating 'two trades'. An inventor
(Gerard Philips) and an innovator (his younger brother Anton
Philips) started a business in a small country with a very limited
domestic market and without a true manufacturing tradition. In
several respects, the First World War was a watershed for their
company. First, Philips' laboratory for basic research was
established in 1914. Ever since that time, R&D has continued to
build a solid base for expansion into new product frontiers. In
addition, the First World War provided the impetus for vertical
integration in production, as foreign sources of materials were cut
off. Finally, economic growth after the war stimulated the establishment of manufacturing operations abroad. These three lines of
development should be placed in a long-term perspective as a
background on which to project Philips' strategies for the future.

During the *inter bellum* decades, the firm widened its scope from
the manufacture of electric light bulbs to X-ray instruments and
radio tubes. Later, Philips developed a versatile range of products
in the fields of professional instruments, domestic appliances, and
consumer electronics. Basic research paved the way to these new
frontiers. Vertical integration is now concerned with manufacturing
components for a wide range of industrial sectors. Many goods and
services are bought in by the company. The threat of vertical cut-
back, entailing the loss of basic manufacturing activities which
would hollow out the corporation, was recognized early by Philips,
in contrast to US firms in this field, as elaborated in Chapter 1.
Philips belongs to the top six firms in the world, both in electronic
products and components (i.e. integrated circuits).

Internationalization of the firm took place during the Depression. The Dutch base shrank between 1929 and 1939 from 27,500 to 18,500 jobs, while the number of employees abroad increased from 12,500 to 26,500. High growth rates in the 1950s and 1960s generated a tremendous increase in the number of jobs (90,000 in 1950; 359,000 in 1970). In 1970 one out of every four of the firm's employees worked in the Netherlands. At an early stage, before the 1960s, foreign competitors were taken over (Mullard, UK; La Radio-Technique, France; Müller, Germany). Outside Europe, Philips has a long tradition of manufacturing, also in Third World countries. North American Philips Corporation (NAPC) has been operational for nearly fifty years and has recently been included in Philips' world-wide operations. During the Second World War, NAPC commanded Philips' production outside occupied Europe.

What kind of strategic options do corporate managers consider? And what impact do their decisions have on a firm's functional and geographical division of activities? The following case study documents the changing geography of Philips in the Netherlands as the firm restructures its domestic base.

Strategic options – avenues for the future

In his Harvard lecture (27 October 1987), Philips President Cor van der Klugt outlined four key trends that have to be faced in his business arena:

1 new patterns of competition (the Japanese challenge);
2 the development of global markets (the fragmentation of the European market) in the face of the rising cost of R&D and shortening product life cycles (PLCs)
3 the concept of centres of excellence in all three core regions of the world;
4 the maintenance of basic technologies in order to meet the complexity of new products, and integration (converging technologies).

There is a need to rethink the structure of a versatile company that is on its way to becoming a global corporation. Its functional and geographical orientation will have to change. Two of the key trends outlined by the president of Philips will be examined here. The corporate strategy of establishing centres of competence comprising international production centres seeks to convert the organizational matrix from a geographically based to a functionally based structure. The second strategy entails concentrating on core strategies that are interconnected with converging technologies in electronics.

Centres of competence

Traditionally Philips has advocated a 'local for local' policy, which entails integrating the company's activities on a geographical basis. This policy did not, however, mean that the production capacity and sales volume of each country were in balance, apart from the fact that the Netherlands, as the home base, was over-represented in terms of production. Each of the countries included in the integration plan was allocated a particular status. 'Key' countries by product division were assigned co-ordination tasks for resources, production, and marketing; small 'local-market countries', where national organizations (NOs) supervise a small range of products, were delegated sales activities.

Conversion of the matrix means that product divisions (PDs) have become more important at the expense of NOs. Centres of competence are the hubs of the new strategic concept. Three main world regions (Europe, North America, and the Far East) are designated as areas with a distinctive set of market potential, distribution channels, know-how, mentality (labour and consumers), infrastructural provisions, capital, and subcontractors. International production centres (IPCs) are pivots in these centres of competence for each product division. IPCs are based on the principle of economies of scale. They provide basic products and components for a range of plants located in different countries or states within a world region. At the same time, they supervise national production centres (NPCs) near the market. For instance, at an IPC for compact discs located in Hasselt (Belgium), logistics management based on 'manufacturing resources planning' implements a flexible production automation and governs the flow of goods through the organization.

IPCs are assisted by 'centres of incorporation', which deliver expertise for research, training and management. IPCs are supposed to be key elements within 'business units', comprising a bundle of horizontally integrated production units and vertically integrated product–market combinations (PMCs), which are characterized by a common product planning and marketing. This is the main frame of the product division. A business unit is a strategic planning organization of profit centres, each responsible for its own strategies under the supervision of product divisions. In the company's own diplomatic language, geographically the concept of business unit is 'a balancing act between global integration and national responsiveness'.

Intrapreneurship is fostered by task forces and project teams, which are management tools to integrate the chain of events from design and development activities towards production and marketing. The old problem of how to integrate the 'two trades' of technology and sales could be tackled in such a manner. Philips – inventor of the compact disc – has always been strong in research and development but weak in marketing. 'Contractual relationships' between business units as well as 'co-makership' with external firms are new elements in the flexible organizational structure (Dekker 1987).

A corporate goal is to trim the organization by deleting several layers from the hierarchy in order to decrease the number of decision-making levels. It is expected that world-wide between ten and twenty thousand staff positions will disappear in order to cut overheads.

Selecting core activities

According to the company's own metaphor, there is a 'Philips tree with components as the trunk and with consumer electronics and information technology and communications as the branches'. The basic proposition is that there is a need for key activities, characterized by interdependent and interlocked activities. The three product divisions mentioned in the metaphor will require such a tremendous amount of research effort and development expenditure that capital could not be allocated to 'stand-alone activities' such as domestic appliances. A major stand-alone activity field, PD lighting – a 'cash cow' thanks to Philips' leading position in this field – has acquired a special company status under the corporate umbrella. Sales and deliveries by product division are shown in Table 3.1. Deliveries by the components division are higher than sales figures due to intracorporate deliveries between divisions (in particular oriented towards consumer electronics and professional equipment). This illustrates the interdependencies of core activities. There is a definite problem in identifying non-core activities, in particular when those activities are major contributors to company profits (a recent example is Phonogram, taking advantage of high CD sales, and not sold for that very reason).

The selection of core activities has been facilitated by the transfer (at the end of 1988) of the white-goods business (PD domestic appliances) to Whirlpool International, a joint venture in which Whirlpool Corporation of the USA has a 53 per cent and Philips a

Table 3.1 Philips. Sales and deliveries by product division, 1988

(m. Dutch guilders)	Net sales	As % of total	Deliveries	As % of total
Lighting	6,910	12	6,974	12
Consumer electronics	18,227	33	18,490	31
Domestic appliances	6,762	12	6,797	11
Professional products and systems	15,084	27	15,359	25
Components	7,792	14	11,199	19
Miscellaneous	1,304	2	1,396	2
Total	56,079	100	60,215	100
Inter-company deliveries*			–4,136	
Net Sales			56,079	

Source: Philips in 1988
Eindhoven, 23 February 1989
Note: *Intra-corporate

47 per cent shareholding. A complete transfer is expected in the years ahead. The strategy to obtain financial resources by building up joint ventures and thereby lowering Philips' investment in unrelated business has failed in the area of medical equipment. In 1980 Duphar was sold to Solvay; in 1988 a promising joint venture with Britain's General Electric Co. did not materialize, as the falling dollar deflated Philips' medical earnings.

Mergers and acquisitions are needed to combat major competitors in core activities. At the end of the 1970s thirty-five colour television manufacturers were producing in Europe, although the ten leading firms in the world controlled 80 per cent of exports (Dicken 1986: 336). Just as in the US one decade earlier, a horizontal integration occurred, whereby Philips took a share in Grundig, a German producer. Now, a new race is on for – as US Congressman Don Ritter told *International Business Week* (30 January 1989) – 'a crown-jewel product', called high-definition TV (HDTV). That article called this technological advance in the world of video 'as sweeping as the replacement of propellor-driven aircraft by jet planes'. It may pave the way to a wide array of electronic products, from home-entertainment systems to medical imaging and even radar defence systems. Chip manufacturers will need a major share of the HDTV market, for it will be a major strategic element in competition for all high-tech industries, in particular the computer business. Philips will have a stake in this, controlling US-based Magnavox and working in its own laboratories at Briarcliff Manor (NY) for HDTV activities. This example illustrates the importance of being linked into the US manufacturing system during a period in which US industrial strategy has to cope with Japanese competition. Furthermore, Philips' US experiences will help keep the firm in the lead in the European market.

Crucial to this core strategy is R&D, cross-fertilizing the cutting edge developments in technology. Micro-electronics is all-pervasive, interconnecting the fields of information-handling by computers with telecommunications (merged into telematics). Components can be delivered by another PD. Vertical integration is re-emphasized in corporate planners' reports in order to reach synergy, and at the same time to avoid becoming fully dependent on Japanese suppliers. The new electronics business needs a great deal of services, in particular software (Muntendam 1989). Interconnections between the electronics industries and other sectors have become of prime importance. Major examples of these trends can be found in bilateral activities with the chemical and automobile industries. A joint venture with Du Pont de Nemours for tapes and optical media is such an example (Table 3.2). In the years ahead the increasing application of electronics will lead to ventures in a sector where European manufacturers face fierce competition: the automobile industry. European co-operation across sectors will grow, at least at the level of corporate R&D.

Philips' managers advocate a European technology and industrial policy themselves taking an active part in European initiatives in these fields (e.g. Esprit, Race, Brite, and on a private basis Eureka and Jessi). This means sharing risks and resources in order to prevent hollowing out European firms and to strengthen the global competitiveness of European-based companies confronted with Japanese MITI strategies. They have set targets: in the 1970s consumer electronics, in the 1980s information technology and components (integrated circuits), and in the 1990s the field of telematics. Philips will face these shifting challenges by investing in centres of competence outside Europe, selecting high-growth core activities and seeking strategic partnerships.

Strategic alliances

The era in which a large number of electronics firms invested in new fields of technology has passed. The same is true for national aims such as the French policy for an integrated electronic sector (*la filière électronique*). Even leading companies have to work together

Product division	Partner firm	Partnership	Year	Activities
Lighting	Compagnie des Lampes	majority share	1982	consumer lighting
	Westinghouse	take-over[a]	1983	consumer lighting
Consumer electronics	Magnavox	majority share	1974	TV
	Grundig	minority share	1979	TV
	Marantz Japan	50% share	1981	Consumer electronics
	Marantz Europe	take-over	1981	Consumer electronics
	Du Pont de Nemours	joint venture	1980	Tapes (PDM)
	Du Pont de Nemours	joint venture	1985	Optical media (PDO)
	Huoyang Prefecture Industrial Development Company	joint venture	1986	Car audio apparatus (via Hong Kong)
	Kyocera	joint venture	1986	Car audio electronics
	Beijing Radio Factory & China Electronics	joint venture	1985	Home Interactive Systems (HIT)
Domestic appliances	Ignis/IRE	joint venture	1985	Consumer electronics
	Bauknecht	take-over[a]	1972	Domestic appliances
	Whirlpool Corporation US	minority share[b]	1984	Domestic appliances
Professional products and systems	ASMI	joint venture	1988	White-goods appliances
	Bosch	joint venture	1984	Semi-conductor lithographic apparatus
	Control Data Corporation	joint venture	1986	Broadcasting TV apparatus
Telecommunication components	AT&T	joint venture[c]	1984	Laser Magnetic Storage Int.
	Matsushita	joint venture	1984	Public telephone and transmission
	RCA and INTEL	agreement	1952	Components (MEC)
	Texas Instruments	agreement	1982	Specific ICs
	Siemens	project partners	1984	Semi-custom ICs
	Sharp	know-how agreement	1984	Submicron (R&D)
	Nippon Chemicon Corp. & Nippon Steel Corp.	joint venture	1985	Liquid crystal displays
			1986	Ceramic electronic components

Source: Philips company reports

Notes: a) As far as specific activities are concerned
 b) Deconsolidating in the years ahead
 c) Minority share (40%) in 1988

in order to finance their enormous R&D expenses (Roobeek 1988; van Tulder and Junne 1988). Furthermore, repayment periods are shrinking in a time of shortening product life cycles (PLCs). In the world of telecommunications the era of electro-mechanical equipment lasted twenty-five years, but digital equipment is supposed to count on a pay-off in eight to twelve years. The bottom line of the market, looking at minimum investments and repayment period, is estimated at 8 per cent. Therefore not more than twelve companies world-wide can take part in this race. Employing ISDN (Integrated Services Digital Network) in the 1990s may double the cost, permitting only six corporate firms to participate.

This means that strategic alliances are needed, spanning a long time, bringing R&D facilities together in this particular field, pushing for standardization of equipment and joining forces in marketing. These strategic partnerships can be focused on R&D efforts, such as the Philips–Siemens megabit chips project. It may also be more market oriented, as illustrated by the venture of Philips and AT&T, undertaken in order to compete on the market of digital telephone exchanges. Combining Japanese management and Philips know-how, Philips entered a joint venture (MEC) with Matsushita to produce components for electronic tubes and semiconductors. The fact that Philips markets compact discs together with Sony illustrates this new era of co-operative competition. Sometimes a former supplier will be included in a joint operation; for instance, Philips involved the US firm Control Data Corporation in the manufacture of optical memories. This complements Philips' optical technology and provides an entry to the market for mainframe systems in the US. A list of major partnerships of Philips is given in Table 3.2.

As Ohmae (1985) pointed out, there is a basic advantage for geographically distant competitors to work together in production and marketing, as each one will have a stronghold in each of the markets. Trade barriers will foster strategic alliances (joint ventures) for production. It is unlikely that a back-door flow of products will develop by just establishing 'screwdriver' (assembly) plants which lack high-value-added activities. A higher 'local content' (suppliers) is sought by European governments. Furthermore, co-operation is needed to meet the competition of Japanese firms pushing products on the market and to offer price levels that could not be reached without a big market share in the future. This 'learning curve' does not give a firm the opportunity to write off R&D expenses in a traditional manner.

The Siemens–Philips case illustrates that neighbours with the same research-based tradition can co-operate in R&D. It is, however, important to stress the significance of keeping in touch with the R&D Meccas in the electronics world, such as Silicon Valley (Philips took over Signetics for that reason in 1976) or Silicon Island (Kinsju, Japan). 'Centres of excellence' within each 'centre of competence', in Philips' terminology, are watch-towers looking for what is new in the electronics business.

Fostering globalization

The strategic options outlined above have consequences for the future prospects of specific countries (NOs) and product divisions (PDs). In centres of competence such as North America and the Far East, offering vast human and technological resources as well as markets, the company will have to grow far much faster than in Europe, which accounted for 61 per cent of sales in 1988. North America (with 22 per cent) and Asia (with 7 per cent) need more attention as markets. At the same time there is a geographical imbalance between figures for sales and deliveries (Table 3.3). A prime goal is to converge sales and deliveries shares for North America while increasing production, whereas the goal for Asia is to intensify marketing (Japanese and NIC competition being fierce). For professional electronics, the US is a very fruitful base; for consumer electronics Japan and NICs are the pacesetters (Muntendam 1987, 1989). Although offering small and fragmented markets and low productivity in comparison with competitors, Philips 'has a particularly extensive international network in developing countries across a whole range of electronic activities' (Dicken 1986:342).

Apart from the imbalance between deliveries and sales, there are other reasons to shift activities to the US and Japan. Markets increasingly determine the production allocation, whereas wage differentiation is of decreasing importance. Assembly based on flexible production is becoming more important, including a market-driven concern for quality and just-in-time delivery. Distribution channels in the Far East are domestically controlled and required for joint ventures. Not only can monetary fluctuations be avoided to some extent, but there is a need to tap major research bases in the world, including software capacities.

World-wide sourcing is a major development. There is some concern that West European suppliers are increasingly unable to meet quality standards. In most multinationals purchasing departments have been underrated. The growing share of components from suppliers based in the Far East can also be illustrated by the case of Philips; the US is the big loser and Europe has a small stake

Table 3.3 Philips. Sales and deliveries by geographical region, 1988

(Million Dutch guilders)	Net sales	As % of total	Deliveries	As % of total
Netherlands	3,714	6	17,054	22
Europe (excluding the Netherlands)	30,629	55	36,463	46
USA, Canada	12,457	22	13,109	17
Latin America	3,311	6	3,293	4
Africa	1,084	2	659	(0.1)
Asia	3,945	7	7,211	12
Australia, New Zealand	939	2	931	(0.1)
Total	56,079	100	78,720	100
Inter-company deliveries*			−22,641	
Net sales			56,079	

Source: Philips in 1988
       Eindhoven, 23 February 1989

Note: *Intra-corporate

Table 3.4   Geography of Philips' corporate purchasing for six components in 1982 and 1986 (estimates in percentages)

	1982			1986		
	Europe	US	Far East	Europe	US	Far East
Testing and measuring apparatus	20	50	30	20	30	50
Automated assembly equipment	20	45	35	20	30	50
Semiconductor equipment	4	66	30	1	59	40
Integrated circuits (ICs)	10	40	50	10	30	60
Discrete electronic components	10	45	45	10	35	55
Electro-mechanical components	25	55	20	40	25	35

Source: Fröling and Zoon 1988

in these sources (in particular for semiconductors and ICs). Europe's share in electro-mechanical equipment is rising, as a result of the establishment of Japanese and US outlets in Europe in recent years (Table 3.4).

Philips' inter-company deliveries comprise 29 per cent of all of the firm's deliveries. This entails a stimulus to international trade and a distinct geographical division of labour within the firm. Intra-PD balance of payments has changed tremendously (de Smidt and van der Voorn 1989). In the years ahead intra-Philips deliveries will increase faster, stimulated by increased vertical integration and growing globalization. Components are the main types of delivery responsible for these new imbalances.

In outlining corporate strategy, the avenues of 'back to basics', alliances, and globalization should be traced in the regional analysis. A long-term view is needed in order to explain the resulting locational pattern. In the following section, recent developments will be confronted with the avenues of corporate strategy.

Philips in the Netherlands

The most striking feature in the geographical portrait of Philips is the share of its domestic base, the Netherlands, in deliveries (22 per cent) compared to sales (6 per cent). In the first half of the 1980s, Philips closed down fifty of its 470 factories world-wide (in 1972 there were 550 factories). A further reduction in Europe will occur: from 170 to 100–120 plants in the 1990s (Muntendam 1989). This restructuring will be particularly relevant for the Netherlands, which is over-represented in nearly all PDs and is the host country for overhead facilities. The role of Philips in the Netherlands will be highlighted in this section, focusing on the growth era and re-structuring phases and at the same time pointing out recent joint ventures. Special attention will be given to regional policy issues and labour upgrading in a geographical perspective.

Decentralization in search of labour: a flashback

In the post-war period up to the beginning of the economic crisis (1973), Philips' establishments in the Netherlands quadrupled in terms of number of employees (from 22,000 to 89,000). In the same period the share of Dutch-based operations in Philips world-wide decreased (from 40 to 25 per cent of the firm's total employment). Which tendencies in the period 1945–73 can be traced that are relevant to the latter stage of restructuring?

Until 1945 over 80 per cent of Philips' employees worked in or around Eindhoven, located in the south-east of the country. In 1960 half of the 75,000 employees in the Netherlands worked in Eindhoven, in 1973 just over 41 per cent. A net growth of 27,000 jobs in the 1950s and of 15,000 up to 1973 has been realized outside this main centre. In the 1950s a long-standing migration to Eindhoven continued – providing a growth of 14,000 jobs – but housing shortages prevented further expansion of Philips in this boom town. Instead of 'workers to the work', the new adage was 'work to the workers'. New production units have been established especially in development areas, both in the Netherlands, and the Flemish-speaking regions of Belgium (cf. Tromp 1958; George 1961; Jansen 1972; and Fischer 1980, Figure 3.1).

Regions struck by unemployment due to agricultural expulsion and/or high population growth, acquired forty-eight out of eighty-six new establishments started in the period 1945–73. Figure 3.1 shows the geographical dispersion of Philips by regional policy areas which coincide with the economically deprived areas of the late 1950s, although regional policy has not been targeted to all regions all the time. The prime motive for the regional shift was the search for unskilled and semi-skilled labour. Large manufacturing plants were started in the peripheral north, e.g. Drachten and Stadskanaal. In the 1960s labour reserves near Eindhoven dried up and new sources had to be tapped. Traditionally Dutch married women did not want a job, in contrast to Flemish women, and expansion across the border to Flemish-speaking Belgium followed this labour market.

During the 1960s new opportunities for recruiting labour opened up. In textile regions, such as Twente (east) and Tilburg (south), many plants closed down. The sole Dutch coal mining region of South Limburg could not meet the competition of new energy sources, and all pits were closed as of 1965. The supply of labour with industrial experience could have provided Philips with opportunities for expansion. But it turned out that a new generation of labour in those restructuring areas offered more suitable recruits. Some new large plants in urban centres have been established. Philips was already very active in the Twente region (defence systems).

From 1965 onwards Philips has attempted to restructure itself nation-wide. Small branch plants, employing women in villages, have been closed down for reasons of economies of scale. The locational pattern of Philips has since become more urbanized.

Upgrading and branch plants during a period of growth

Decentralization in the organization of Philips does not imply that the large cities of the Randstad Holland dropped out of the picture. In fact, they became attractive for two labour segments: skilled

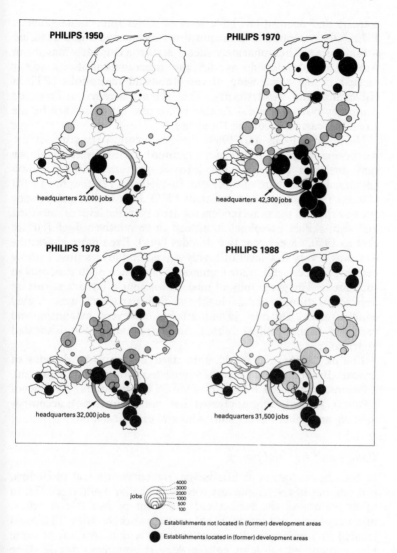

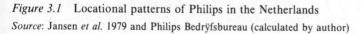

Figure 3.1 Locational patterns of Philips in the Netherlands
Source: Jansen *et al.* 1979 and Philips Bedrÿfsbureau (calculated by author)

males and unskilled girls. The saga of Philips' growth in the Netherlands has largely been a matter of internal growth, and mergers and acquisitions have been of minor importance (Jansen 1972). One exception is the acquisition of Randstad-based qualified subsidiaries. The pharmaceutical sector (Duphar) based in Amsterdam developed, as did the telecommunications sector located in the same wing of the Randstad metropolis (PTI in Hilversum and Amersfoort). The Hague became a base for computer systems, as did Apeldoorn, a new centre chosen for its amenities eastwards of the Randstad.

During the 1950s and 1960s the qualification structure of the work-force employed by Philips changed nationally from 51 per cent unskilled and semi-skilled to 42 per cent. Highly skilled personnel had a share of 5 per cent in 1950 and 12 per cent in 1970 (Jansen 1972; Jansen and de Smidt 1975). Economically depressed regions showed the same tendencies. However, the level of unskilled and semi-skilled personnel continued to be relatively high (80 per cent in 1950, 68 per cent two decades later). Even more characteristic was a very low level of highly skilled employees (just 1 and 4 per cent respectively), quite common for a branch plant economy in such areas. The geography of unskilled labour offered a picture of deconcentration, whereas highly skilled personnel were highly concentrated. Outside headquarters, however, establishments recruited highly skilled labour, in particular in the Randstad metropolis.

Philips has been a world unto itself during these decades of growth. Branch plants were interconnected within separate product divisions, controlled by the Eindhoven headquarters. As Fischer (1980:587) stated, 'Philips created jobs, not a growth pole accompanied by multiplier effects and industrial diversification.'

Philips and regional policy

In the agglomeration of Eindhoven, the corporate seat of Philips, just one out of five employees was a blue-collar worker in 1978, in other regions of the Netherlands, one out of two. Nevertheless, nowadays one out of four blue-collar workers with Philips is located in Eindhoven. But most striking is that two out of three highly qualified (at least college degree) employees reside there (Figure 3.2). These figures could give the impression that outside the headquarters location a low standard of qualification and a low level of tertiarization characterize the status of plants as mere production units.

Is there any tertiarization in plants located in regional policy target areas? The important contribution of Philips to Dutch regional policy in the 1950s and 1960s could be eroded by the

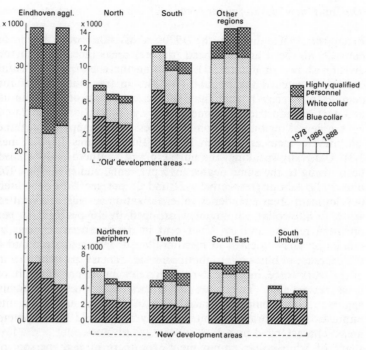

Figure 3.2 legend:
- Highly qualified personnel
- White collar
- Blue collar

1978 1986 1988

(excluding jobs in establishments or joint ventures that have been (partly) dissolved)

Figure 3.2 Number of jobs by segments of labour market in 'old' and 'new' development areas, in Eindhoven agglomeration and in other regions

Source: own research and Philips data

upgrading of the labour supply which does not coincide with an increased demand for more qualified labour in those regions. Furthermore, the position of those branch plants in the PLC (product life cycle) could be undermined by either runaway effects to newly industrializing countries or shortening of PLCs, keeping production nearby higher qualified production centres outside development areas.

These hypotheses should be tested for two typologies of regions, taking a division according to blue- and white-collar labour, as well as highly skilled personnel as a rough yardstick (unfortunately, a division by skill levels could not be made). What has been the impact of restructuring on the geography of Philips in recent years?

Marc de Smidt

'Old' and 'new' development areas

From the 1950s through the 1970s a division could be made between northern and southern problem areas (according to the division shown in Figure 3.1). In the northern periphery, a rural exodus threatened the population base. In the southern regions demographic growth and, later on, restructuring of coal-mining and textile industries in some urban agglomerations stimulated governmental regional economic policies. What happened in these 'old' development areas from 1978 to 1988 (Figures 3.1, 3.2, and 3.3)? Generally speaking, the northern and southern regions have been losing to the same degree (-15 per cent), and even more for blue-collar labour (respectively 21 and 28 per cent). For the 'old' development areas a tendency to tertiarization is weak in a relative sense. White-collar employment dropped by 16 per cent in the northern regions and by 7 per cent in the southern regions. In remaining areas, located in metropolitan or intermediate regions, the decrease in blue-collar labour and the increase in tertiarization of the work-force, in particular the share of higher personnel, have been remarkable. The same tendencies as in the Eindhoven agglomeration could be traced. These findings underline the impression of a branch plant economy in the 'old' development areas, characterized by a high percentage of blue-collar and a low share of white-collar employment. Numbers of high personnel, however, have grown by one-third (increasing from 7.5 to 12 per cent in those regions).

It is questionable if this definition of old development areas is too rough, in view of the 'new' development and restructuring regions emerged in the 1970s inside and outside the 'old' regions. Some 'old' development areas should not be regarded problematic at all (e.g. some North Brabant regions and the south-western port areas).

Taking a 'new' map of problem regions, it turns out that there is a contrast in level as well as dynamics within these areas. On the one side in the northern periphery and the former coal-mining region of South Limburg, a great many blue-collar workers are concentrated (Figures 3.2 and 3.3). Between 1978 and 1988 one out of four blue-collar jobs in the northern periphery and nearly one out of three blue-collar jobs in South Limburg have been lost. In the south-eastern regions and Twente – mostly urbanized industrial restructuring areas – white-collar jobs are relatively strongly represented. In those regions highly qualified plants have been established. Sometimes these plants have a long tradition, e.g. the defence equipment centre at Hengelo (Twente), but recent initiatives may also be mentioned (the Nijmegen megachips centre, a joint venture with Siemens). The decrease in blue-collar jobs has

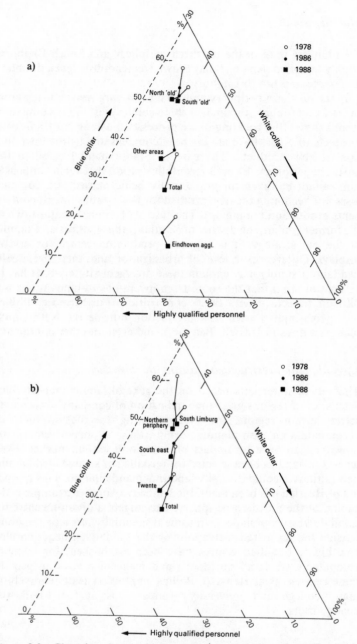

Figure 3.3 Changing shares of labour-market segments in 'old' and 'new' development areas, in Eindhoven agglomeration and in other regions

Source: own research and Philips data

been far less than in the northern periphery and South Limburg. Highly qualified personnel has grown tremendously (even doubling in Twente and South Limburg).

In the northern periphery and South Limburg restructuring area, the PLC problem threatened blue-collar jobs. The company's record shows that trickling-down processes, pushing out traditional products to NICs, have always been compensated by the introduction of new products. The case of Stadskanaal, located in the northern periphery, forms a recent illustration that such compensation cannot be taken for granted (TV being phased out, compact discs not becoming the new product for this establishment; components production remaining). The case of Heerlen, a major town in the former coalmining district of South Limburg, offers an example of the old strategy; it is the new production centre for crystal displays. Differences in level of urbanization and, therefore, qualified labour supply may explain these divergent strategies. It has to be kept in mind that the route from inventions to innovations is a difficult trajectory with fierce competition. Furthermore, Philips has increasingly started new production outside the Netherlands (compact discs in Hasselt, Belgium), and even on other continents.

Upgrading and restructuring during the last decade

Theoretical statements based on the general labour market characteristics of regions give some indication of company's reasons to select certain regions for manufacturing specific products or accommodating non-manufacturing tasks. A major enterprise, however, can have an impact on a region's labour market. Even when a region has been selected for unskilled or semi-skilled labour, new initiatives could diversify labour demand later on. The upgrading of Heerlen has been mentioned already. Another example is the capital of the northern periphery, Groningen, a division centre for small domestic appliances. In some residentially attractive regions, outside the Randstad metropolis or the Eindhoven headquarters, new highly qualified centres have been established, for instance computer systems at Apeldoorn and megachips at Nijmegen. In these centres, as at Hengelo, Philips employs at least relatively as many college and university graduates as at the Eindhoven headquarters.

Reshuffling for strategic reasons

A very complicated selection within the locational pattern has been the result of the company's strategy to concentrate on core activities and to become engaged in strategic alliances. This strategy has exerted a major impact on highly qualified establishments, in particular in the Randstad metropolis. With the exception of these joint ventures and deconsolidations, the qualification level of the few remaining Philips establishments is quite low! Some qualified activities have been preserved at some locations after a reshuffling precipitated by a joint venture. This is the case for the joint-venture APT, in 1984 started as a fifty–fifty partnership of Philips with AT&T in telecommunications (3,781 jobs), recently converted into a 15 per cent share of Philips. A remaining part of the central Hilversum establishment has been related to the Apeldoorn centre (already supervising two locations in peripheral regions). At The Hague professional data systems (software) have been left out and remain under Philips' umbrella. A comparable case is the transfer (in 1980) of Duphar to the Belgian chemical company Solvay, whereby some qualified activities for other electronic equipment were maintained by Philips at Amsterdam. In the figures presented here, joint ventures and deconsolidations are not included.

Product divisions: regional labour market impact

Although the turnover of the matrix from national organizations of Philips to product divisions is a major strategic choice, it is not easy to acquire good insight into the regional impact of product divisions (for a historical account, see Fischer 1980). Officially these figures are not available. In practice there is some difficulty in incorporating figures for some establishments into product divisions due to the fact that a broader range of products is made, cross-fertilizing activities are carried out, or support is given to several product divisions (machinery production). Outside Eindhoven and excluding some establishments for reasons just given, our estimates of the regional impact of product divisions can be summarized as follows.

Lighting is a corporate activity dating back to the early days of regional expansion near the headquarters in the southern and south-western regions. The number of jobs remained rather stable during the recent decade, half of these jobs being blue-collar. Consumer electronics decreased as a production activity and just a few large plants in the south-west are left. Highly qualified activities are growing in the Eindhoven agglomeration in or near division headquarters. Components manufacturing is the most important and stable activity outside Eindhoven (one out of three jobs) and was recently stimulated by the Nijmegen megachip centre. Most of these plants are located in the south-east and South Limburg. The percentage of blue-collar jobs is somewhat lower than for lighting, and highly qualified personnel is better represented. More comparable with lighting is the sector of (small) domestic appliances, manufactured in the peripheral north. There is, however, a difference due to the fact that Groningen is a divisional centre and therefore has a higher level of job qualification. Some products have been taken over by Philips' establishments in NICs (e.g. Singapore).

The most qualified activities are located in Twente (Hengelo) and in some attractive urban centres outside regional policy regions (Apeldoorn, The Hague, Hilversum). Professional instruments and systems are manufactured or developed on these premises. Highly qualified jobs outnumber blue-collar jobs (29 and 22 per cent respectively)! Strategic options like 'back to basics', alliances and globalization have been formulated recently, a longer time horizon for evaluating impacts on a regional scale is needed. 'Low grade' activities will be relocated to NICs and 'high grade' activities will be developed in other firms ('non-core') in Europe, the US or the Far East (alliances and globalization).

Conclusions

Philips is coping with a restructuring process, selecting core activities, and striving to become a global company. Centres of competence supported by centres of excellence are basic elements in this global strategy. National organizations ('local for local') will become of less importance, and product divisions organized on a continental basis will take the lead. There will be a 'Philips tree with the components trunks and consumer electronics, and information technology and communications as the branches', apart from lighting as a separate corporate activity.

Strategic alliances are and will be built up, in particular in the fields of components, informatics, and telecommunications. How vulnerable such an alliance can be is illustrated by the case of AT&T, which seeks European market expansion. APT, the joint venture with Philips, has been rebaptized as AT&T Network Systems International. Philips' minority share per cent will decrease from 40 to 15 if Itatel or Spanish Telefonica become new partners of AT&T. As pointed out above, the economies of scale, shortening of the PLC, and the tremendous R&D costs require the co-operation of major firms.

Globalization means restructuring in a geographical sense. European plants have to close down for reasons of economies of scale and for strategic motives to bring production and market shares into a balance. Apart from the location of the headquarters and major R&D facilities, the Netherlands' share of 22 per cent in deliveries compared to 6 per cent in sales illustrates such an imbalance. It turns out that the number of jobs provided by Philips in this country decreased in the 1980s and recently stabilized (1978:77,470; 1986:69,812; 1988:70,656). Most of these job losses are due to the fact that joint ventures (with AT&T and Dupont de Nemours) or acquisitions by other firms (Duphar) occurred. Reshuffling of jobs between establishments means a selection of locations. Some establishments have lost part of their functions to Philips' subsidiaries in newly industrializing countries or phasing out of the life cycle of the product involved. By not replacing blue-collar jobs, employment is gradually decreasing, but up to now this has been compensated by the growth in white-collar jobs and, almost everywhere, highly qualified personnel. The relative significance of headquarters functions, including product division head offices and R&D laboratories, is growing. At the same time higher qualified production makes it imperative to recruit people with a higher education.

Philips in the Netherlands may be an example of a global corporate firm that is restructuring its domestic base by cutting blue-collar jobs and decreasing white-collar jobs in a leaner organization, but highly qualified tasks will require continual recruitment of highly qualified people. In Europe after 1992 these jobs will be filled not only by Dutchmen.

References

Dekker, W. (1987) 'Leiden in last, nieuwe dimensies van management', inaugural lecture, Leiden University.

Dicken, P. (1986) *Global Shift. Industrial Change in a Turbulent World*, London: Harper & Row.

Fischer, A. (1980) 'L'industrialisation contemporaine des Pays-Bas. Recherche sur l'évolution des régions périphériques', *Sorbonne N.I. Recherches* 41, Paris.

Fröling, A. and Zoon, K. (1988) 'Ruimtelijke Gevolgen van Veranderingen in het Strategisch Management van Philips', Geografisch Instituut (MA thesis), Utrecht.

George, P. (1961) 'L'établissements Philips aux Pays-Bas, une politique de la répartition géographique des usines', *Bulletin d'association des géographes françaises* no. 301-2: 198-205.

Jansen, A. C. M. (1972) 'Enkele aspekten van het ruimtelijk gedrag van grote industriële concerns in Nederland, 1950-1971', *Tijdschrift voor Economische en Sociale Geografie*, 63: 411-25.

Marc de Smidt

Jansen, A. C. M. and De Smidt, M. (1975) *Industrie en Ruimte*, Assen: Van Gorcum.

Muntendam, J. (1989) 'Transnational companies are going global. The case of Philips', *Tijdschrift voor Economische en Sociale Geografie*, 80 (forthcoming).

Ohmae, K. (1985) *Triad Power: The Coming Shape of Global Competition*, New York: Free Press.

Roobeek, A. J. M. (1988) *Een race zonder finish. De rol van de overheid in de technologiewedloop*, Amsterdam: VU uitgeverij.

Smidt, M. de and van der Voorn, A. G. F. J. (1989) 'Philips in the UK', *Area 21*, 2: 145–9.

Smidt, M. de and Wever, E. (1989) *An Industrial Geography of the Netherlands. An International Perspective*, London: Routledge.

Tromp, Th.P. (1958) 'Les usines Philips et la décentralisation industrielle', *Cahiers de Bruges*, 2.

Tulder, R. van and Junne, G. (1988) *European Multinationals in Core Technologies*, London: Wiley.

Chapter four

Standard Elektrik Lorenz
Introducing CAD into
a telecommunications firm:
its impact on labour

Martina Fuchs and Eike Schamp

Introduction

The formation of a new long wave of economic development is currently said to be based on the 'Fifth Kondratieff' (Hall 1985). Long waves of economic and technological development previously needed their own specific infrastructure. Modern telecommunications systems are considered the basic infrastructure of the 'Fifth Kondratieff'. Only by means of modern telecommunications systems can digital transmission-based computers at different locations and workplaces be connected. This connection is termed 'telematics'.

A corporation involved in the creation of the basic infrastructure of a long wave by means of new products may be labelled a high-tech corporation. With its high-tech products, especially its communication systems, the Standard Elektrik Lorenz Company (SEL AG) belongs to the key sector of future industrial development. With a turnover of about 4 billion German marks and approximately 22,000 employees, SEL may be considered a medium-sized West German company. Development expenses within the company totalled 601m. DM, roughly 12.5 per cent of the turnover in 1987. One novelty in the manufacturing of new goods based on microchips is the necessity of a simultaneous organizational change, i.e. a new development of production flow and manufacturing process. Unlike former innovation cycles, where a time-lag existed between product-innovation and process-innovation, necessary investments now have to be made simultaneously. This brings about two results: first, it requires a learning phase in which the new product and process must be mastered, which forces the user to seek advice and support outside of the corporation; and second, it produces a need for financing, which often can only be met by large corporations.

Among the innovations in the field of computer-aided manufacturing processes, computer aided design (CAD) is considered a key technology. Generally high-tech products are highly complex. The expense of the design of such goods rises in relation to the lead time. This is counteracted by the acceleration of the design process with CAD. In addition, the product can be designed more simply by the use of CAD, so that even the lead time of manufacturing can be reduced. Finally, the work steps preceding the manufacture itself are shortened, for example, the making of parts lists and of workshop drawings, as well as inventories for storage and material acquisition. In this case, further opportunities are opened for an information linkage to CAD/CAM.

Industry made its first attempts at introducing CAD in the late 1960s. By now, more than 200 different CAD systems are offered in West Germany. CAD is gradually beginning to succeed in industry, with its first users being the automobile, mechanical, engineering, aerospace, and, especially, the electronics and telecommunications industries.

In the following sections we will analyse the possible consequences of the introduction of CAD into the internal corporate labour market of SEL. At present, there is still great uncertainty about possible job-related effects of CAD in industrialized countries. Ebel and Ulrich (1987:351), for example, remark in their latest report on an eight-country comparison: 'It is too early to try to reach definite conclusions on the subject: experience is still too limited.' Therefore, a very acute need for further experience with the introduction of CAD exists. The geography of enterprise has not yet contributed much to this subject. In their survey Hayter and Watts (1983) showed that nearly all essays are viewed from the management's perspective. Choices of location in a hierarchy of establishments and linkages are in the forefront of examination by the geography of enterprise. Detailed studies of the consequences of technological change on present jobs in multi-plant companies are lacking. Ellegard and Alvstam (1987) made a first step in that direction by analysing the fragmentation of tasks with increasing automation at the Volvo Corporation. Below we will show that the introduction of computers into design can also lead to other types of rationalization. What effects will this have on jobs? Furthermore, Massey and Meegan (1982) discussed the consequences of investments on technological change in companies. In relation to our study, theirs is limited to the quantitative aspects of job losses, which are largely connected with a change of location pattern. In this study we want to demonstrate how jobs within an existing location pattern change with the introduction of a new key-technology to a new generation of corporate structures. Even this study can examine only a fraction of the possible consequences of technological alteration on jobs. This appears to justify even more a geography of enterprise from the perspective of labour.

Internal corporate labour market and technological change

Among the different theories of the labour market (de Smidt 1987) the conception of a segmented labour market appears best to describe the reality within a large corporation. The functional segmentation creates two labour markets. These differ in qualification requirements, job safety, and level of wages. In the primary segment, higher requirements are directed to the formal qualification of employees, and the employees are rewarded with greater job safety and higher income. In the secondary segment, so-called 'everybody' qualifications are demanded; this segment is connected with uncertain employment and low wages. The division into primary and secondary segments results from the asymmetrical distribution of power on the labour market, which in the capitalistic system exists between the owners of the means of production and the dependent employees. The owners of the means of production maximize their profits by dividing their staff and playing the segments against one another. This cuts the wage costs. If competition between the two segments arises, the secondary segment will lose (Offe and Hinrichs 1977).

The locational segmentation can be derived from the different working conditions in corporate functions. The main functions are dominated by primary activities such as central management, R&D, design, and manufacture of high-quality products. One or more main locations of a corporation can thus be identified. Secondary activities dominate in the peripheral functions of the corporation, especially in manufacturing low-quality products, mass production or subcontracting (Buttler, Gerlach, and Liepmann 1977:118). This defines the peripheral locations of a corporation.

To some extent, these ideas of a corporate labour market are static. Indeed, the concept must take economic and technological change into consideration (de Smidt 1987:5). This is what our case study of the introduction of CAD into SEL tries to achieve. As design is one of the core activities of an industrial corporation, the introduction of CAD directly affects the primary segment of the corporate labour market. If and how the secondary segment of employees is changed by CAD must also be examined.

The introduction of CAD is an important element of an

overlapping corporation strategy, which Baethge and Oberbeck (1986:22) characterize as 'systemic rationalization'. The characteristic of systemic rationalization is the restructuring of the entire manufacturing process instead of the automation of single sectors of the process. To achieve this in one movement of rationalization, corporations are combining operative and administrative functions simultaneously with computer networks. These computer networks are supposed to improve the flow of material and data. In some corporations, these measures reach a new quality of rationalization, which Kern and Schumann (1984:19, 317) call 'new production conceptions'. Until now, rationalization has pursued the Tayloristic principle of increasing labour division followed by a minimization of human labour. Yet important potential productivity is wasted by applying these principles today. For this reason, a new form of rationalization is developing. With these new production conceptions the management is trying to develop productivity by using human labour more efficiently by integrating tasks and further qualifications. The direct and indirect effects of CAD on staff segments opened up a field of analysis where the process of change has not yet been completed. Various tendencies are visible. In order to evaluate the probability of occurrence for each, we interviewed experts, managers, and staff representatives, as well as employees already working with the new technologies. These interviews were supplemented by observations at the workplace.

The telecommunications market

The scope of action of a telecommunications corporation is determined primarily by the following parameters: the markets change fast, the markets are regionally segmented, and they are governed by only a few competitors, i.e. there is an oligopoly.

The telecommunications industry is commonly characterized as one of the most dynamic industries. Production in this sector grows annually by approximately 8 per cent. Between 1978 and 1984, the world-wide export growth averaged 11.3 per cent (Hess 1988:17). This growth is connected to a strong innovative push from electromechanics to digital technology. Therefore, a structural change takes place on the supply as well as the demand side. The use of electronics makes communication and data processing possible, but at the same time requires their synthesis. The suppliers are forced to increase expenditure for innovation. In the past many corporations have tried to develop digital telecommunication exchange systems. Some failed because of the duration and the high cost of development. In 1983, Switzerland, for example, discon-

Table 4.1 Market sharing by some large suppliers of digital exchange systems in Europe

Country	Company	System	%
W Germany	Siemens	EWS-D	60
	ITT (SEL)	System 12	40
France	CIT-Alcatel, Thomson	E10, E12	84
	CGCT (1987: Ericsson)	Axe	16
UK	Plessey, GEC	System X	100
Sweden	Ericsson	Axe	100
Spain	ITT	System 12	70
	Ericsson	Axe	30

Source: Dang Nguyen 1985:97

tinued its development after fourteen years and an expenditure of 300m. SF. The Swiss postal system now uses devices made by Siemens, SEL, and Ericsson. As a matter of fact, the present digital exchange systems cost between $US0.5 and $1.4bn for research and development (Dang Nguyen 1985:108).

The high expenditures create pressure to sell great quantities, yet this is complicated by the strong regionalism of the markets. Most private and public postal corporations have a monopoly within their territory and have developed terms of purchase with national telecommunications corporations over a long period of time. This is shown in Table 4.1.

Telecommunications corporations can, on the one hand, try to lower the costs of production. On the other hand, they have to try to win new markets through co-operation and merger. Both strategies need capital. Actually, probably only half of the now-existing important world-wide telecommunications corporations can survive. An intensification of the world-wide oligopoly is beginning to appear. Among the European telecommunications corporations a concentration by means of take-overs can presently be observed. In 1989, Siemens, for instance, is trying to take over Plessey in Great Britain and Italtel in Italy. The Swedish corporation Ericsson took over the French CGCT in 1987. As early as 1988, financial instability forced the corporation to sell its computer and office equipment sectors. Consequently the principal strategies are both internationalization and concentration on core capacities, i.e. on particular manufacturing processes and products which embody the special expertise of the firm.

Standard-Elektrik Lorenz (SEL)

The German firm SEL is affected by similar corporate strategies. The SEL company resulted from a fusion of the Mix and Genest GmbH, which belongs to the American ITT Corporation, and Lorenz AG in Stuttgart in 1958. The new company was active in three sectors: communications technology with headquarters in Stuttgart; entertainment electronics with headquarters in Pforzheim, and component manufacture with headquarters in Nuremberg. SEL was not the market leader in any of these three sectors. In the 1970s, the entertainment electronics section was already suffering considerable losses, but up until 1986 only few plants had been sold or closed down. Figure 4.1 shows the development of the corporate location pattern in West Germany between 1977 and 1988.

The company tried to take a leading position in all three sectors. SEL played a significant role in the world-wide development of the digital exchange system 'System 12' within the ITT Corporation. However, the system was not sold in the USA as originally planned. Financial difficulties induced the ITT Corporation to yield all communicational activities in Europe, including SEL, to a joint venture with the French corporation CGE, called Alcatel SA in 1986. ITT renounced its majority in this new corporation. SEL lost the extensive corporate freedom of decision it had under ITT. This take-over enabled the French corporation to gain a foothold in the German and other European markets. Today Alcatel is the largest European supplier of telecommunications systems. A manufacturing reorganization and co-ordination is advisable, because the two exchange systems offered by the new corporation are fundamentally different. Actually, the company is aiming at the manufacture of the same components and the same software. The competition of two systems within the new company may become pronounced with the development of a European internal market.

The new owner of SEL immediately enforced a strategy of rationalization and modernization. In 1987, the entertainment electronics division, which was running at a loss, was sold to the Finnish corporation Nokia. Two thousand jobs were lost due to rationalization in the remaining plants: the production of components in Nuremberg was concentrated from three plants into one. Even in 1987 the organizational structure of the company was

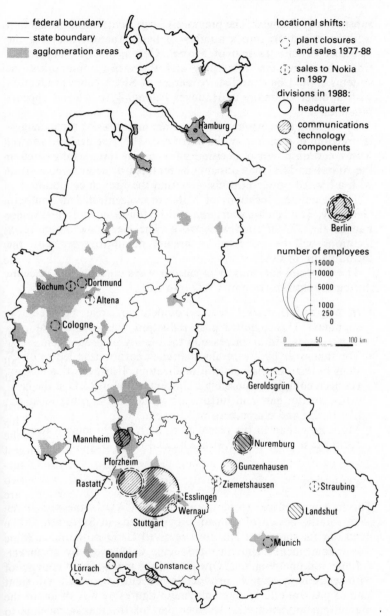

Figure 4.1 Development of the location pattern of SEL in West Germany, 1977–88

substantially changed. The previously large divisions of production were branched off into a number of fields, thereby adapting the structure of SEL to that of Alcatel. Currently SEL's separation from the computer technology and the office communications systems should be expected. A merger of SEL's cable production with another company in Hanover belonging to Alcatel appears possible.

By limiting the corporation to certain major tasks, the managerial freedom of decision will be narrowed. The decentralized control with a certain power of decision on company level, as it existed in the American ITT, may possibly be replaced by centralized control with a limited power of decision within the French corporation.

The remaining locations of SEL are concentrated in southern Germany. The headquarters can still be found in Stuttgart, where half of the 22,800 employees work. The hierarchic structure of locations will be discussed in greater detail together with the introduction of CAD.

The environment, thus, is in various ways unstable and insecure during the introduction of CAD into SEL.

- In a growing market severe competition exists between few suppliers. This requires cost reduction with the aid of new technologies and an increase in the quality of production.
- The take-over by a centralized French corporation led to quick steps in restructuring and rationalization. However, this has not yet been completed; possibly a concentration of R&D at the head office in Stuttgart and further job reductions at other locations like Berlin and Nuremberg will follow.
- More now than in the recent past, SEL will become a regional multi-plant corporation with a limited range of products.

CAD in SEL

The first workplaces to be installed with CAD in the mid-1970s were for the design of printed circuit boards in Stuttgart. Other departments and other locations received CAD in the mid-1980s. The management's aims in introducing CAD were by no means definite and unambiguous. One part of the management concerned with technology expects product improvements, which will then lead to positive effects on employment figures by way of improved marketing opportunities. Another part of the management concerned with business expects CAD to reduce employment. The accountancy department only approves of investments in new technologies if this will lead to a decrease in manpower.

Furthermore, differences emerge between the goals of central management in Stuttgart and management at other locations. Although the common aim is to reduce the lead time by introducing CAD, this goal must be implemented by the various sectors. Central management in Stuttgart would like to optimize the production process in the entire company, whereas most of the management at other locations seeks a reduction in the lead time only for their own establishment. Managers of the other sub-centres form an exception: they would like to promote computer-aided integration in various sectors of the company by use of CAD together with the central management in Stuttgart. Firstly, an integration of CAD into other technological innovations at local level is pursued, e.g. CAD in conjunction with computer-aided manufacturing (CAM), computer-aided planning (CAP) and computer-aided quality control (CAQ). And secondly, the linkage between individual locations is sought. In practice, this means a computer-aided integration corresponding to the term 'systemic rationalization' used by Baethge and Oberbeck (1986).

Corresponding to the respective goals, four methods of introducing CAD emerge at the various locations. The criteria for differentiation can be found, first, in the level and further growth of computer-aided integration, and, second, in the level and growth of CAD. In our case study, the level and further growth are related: a low level is accompanied by a small growth, and vice versa. At the central locations (Stuttgart, Nuremberg, Pforzheim and Mannheim) level and growth of both computer-aided integration and use of CAD are quite high. In Constance and Gunzenhausen, computer-aided integration is strongly established, but the use of CAD is small and limited to a few processing sections, or not present at all. Yet in Landshut, Hamburg, and Berlin, CAD is significant; computer-aided integration, on the other hand, has no importance. In Wernau and Bonndorf (Black Forest), computer-aided integration exists at a low level, and CAD does not even exist.

It is remarkable that the first-mentioned method, which involves computer-aided integration and CAD, is characterized by a high level of centralization (i.e. strong power of decision) and by modernized machinery. Stuttgart is the location with the highest degree of centralization, being SEL's headquarters as well as the head office of the division of communications technology. Other locations have to survive with older production technologies or in markets with very strong competition (Figure 4.2).

Nuremberg, Pforzheim and Mannheim do not belong to such peripheral locations; they are sub-centres. The head office of the components division is located in Nuremberg. Mannheim is in a

Martina Fuchs and Eike W. Schamp

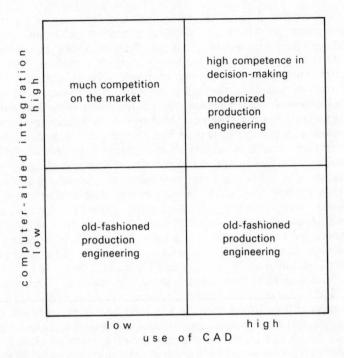

Figure 4.2 Typology of the SEL locations after use of CAD and computer-aided integration

strong position because of its concentration on military production. These sub-centres and the Stuttgart centre possess the following four characteristics:

- products of digital technology are manufactured with digitally controlled machinery;
- wage costs form only a small percentage of overall costs; for the most part, less than 3 per cent;
- technical organizational innovations have been made, including the introduction of systems for control and production engineering, computer-aided information systems for transferring quality data from all phases of manufacturing into planning as well as data records;
- an intra-locational linkage system between individual departments for development and design within the corporation has been introduced (Figure 4.3).

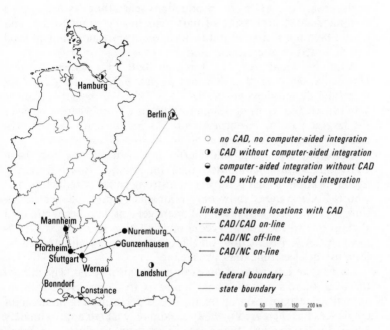

Figure 4.3   Location-combining computer integration of SEL, 1988

As a site, Constance represents the method of using computer-aided integration, but without a significant use of CAD. Although processing technologies have been modernized, the investment in CAD is limited by insufficient freedom for action. The location of Constance, although legally independent, is connected by a 100 per cent capital link with SEL. The concerted pressure by central management for a short-term improvement of balance has increased the willingness of the local management in Constance to take immediate steps to improve efficiency.

With its relatively mono-structured production of 'personal systems' (multi-applicable personal computers) the local company has to operate within markets with severe price competition. The management's policy is not oriented towards an increase in the range of products by means of innovation, but towards a decrease in development capacities. The number of jobs in development and design is being reduced, and previously intended investments in CAD did not take place, whereas the computer-aided integration outside development and design is promoted. In industrial

87

engineering, a system of production scheduling as well as a computer-aided processing of parts lists has been put to use, and from 1989 on a system of data collection at the establishment level will be tested in a feasibility study.

Another example of this method is Gunzenhausen. Gunzenhausen, however, does not possess either its own development and design department or CAD. Like Wernau, this plant is subordinated in terms of design to Stuttgart, from where it receives the largest part of its information. As in Stuttgart, labour productivity and level of integration are high in Gunzenhausen.

Landshut, Hamburg, and Berlin represent the method using CAD but without computer-aided integration. Apart from the Berlin location, which is subject to a strong capacity reduction and whose CAD systems show only remnants of previous centralization, by this method the local management has been enlarged slightly due to the positive economic situation and to new investment in CAD. Production, on the other hand, is characterized by little use of electronic data processing.

Let us take Landshut as an example of this method. The annual turnover of this establishment amounts to 120m. DM, with an annual net capital gain of up to 5 to 6 per cent. The number of employees has increased from approximately 800 to approximately 1,000 during the last two years. The main products are small engines and ventilators for use in e.g. hot-air ovens, gas-heating and office equipment; only primary products are manufactured in Landshut. The production is oriented towards the customer: products will be redesigned completely according to the requirements of the customers. Considering an average daily output of 30,000 units, the predominant batch sizes of a few hundred or even a few thousand units are small. In Landshut, a flexible production based upon conventional technology prevails; the only effort towards integration concerns the projected system for production planning. Above all, the CAD systems serve to generate sketches; they do not serve interconnection.

In Wernau and in Bonndorf we find the method with neither computer-aided integration nor use of CAD. The site in Wernau produces mostly coils and other wound goods. Because it is merely a removed manufacturing section, this plant depends on the Stuttgart site. The establishment in Bonndorf belongs to the motor-producing section of the components division, like the one in Landshut. The orientation towards customers' requirements is even stronger in Bonndorf, and some very specific designs are executed. The number of repeated parts is an important factor of profitability in the use of computers for drawing. However, this number is so small at Bonndorf, that the management rejected the introduction of CAD in spite of its financial advantages.

As we can see, the organizational structure of centre and periphery determines the use of CAD. Depending on the level of centralization and modernization, which differs even within a 'high-tech' corporation, the use of CAD and its contribution to computer-aided integration varies. Viewed in a spatial perspective, the concentration on Stuttgart, Nuremberg, Mannheim, and Pforzheim proves to be a continuation of the central management's general location policy to keep and promote modernized, efficient production of investment goods in southern Germany.

Effects on labour

The introduction of CAD shows immediate effects on the quality of work in development and design. Despite the relatively short time span that has elapsed since the introduction of CAD, these changes can be assessed at least roughly. But we should also ask what significance the current change will have in the long term.

The indirect effects on other functional sectors of the firm and locations will increase significantly in the course of extended computer-aided integration. But the measurement of those effects is much more complicated. For one thing, these effects will become apparent in the entire company with a 'time-lag', and CAD is simply too young a system for its users to foresee its exact consequences. And then, the relation between specific causes and indirect effects in the study of effectiveness has always proved to be a fundamentally problematic question.

Immediate effects

The introduction of CAD does not always mark a technological leap from the drawing-board to CAD. It may also play a part in a long-term process of change of employment and job profiles, as is the case in Stuttgart. There, technological change set in early and resulted in restructuring the development and design departments even before the introduction of CAD.

In the SEL company, development and design are split up into four sections:

- the development of software: here the CAD software is designed;
- the design of printed circuit boards: here the layout for electronic circuits and their connections is created;

89

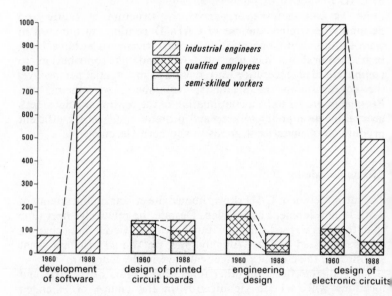

Figure 4.4 Change in employment categories in development and design according to the level of education

- the engineering design: here the encasement and all other parts of the appliances are designed;
- the design of electronic circuits.

Between 1960 and 1988 there was a significant relative and absolute decrease in the number of semi-skilled workers and qualified personnel working in the design of printed circuit boards, the engineering design, and the design of electronic circuits (Figure 4.4). There was an increase in the relative and absolute number of industrial engineers (with university degrees) who design printed circuit boards; in engineering design, only their relative number increased. Only in the design of electronic circuits, which was diminished to half the number of its former employees, did the number of industrial engineers decline absolutely, although they maintained their high quota of 90 per cent. With no exception, only industrial engineers are working on the development of software, and their number has risen ten-fold in this period.

Such shifts must be attributed to changing work profiles. The gradual change will be explained with an example from the design of printed circuit boards. Well into the 1960s the employees still drew the printed circuit boards with pen and ink. Laboratory assistants made high-contrast photographs of these sketches, which were then used to produce slides. Few industrial engineers but many technical designers were employed. Some had been trained as technicians, but most were only semi-skilled.

Since the mid-1960s, an adhesive technique has been applied: the designers stuck the circuits and solder points on paper with adhesive tape and rings. Afterwards, these collages were photographed as slides. For this task, SEL continued to employ semi-skilled workers to a large extent. For the most part, SEL hired additional female foreign workers, as the wage costs for this group were relatively low.

The adhesive technique had a high susceptibility to error; sometimes the glued-on elements would fall off unnoticed. Therefore, in the mid-1970s the transition to digital methods was made. By putting pressure on certain points of the co-ordinate system of the digitizer the designer would put the data in; it was then transferred to a light drawing device by means of punched tapes. The employees were able to read the symbols of the punched tapes and to correct errors. Fewer semi-skilled workers were needed to perform this task, which required qualified personnel instead.

Higher resolution monitors and greater precision became more and more necessary. In the 1970s, SEL introduced the first CAD system, but because of the intricate application the effects on employment figures remained small. This changed only when SEL started to use more efficient systems in the individual departments on a decentralized basis. Above all, the semi-skilled workers disappeared; the qualified workers were able to qualify themselves further and possibly advance to the position of designers-by-trade.

With the implementation of new CAD systems since the mid-1980s, especially for overall integration, many qualified workers were no longer able to perform the necessary tasks. The chosen systems and most of the tasks demanded university graduates. When hiring new personnel, SEL preferred applicants with university degrees. The new systems opened up a whole range of procedural methods for users and could therefore be considered as promoting learning. This was primarily an advantage for university graduates with some knowledge of data processing.

In the corporate centre semi-skilled workers disappeared first, due to the innovations in processing. Currently, the job requirements even surpass the abilities of many qualified workers, and especially older employees are being forced out of work. To begin with, the development bore negative effects primarily on the secondary segment. Along with this, the percentage of industrial engineering jobs increased. Since the work load will become less after a few adjustment difficulties, the number of jobs in some departments of development and design is already decreasing. Here CAD does not only compensate for a theoretically required number of new jobs. For even beyond such fictitious staff reductions, some real reductions have to be attributed to the introduction of CAD.

Contrary to the situation in Stuttgart, with its gradual change, in all other locations introducing CAD the substitution of drawing-boards by CAD systems came about as a technological leap. In general, we can distinguish two phases. During the first phase, a number of technical problems will occur, and the employees have to deal with a high additional work load due to adjustment. No rationalization effects will occur during this 'learning phase'. These effects only begin to produce results with the routine use of the new production devices (Wildemann 1986:344). Except for Stuttgart, CAD was introduced to all sites in the mid-1980s, and therefore these sites are still in the 'learning phase'. Effects on quantity or even shifts in employment categories can therefore not be found yet at these sites. Nevertheless, a major change in the task requirements is taking place, which both primary and secondary segments have to master. The employees are required to adapt to sudden changes in working conditions; thereby the peripheral role of work on these sites becomes quite clear.

What are the specific consequences that followed the technological leap in development and design? The employee no longer has the entire sketch in view, but instead only sees the sections specifically called-up on the monitor. He has to imagine this section fitting into the context abstractly. The employees used to work with pen, ink, and ruler, whereas they now have to deal with an input device (mouse, puck) and a keyboard similar to a typewriter's. Using the conventional technique, they were able to develop their object step by step starting off from the centre line. They now have to visualize the entire object right from the start when working with CAD and then imagine the procedure leading towards the final drawing.

Working with systems giving representations of appliances and their mechanical components in three dimensions is even more difficult when using CAD. The individual views in two dimensions can no longer be separately designed, but instead all three dimensions have to be taken into consideration simultaneously. By linking CAD systems to actual manufacturing, this task requires more knowledge of the production procedures. Last but not least, insufficient knowledge of the English language poses a serious problem. As usual, the manuals are written in English. In addition, working with CAD itself requires a comprehensive knowledge of English, especially when using the system for representations in three dimensions, which has just been brought onto the market. If, for example, a line is to be drawn with one of these new CAD systems, the command is 'lbp' ('line between points'). For employees with little knowledge of English this abbreviation makes no sense, and they simply have to memorize the term – like a great many others – without understanding it.

The gap between the corporate centre and peripheral locations is also manifest in training sessions. With the exception of Stuttgart, training will take place at the workplace itself or in an adjoining room. In groups or alone, participants selected by their department head will be trained – this training will generally be shorter than in Stuttgart. Their subject is limited to a short instruction in better use of the new tool for specific procedures. In Stuttgart, however, participants will be trained in a separate building, since they come from various sections in development and design. Because of the spatial division between training and workplace, disturbances caused by work processes can be avoided. The heterogeneous structure of the course promotes exchange of experience between departments and simplifies co-ordinated work processes. These courses not only take more time but give more detailed information. For example, they discuss problematic aspects of data protection, the integration of the new CAD system into other electronic data processing within the company, the level of extension, and future aims in the use of CAD. This makes it easier for employees to understand the overall production process more clearly and enables them to deal better with future technological changes. Primary and secondary segments therefore profit more from extended training measures in Stuttgart than in other locations. Such restructuring of qualifications corresponds to the 'new production conceptions' described by Kern and Schumann (1984).

Indirect effects

The indirect effects of introducing CAD are mainly visible in Stuttgart, but to some extent also in other sites that introduced computer-aided integration along with CAD. In Stuttgart, some sections directly related to development and design have disappeared, such as the photo laboratory and blueprint department.

At present, digital records are being assembled; thus, conventional documentary functions are becoming superfluous. In Stuttgart, and to some extent in Pforzheim, Nuremberg, and Mannheim, effects on model construction and manufacturing of samples should follow. A decrease in the need for models and manufacturing samples seems possible, especially because of the improved vivid graphic simulation in the new systems. All of these sections at the locations with computer-aided integration demand qualified personnel.

The connection between the different developmental departments using CAD is still too new to show results. One possible outcome should be the effect of rationalization on various developmental departments. This occurs less at the company level than at the corporate level, where the integration within the Alcatel union has only just begun.

With regard to the interconnection on location level at sites using this method of introduction, the linkage of CAD and CAM was predominant. Above all, the future should bring about the integration of quality control, assembly, and distribution. The flow of material and information from supplier to customer should be computer-aided. Stuttgart is holding a leading position at present and is currently developing a 'factory 2000' for printed circuit boards.

Effects of the existing CAD/CAM linkage can already be observed in the additional qualification requirements and training. Quantitative changes and social restructuring are influenced by changes preceding the introduction of CAD/CAM. For example, the shift from electro-mechanics to digital products and production methods was accompanied in Stuttgart by standardization, miniaturization, and combination of individual work steps. This also entailed a reduction in jobs, especially for foreign female workers with lower qualifications.

Not only does the secondary segment of the labour market suffer negative effects, but to some extent also the primary segment suffers, particularly as far as qualifications are concerned.

Changes corresponding to the 'new production conceptions' described by Kern and Schumann (1984) are manifest in Stuttgart in their indirect as well as immediate effects. For the first time in SEL, semi-skilled female workers in manufacturing will be given training that is more detailed than 'on the job' instruction. The flexibility in the employment of staff will thereby increase by the formation of three groups of female workers: one group will still be instructed specifically for their task, the second should also be able to work in procedures closely related to the tasks they were trained for, and the third group can be employed both in closely and remotely related tasks.

Immediate changes connected with CAD/CAM have also confronted the qualified personnel. On the shop floor, the foremen need more comprehensive knowledge of data processing than before, as does the personnel who set up machines; in addition their knowledge needs to apply to checking for and repairing defects. The production engineers' knowledge of machines may decrease, whereas their critical use of electronic data as well as their overall view of the entire production process must increase. While the employees in industrial engineering often used to advance from manufacturing, this has now become extremely difficult since they seldom possess sufficient knowledge of data processing. Their experience cannot always compensate for this lack of knowledge.

As we can see, the centre-periphery structure of the organization corresponds only partially to the effects of CAD on employment categories and job profiles at the various sites. The differentiation of job categories and work profiles occurs at locations that have implemented computer-aided integration and CAD. Differences can be explained by the dominant influence of the Stuttgart location, where changes began early.

An evaluation of both direct and indirect effects in Stuttgart should take into account the rationalization measures already executed, from which primarily the secondary segment of the internal labour market has suffered. After the learning phase, real job reductions in the company's centre have already affected the primary and secondary segments. Especially qualified workers lose their status to some extent; there is a tendency for this group of employees to descend into the secondary segment. Rationalization effects at other locations will surely entail a further expansion of this pattern of segmentation. Concerning their qualifications, the employees of both segments in Stuttgart can profit from formulating measures that correspond to the 'new production conceptions'. The diffusion of such conceptions and measures into the other company locations is probably impeded by the narrow financial scope of these locations. Therefore, in this multi-plant company a segmentation into locations with a traditional Tayloristic and systemic rationalization has taken place. Only in the corporate centre have 'new production conceptions' been realized.

Feedback from employees and their representatives

The dependent employees cannot simply be considered passive objects afflicted by technological change. They are individually and

95

collectively active subjects as well. Their action radius is circumscribed to a large extent by institutions. In West Germany, for example, the Works Constitution Act, the decisive legal framework, is supplemented by collective agreements after negotiations between employers' associations and trade unions. These form the basis for negotiations on a company level, which will be enforced as basic agreements for the entire company or as individual agreements for specific locations.

First, we will discuss the reactions to the direct effects; these are of a similar nature at all sites. First of all, the employees will react individually either in a defensive way – e.g. some employees will simply continue to work with the drawing-boards – or in an offensive way to improve the individual working conditions, e.g. by participating in user groups. In these user groups, established by executives in order to increase the acceptance of the new technology, work-related technical problems in the use of CAD are discussed. Reactions tend to be of a more defensive nature in the secondary and of more offensive nature in the primary segment.

Second, collective reactions will occur. Staff representatives stand for the interests of both segments. Particularly when discussing the equipment of the workplace – e.g. furniture adapted to the human body – or the development of software – e.g. setting a time frame for the appearance of the next mask – the works council's demands may be met to a large extent, because these demands run more or less parallel to the interests of management. Management seeks an increase in job performance. Questions of working hours cause more conflicts. Management of other corporations have succeeded in introducing shift work in development and design along with CAD, but the SEL management has not. It proved even more difficult for the works council to achieve regulations against supervision and, above all, to control the observance of these regulations. Regarding this, the following agreement was made: the works council may execute random samples to check if performance and behaviour are being monitored via data processing.

The biggest problem with CAD is its function in computer-aided integration and therefore its indirect effects. It is exactly here that the legal foundation provides a weak basis for representing interests. The Works Constitution Act prescribes that management only has to inform the works council if new technologies are being introduced. Opportunities for workers' participation exist only if the introduction of new technologies result in a restructuring on the whole plant level. And even the duty to inform is generally interpreted in a limited way by management, as occurred at SEL.

Although from a legal standpoint management has to inform the workers of its intention itself, the works council received a number of important details only after inquiry. In order to be able to intervene, the workers have to give evidence of decisions made previously, and this often proves difficult.

The question of effective inter-locational policies of the works council concerning systemic rationalization, however, has not yet been solved. If at location A a technology is introduced that also concerns location B, neither the works council A nor the works council B has the right to intervene in relation to its effects on B. This drawback can only be compensated to a limited extent by basic agreements, because these documents are formulated in general terms and rarely cover the specific case.

Therefore, the dependent employees and their representatives are confronted with two problems. First, a segmentation exists between the various company locations; the various rationalization grades, requiring different procedures, correspond to these segments. Second, concerning this new type of rationalization currently being developed, regulations are lacking, in particular those covering inter-locational, indirect effects.

Conclusion

The case study provided a detailed demonstration that some of the conceptions used in industrial geography and labour market research have to be differentiated. The conception of locational hierarchy of sites or the conceptions of spatial division of labour in a multi-plant corporation, for example, are sufficient to explain the different strategies applied in the introduction of CAD. However, they are not sufficient to explain the direct and indirect effects of the introduction of CAD on the jobs of primary and secondary segments. In addition, the conception of a dual labour market itself needs further revision, since a segmentation of the locations into central locations with systemic rationalization and peripheral locations with Tayloristic rationalization can be observed. Within the group with systemic rationalization, the dividing lines in social differentiation change, as seen in the loss of status for qualified workers. Exclusively in the company centre in Stuttgart, not in sub-centres, some advantages related to additional training can be found for employees in the shape of 'new production conceptions'.

We should discern whether the formation of a new rationalization phase accompanying the 'Fifth Kondratieff', characterized by a change of the segmentation patterns in the corporate structure and internal labour market, is actually a typical phenomenon. If so, then the question arises about the connection between the internal processes and what happens on the regional labour market. In this case study we merely considered the job market within SEL. It seems possible that employees negatively affected by the introduction of a new technology will find an opportunity to avoid such negative effects on their respective regional labour markets. Yet this opportunity does not exist in peripheral regions with a high level of unemployment. However, what is the situation of dependent employees in regions with high economic growth? The region around Stuttgart, with the centre of SEL, is currently considered a prospering region with a low level of unemployment. More recent studies about the future perspectives of the labour market in Stuttgart, however, predict a growing deterioration of this situation, both by capacity reduction along with already implemented modernization, and by rationalization along with neglected modernization (Richter et al. 1988). The effects of the introduction of CAD within the company may currently hold no significance for the local labour market in Stuttgart, but this may still change.

References

Baethge, M. and Oberbeck, H. (1986) *Die Zukunft der Angestellten: neue Technologien und berufliche Perspektiven in Büro und Verwaltung*, Frankfurt/Main: Campus.

Buttler, F., Gerlach, K. and Liepmann, P. (1977) *Grundlagen der Regionalökonomie*, Reinbek bei Hamburg: Rowohlt.

Dang Nguyen, G. (1985) 'Telecommunications: a challenge to the old order, in M. Sharp (ed.) *Europe and New Technologies. Six Case Studies in Innovation and Adjustment*, London: Pinter.

Ebel, K. H. and Ulrich, E. (1987) 'Some workplace effects of CAD and CAM', *International Labour Review* 126: 351–70.

Ellegard, K. and Alvstam, C. (1987) 'People – Production – International Division of Labour', in F. E. I. Hamilton (ed.) *Industrial Change in Advanced Economies*, London: Croom Helm: 23–44.

Hall, P. (1985) 'The geography of the Fifth Kondratieff', in P. Hall (ed.) *Silicon Landscapes*, Boston, London, Sydney: Allen & Unwin: 1–19.

Handelsblatt, different articles.

Hayter, R. and Watts, H. D. (1983) 'The geography of enterprise: a reappraisal', in *Progress in Human Geography* 7: 157–81.

Hess, K. P. (1988) 'Ein Markt im Wandel: Die Telekommunikation', *Technology and Management* 1, 1988: 12–22.

Kern, H. and Schumann, S. (1984) *Das Ende der Arbeitsteilung? Rationalisierung in der industriellen Produktion: Bestandsaufnahme, Trendbestimmung*, München: Beck.

Massey, D. and Meegan, R. (1982) *The Anatomy of Job Loss: The How, Why and Where of Employment Decline*, London: Methuen.

Offe, C. and Hinrichs, K. (1977) 'Sozialökonomie des Arbeitsmarktes und die Lage "benachteiligter" Gruppen von Arbeitnehmern', in C. Offe (ed.) *Projekt Arbeitsmarktpolitik*, Neuwied, Darmstadt: Luchterhand: 3–61.

Richter, G. et al. (1988) *Stuttgart - Problemregion der 90er Jahre?* München (=IMU-Institut für Medienforschung und Urbanistik, Studien 7).

Smidt, M. de (1987) 'A taxonomy of labour market theories - geographical perspectives', paper presented at the Rabka Conference, IGU Commission on Industrial Change.

SEL - company reports.

Wildemann, H. (1986) 'Einführungsstrategien für neue Produktionstechnologien - dargestellt an CAD/CAM-Systemen und Flexiblen Fertigungssystemen', *Zeitschrift für Betriebswirtschaft* 56, 1986, 4/5: 337–69.

Wirtschaftswoche, different articles.

Chapter five

Goodman Fielder Wattie
Good Food World-wide?
Internationalization and performance

Richard Le Heron

Introduction

Several antipodean companies, amongst them Goodman Fielder Wattie Ltd (hereafter GFW), are ranked in the Fortune 500 list of world multinational corporations (MNCs). GFW recently attracted international attention in 1988 when it launched a £3.2m. take-over bid for Rank Hovis McDougall (RHM), a British-based food conglomerate. Ten years earlier the companies now merged under the GFW label were modest enterprises, operating mainly in Australia (Fielder and Allied Mills), and New Zealand (Goodman Group Ltd and Wattie Industries Ltd). The internationalization of the companies and the accompanying geography of restructuring form the subject of this chapter.

The chapter argues that a geography of enterprise perspective can be more fully developed from a deeper understanding of the internationalization and regulation of capital. Internationalization is defined as the tendency of capital to attain the global level in (1) sale of output (2) source of finance (3) location and organization of production. Internationalization as a phenomenon is poorly covered in the literature. And yet, one pathway to giving added coherence to geographers' efforts in the enterprise field is to attempt an integration of internationalization into the geography of enterprise theme. This chapter tentatively starts on this route. The evolution of GFW is used as a vehicle to discuss deficiencies in approaches to the geography of enterprise and to sketch a preliminary framework for studying the emergence of capitalist organizations and their geography. The account of GFW is by no means comprehensive and is biased towards New Zealand sources. Nevertheless as an example of internationalization GFW has special value because it illustrates that internationalization as a general process is expressed at the concrete level in many ways, including apparently 'counter-directional' geographies of corporate evolution from 'semi-peripheral' to 'core' industrial economies.

Framework

The geography of enterprise literature has developed in two main phases: a period from McNee's (1958) contribution to the mid-1970s and the period from then to the present. Broadly these phases span years of high state intervention and regulation, and a time when an earlier regulatory order was being eroded. The difference in structural context is potentially very significant, depending on how phenomena chosen for study are theorized. It is suggested that the dimensions emphasized in the two phases would gain added potency if they were fused with the notion of internationalization.

During the first phase, concern was mainly with the evolution of company structure, changes in company strategy, and decision-making processes involved in new plant location, relocation, closure, and expansion (Krumme 1969; Thomas 1980; Watts 1980). These threads often coalesced under the heading of corporation and environment (McDermott and Taylor 1982). Both the internal milieu of companies and the interaction with the environment were emphasized. The external environment was downplayed on the grounds that systematic knowledge of wider forces was unnecessary to an understanding of corporate behaviour and geography (Hayter and Watts 1983). This assumption was not a problem when the central and local state in many actions provided a relatively stable and expansionary business environment. Treating the context in which individual companies grew as unproblematic encouraged a view that company growth arose largely, if not entirely, from company efforts. The geography of growth was typically collapsed into models of changing spatial scales of operation with only limited regard to a potentially complex causality that underpinned the geographic progression specified by the models.

Rapid international and national restructuring in the 1970s prompted a redirection of empirical and theoretical effort (Massey and Meegan 1985; Taylor and Thrift 1982, 1985). The obvious importance of MNCs steered work towards more complex location practices and to retheorizing the study of enterprises and their organization of space. Taylor and Thrift (1985) review the contributions of Marxist theory, industrial economics, organization theory, and urban and regional research to the study of MNCs, and identify the restricted domain of each literature. They suggest that geographic research is strategic because it is the spatial organization of multinationals as a problem set that ties together the structural competitive, corporate, and local contexts covered respectively by these literatures. Recent political economy work on the structural context (Fagan 1988; Le Heron 1988a) provides several leads that enable the Taylor and Thrift architecture to be extended across each context.

Increasingly the 'natural' scale of capital is being viewed as global. This has an important consequence. Whereas conventional thinking stresses a progression from local to global, the alternative position holds that capitalism should be thought of as global in nature and that attention should focus on both pressures and barriers, such as the role of the state, to this global expression in the enterprise, at the concrete level. Significantly, internationalization is conceptualized in terms of production, realization, and finance reflecting the three moments through which capital circulates. What is critical in any individual enterprise is the nature of internationalization of each dimension and their combined form. Bryan (1987) proposes a general classification of capital covering global, investment-constrained, market-constrained, and national capital. The general questions for each dimension are as follows. For the realization dimension, concern is with the scope of marketing and the extent of production for domestic or export markets. The financial dimension involves determining which foreign currency markets are used for short- and long-term funds and how they are deployed. Production can be approached by focusing on the location of production and the integration of production across economies. In all three dimensions the state has a central place, acting deliberately or unwittingly to encourage or discourage internationalization through state policy. The three dimensions can thus trace the development of global marketing, global financing, and global reinvestment in companies operating on an enlarging spatial scale.

However, since few corporations have fully attained or even maintained a global posture for lengthy periods, there is urgency to conceptualizing internationalization as a tendency exemplified by a range of empirical outcomes and to investigating instances of internationalization. This shifts the orbit of interest to the competitive and corporate domains. Many aspects influence how these contexts constrain and enable corporate evolution. Three ideas can be singled out as especially useful in orienting empirical work at the moment. First, recognition that companies must be set in the wider circuits of industrial and finance capital leads onto consideration of the production–consumption relations and the impact that re-structuring of particular commodity chains (e.g. steel, meat) has on corporate strategy. In the latest era of capitalism old production–

consumption links are breaking down and new links from the market back to production appearing. Pressures are building for instance on food manufacturing companies to take strategic holdings in retailing and distribution, in order to reduce the uncertainty of this structural development to risk that can be managed. Second, corporate strategy is increasingly concerned with control and co-ordination of existing and new investments to meet only financial objectives. Importantly a number of strategies may be available which would allow companies to explore opportunities using existing and planned company strengths, and reduce risks by targeting weaknesses. Likewise the set of investments which would satisfy company strategy and so hold or improve performance may be wide. Moreover companies often alter their administrative form in an attempt to manage the particular risk of their strategy. To accommodate this variety the content, circumstances, and invest-ment flow of strategies and organizational structures need to be charted. Third, the state needs to be explicitly recognized in analysis. This can include changes in regulation but also geo-political initiatives to open or close doors for trade and various forms of investment.

The broad approach to internationalization outlined above calls for a blending of structural knowledge with the finer details of individual company experience. Space does not permit further elaboration of the preliminary framework sketched so far. How-ever, sufficient signposts have been given to indicate the ideas guiding the chapter's corporate study.

Setting the scene

In the Australian and New Zealand setting the GFW story is both one of company restructuring and food sector restructuring. Even in 1980, the size of at least one company was such that were it transferred proportionately to the United States economy it would have exceeded most companies there. From an analytical stand-point this has an interesting advantage in that company strategy can be meaningfully assessed in relation to industry pressures. The history and geography of GFW internationalization are discussed below in four sections. Each section attempts to portray the character of internationalization arising from company investment behaviours and convey the potential inherent in the enterprise at that stage.

Consolidating in the New Zealand economy

By the 1980s Goodman and Wattie were major New Zealand

companies. Each had grown through a significant merger. In the Wattie case the 1968 union of J. Watties Canneries Ltd, Cropper NRM Ltd, and General Foods Ltd brought together three complementing food interests. Goodman had grown by a different track, using a listed Wellington-based company as the vehicle for backward links from baking into milling and diversification. With turnovers of $NZ98.9m. and $385m. Goodman and Wattie were ranked 50th and 5th in the country.

Several similarities and differences were noticeable. Goodman's baking interests had a high cash turnover, 'with reliable income and little debt lasting beyond a month . . . (allowing) for aggressive borrowing but always with a consistent goal, especially in the food business' (Cave 1987:13). Goodman had by 1980 gained a reputation for market-oriented strategy. The consolidated group was organized into units operating with clearly defined financial and other parameters but with maximum freedom on operational matters. Wattie (1977:6) acknowledged that it was affected by 'seasonal production or purchase of raw ingredients on a seasonal basis and there is a limited degree to which the money involved in inventories can be reduced'. These attributes were to influence corporate strategy in the early 1980s.

While differences were acute in terms of how the companies would approach growth, the options open to apply strategy were very similar. Both companies had vertically integrated. Goodman, principally a baking enterprise and mindful of the United States experience with millers acquiring bakeries, embarked on purchases of regional bakeries throughout New Zealand. Wattie acquired the Kentucky Fried Chicken franchise and built up poultry interests and controlled distribution of its grocery products through a national freight company. Diversification beyond food was also evident during the 1970s (Le Heron 1980a). Finally exporting was actively pursued, despite mixed fortunes and modest contributions to sales and profits.

To a large extent the investment openings in New Zealand were limited by government policy which reduced capital flows in and out of New Zealand and the slow growth of a small economy (Le Heron 1988b). High levels of protection and regulation had fostered domestically oriented production but in the 1970s competition intensified. With an already heavy representation in the food sector scope for growth was narrowing. Three pathways were seen to confer promise. First, rationalizing company activities in New Zealand to raise performance of existing assets. Second, continued acquisition and investment in the food area, and third, greater exporting. Not surprisingly the trajectory traced by Goodman and

Table 5.1 Activity profile Wattie Industries Ltd and Goodman Group Ltd in early 1980s

Activity	1980	1981	% 1982	1983	1984
Wattie Industries Ltd[a]					
Canned food	21.7	21.4	20.6	19.8	20.6
Frozen foods	26.4	27.0	26.3	25.9	20.0
Dry foods	7.2	7.0	8.0	8.5	12.2
Milling and feeds	19.4	20.1	20.4	20.4	21.7
Industrial	11.3	9.7	11.6	13.5	10.5
Service industries	8.0	7.6	4.9	4.7	6.3
Other	6.0	7.2	8.2	7.2	8.7
Goodman Group Ltd[b]					
Flour milling	9.0	7.8	7.5	7.1	—
Bakeries	28.5	34.3	36.1	52.0	—
Textiles	34.5	33.9	32.2	23.6	—
Biscuits	23.1	20.2	20.5	18.7	—
Other	4.7	3.5	3.4	3.1	—

Source: Calculated from company annual reports

Notes: a) Based on sales data.
　　　 b) Based on employment figures. Figures only available for 1980–3.

Wattie to common structural and competitive pressures reflected the differing corporate constraints confronting management. For several years merger and investment activity was confined to New Zealand (Table 5.1). Goodman embarked on further consolidation of their already sizeable baking arm. Table 5.2 shows how this strategy changed the Goodman profile. The table also reveals minimal change to Wattie. This is to a degree misleading as significant geographical restructuring took place at two levels in the Wattie group. Within the core canning/frozen food activities, Hastings, Gisborne, and Timaru were favoured locations for added investment, a pattern augmenting that documented by Le Heron and Warr (1976). Over the whole Wattie group, the home base of Hawkes Bay declined gradually in percentage of staff employed. Indeed the company saluted the centrality of the New Zealand economy by holding its 1984 and 1985 AGMs in Auckland and Wellington.

The association between Goodman and Wattie began in 1981 when the two firms entered into a joint baking venture. Goodman felt a closer arrangement would be beneficial to both companies (a sentiment reiterated in Wattie publicity) and Goodman stood in the market to obtain a 24.0 per cent share of Wattie. Wattie then

Richard Le Heron

Table 5.2 Major mergers, acquisitions, investments, and divestments, 1979–88 (divestments in brackets)

	Wattie Industries Ltd			Goodman Group Ltd		
	NZ	A	Elsewhere	NZ	A	Elsewhere
1979	5(1)	–(1)	–	3	–	–
1980	1	–	–	6	–	–
1981	2	–	2	3	–	–
1982	3	–	1	4(1)	–	–
1983	–	–	–	6(1)	–	–
1984	5	–	2	1	1	–
1985	5	–	–	1(1)	2	–
				Goodman Fielder Ltd		
1986	3(3)	–	–	–(1)	–(1)	1
1987	1(2)	–	2	–	–(1)	–
				Goodman Fielder Wattie Ltd		
1988				–	–	1

Source: Company annual reports

Note: Some acquisitions and investments in the early 1980s were joint ventures between Wattie Industries and the Goodman Group. These are included in both company totals. They do not distort the general picture of spatial strategy.

obtained a 24.9 per cent holding in Goodman. An exchange of directors occurred, including the Goodman Chairman joining the Wattie board. Later P. L. B. Goodman also became Chairman of Wattie, Goodman Fielder (GF), and GFW. The Goodman aim was to pursue real growth in the food processing industry, moving beyond flour milling and related industries by providing commercial leadership (Goodman Group 1983). At least for Wattie, the extension of the original alliance was dubious. Indeed, D. McLeod, Wattie chairman at the time, stated in a retirement speech that, 'In the event, the Goodman Directors chose to advance the concept in a way which brought into play a series of moves . . . which cut across your Board's concept of the manner in which any such relationship . . . would be developed' (*Wattie Group News* 1981:2). He perceptively noted, however, that Wattie had made 'an investment in a dynamic organization'. While Goodman opportunism forged the Goodman–Wattie alliance, Wattie opportunism took a different direction, into the New Zealand meat freezing industry, with a purchase of 24.9 per cent of Waitaki Industries Ltd. Wattie (1982:6) qualified the move, 'Our investment was made in the context of the overall strategy of our future expansion and

106

Table 5.3 Wattie Industries export sales profile, 1980–6

% by market areas

Area	1980	1981	1982	1983	1984	1985	1986
America	1.1	0.1	0.1	2.5	5.0	6.9	8.3
Europe	1.9	2.8	4.1	3.4	1.9	2.7	5.1
Middle East	10.5	7.0	7.8	7.8	6.6	4.2	2.3
Far East	35.7	44.7	41.8	43.8	37.8	33.7	26.4
Australia	22.8	20.3	20.9	16.6	23.4	22.3	27.2
South Pacific	25.0	21.8	20.5	21.6	18.4	24.1	25.0
Other	3.0	3.3	4.8	4.3	6.9	6.1	5.7
CIF export sales ($m.)	28.3	39.3	52.8	50.8	64.6	88.6	79.0
% sales from exports	7.4	7.4	11.5	8.8	10.0	11.8	9.8

Source: Company annual reports

development which lies mainly in the food processing industry with emphasis on export marketing . . . investment was made long term.' The development of exporting overlaid the company consolidations. Again management thinking diverged. Wattie had a long tradition of exporting and memories of an unsuccessful eight years direct investment in Wattie–Pict Australia (a significant operation in Victoria) (Le Heron and Warr 1976; Le Heron 1980b). In spite of a number of overseas joint ventures, the external link was predominantly through exports. The geographical pattern was clear. Sir James Wattie (1971:12) mentioned that until 1968 'Wattie's traditional overseas markets were in the United Kingdom and Europe. . . . It was decided to have a closer look at the Pacific area where trade was developing, particularly with Japan and Australia.' Table 5.3 summarizes the effect of the long-term switch to the Pacific Rim and the moderate though still important percentage of export to Australia.

The internationalization outlined thus far indicates a concentration of production activity in New Zealand but also a commitment to realize some sales abroad. Finance for growth was raised mainly in the New Zealand debenture market or through equity issues. Foreign loans were permitted only occasionally by government. This situation held for each group and divisions in each company. Goodman and Wattie could both appropriately be regarded as investment-constrained companies, facing impediments, both internal and external, to the fuller internationalization

Richard Le Heron

of their activities.

The abrupt change in the style of government management of the economy in 1984 completely altered the structural context in which the companies operated. Goodman and Wattie, like many other New Zealand companies, suddenly found they had to reassess how and where they grew. The Goodman–Wattie alliance in New Zealand laid aside inter-company competitive issues and permitted company attention to turn offshore, in Goodman's case to Australia and Wattie's, the Pacific and beyond. A reorientation in philosophy and operational strategy soon followed.

Outgrowing the New Zealand economy

Perhaps the most strategic move exercised by Goodman was the joint shareholding with Elders IXL Ltd, one of Australia's more rapidly growing companies. Accompanying the ownership change was the negotiation by Goodman to manage under contract Elders Food Division and the financing of the Elders Food Group. Goodman foresaw three benefits: short-term revenue, medium-term access to a ready-made distribution system in Australia, and longer-term global trading opportunities through access to Elders network of international offices and experience with counter trade and other techniques. The Goodman–Elders relationship quickly inducted Goodman into the Australian scene, where it was sensed 'Australasian food processors would come under increasing threat from large Northern Hemisphere operators' (Goodman Group 1985:10).

More immediate uncertainty arose when Allied Mills Ltd, regarded by Goodman as 'one of the major Australian food marketers . . . with interests most closely aligned to Goodman' (Goodman Group 1985:5) was threatened with a take-over bid. The ensuing merger of Goodman, Fielder Ltd, and Allied Mills completed in May 1986, with a Sydney head office, overlapped cereal-based production and edible oils in the three companies. Moreover it was one that apparently fitted the plan, but not the timing of choosing. A unique geographic fit was a feature of the merger. Previously Goodman operated primarily in New Zealand markets, Allied across Australia, and Fielder had concentrated business in New South Wales and at a number of overseas locations, particularly through its gelatine and food stabilizer business. Management comment on the merger was revealing.

The food sector, where the majority of our wholly owned businesses and investments are concentrated, is generally perceived as a low-risk area for investment that maintains its

108

viability even in periods of economic downturn. The low-risk nature of our wholly-owned divisions has allowed us to adopt the aggressive financing policy that has been used to lever the company into its strategic holding in companies which are equally low-risk in nature.

(Goodman Group 1985:5)

That the expansion should be in Australia was almost uncontentious. The 1984 Goodman Group Annual Report had symbolized the new frontier with a map of Australia and New Zealand on the cover!

During this period Wattie offshore expansion was less exceptional (Torrance 1986). The company, as part of a major review of its activity, set down a strategy to adapt to the business environment of the 1980s. A major part of the growth thrust was offshore. Australia was first priority. As a matter of philosophy the Australian market was regarded as part of the domestic market for each consumer food business unit rather than a market serviced by the Wattie export division. Moreover Wattie started to establish bases in foreign countries with growth potential. One investment in particular stood out. The investment in Cold Storage Holdings PLC in Singapore with nine supermarkets and a 20 per cent market share gave a substantial foothold in South East Asian food retailing.

By 1984 the food industry in at least New Zealand was widely penetrated by Goodman and Wattie. Goodman held interests in Wattie and New Zealand Forest Products Ltd (via Dominion Industries Ltd, a joint Goodman–Wattie venture). Wattie had invested in Goodman, New Zealand Dairy Board businesses, and Waitaki International Ltd. Goodman assessed the situation as one with limited long-term growth potential but not without prospects. Their twin strategy was:

to realise our ambition to play a larger role in the Australian and New Zealand market place using our food expertise as a base, while seeking to invest in companies and industries involved in processing and/or marketing of natural resources, preferably on an international scale.

(Goodman Group 1983:5)

The statement highlighted the growing gap between Australasian and global plans and a narrow New Zealand-centred growth strategy. The former consisted of investing in added value production in New Zealand's agricultural and horticultural sectors. Some investments were consistent with such a policy. However the weight of total investment was in market development and production offshore and then principally through acquisition of existing businesses. Maintaining growth in and from New Zealand was also made more difficult by high inflation, high value of the New Zealand dollar (depressing export earnings), elimination of export incentives and increased competition from imported food lines produced for much larger markets than New Zealand. The effect of this was a steady change in the centre of gravity of the emerging companies. How far down this route the companies had travelled by the mid-1980s is addressed next.

An Australasian food company (and industry)

The merger proposal of Goodman–Fielder and Wattie was registered in November 1986 with New Zealand's Commerce Commission, only six months after the GF union. Seen against the background of market and production internationalization outlined already, the step to merge made corporate and structural sense. The combined group would approach its investment strategy in a way that none of the individual companies could have achieved on their own. With the completion of an Australasian base the perceived threat of international competitors in Australia could be addressed and the fuller development of production to market linkages undertaken.

But attractive though the merger was to the companies, the move cut across legislated restrictions in New Zealand on company dominance. Table 5.4 outlines the breadth and depth in particular market segments. Several points stand out. First, the flour, bread-baking, and other bakery rows depict a highly integrated milling–baking complex. Second, GF and Wattie consumer foods were estimated by the commission to amount to 20 per cent of New Zealand supermarket turnover. This calculation was, however, an underestimate as it did not include meat supplies. Third, the Australian dimension is not revealed. There fats and oils formed a third of the large consumer food group of GF. Imports to New Zealand and arrangements with the New Zealand Dairy Board extended penetration of this segment. Poultry production was also a growing component in Australia.

In May 1987 the commission judged that the proposed company meant dominance in flour-milling, baking, fresh pastry, poultry meat, and poultry feeds markets. A protracted court battle ensued. Resolution was reached when GFW agreed to divest a number of companies. When sold, these went to George Weston Ltd, a major Australian firm. The publicity surrounding the merger exposed the

Table 5.4 Pre-merger New Zealand market shares of Goodman Fielder
Ltd and Wattie Industries Ltd (%)

	Wattie Industries Ltd	*Goodman Fielder Ltd*
Fats and oils	indirect	none
Consumer foods		
Cakes mixes	98	0
Ice-cream	68	20
Pasta	0	60
Pet food	62	11
Poultry and stock feed		
Day-old chicks	indirect	0
Feed	53	0
Brau and pullard	69	0
Retail chicken	73	0
Starch	90	0
Flour	41	28
Bread baking	indirect	43
Other bakery	50	10

Source: Compiled from Commerce Commission Decision No. 206A

conflict between the objective of preventing dominance in the New
Zealand market and that of fostering growth of an international
company, presumably with employment growth, in the company
(and industry). Significantly the grounds of debate were subtly
shifted. An economics seminar in Australia for instance elevated
economic efficiency rather than market definition, market concentration or market entry conditions as the appropriate basis on which
to assess mergers (Tuxford 1988). Such a framework for regulating
the growth of individual corporations requires no proof, aside from
company claims, that economic efficiency will be gained. The
commission, in reversing its decision, appeared to endorse the new
ethos, stating 'some reasonable flexibility must be justified in the
commercial context' (Weir 1987:3).

Superficially the creation of GFW appeared as just the next stage
in the evolution of the Australasian food industry. In actuality this
view contains two elements. First, the merger of the two companies
with near dominant positions in many segments of the food
industry reinforced concentration of production, distribution, and
marketing in their hands. Second, discussion of the food industry
must be more than prefaced by reference to key organizations; in
fact, it is a discussion about a few organizations. What then does
the full expression of economic efficiency mean in a company such
as GFW?

GFW stated that post-merger adjustments would aim to integrate business activities, realize benefits of rationalization, and make the company the lowest cost producer in each product line. To achieve its objectives GFW continued with the GF reorganization into relatively independent groups (Ryan 1987). This approach was grounded in the principle that 'structure follows strategy' (Goodman Fielder Ltd 1987:5). The basic effect of this structure is to sharpen attention to financial parameters. Table 5.5 summarizes GFW's activities in 1988. The 90 per cent concentration of sales and profits from food is discernible. Three of the food groups are represented in both countries. Base figures used to prepare Table 5.5 also allow calculation of cross country employee productivity. A sharp contrast between Australia and New Zealand can be seen in Table 5.6, suggesting more restructuring in consumer foods and milling in New Zealand and bakeries in Australia. This may be masked by other developments. Watties for instance have retrenched their canning operations following collapse of can-making orders from breweries and faltering export demand.

The arrival of GFW, seven years after the initial relationship, redefined the Australasian food arena. GFW was at least latently a global company, with an often voiced global growth strategy (Steel 1987). Early developments in a new phase of internationalization are now covered.

New food axes on a world map

An internationalization strategy beyond Australia and New Zealand implied several changes in competitive context and corporate practice. In the short run acquisitions on a scale not previously attempted and commensurate funding requirements of a different order and potentially different kind had to be faced. If successful, longer-run questions would ensue. Should the company focus on marketing products processed in its home-base or opt for independent management and growth of subsidiaries without striving for integration amongst units in various countries? In large measure, short- and long-term strategies were inseparable. For GFW, a strong history of exporting suggested that growth was probably best centred on creating intra- and inter-company links in the world's economies.

GFW's view that it could accomplish a global expansion necessitates a brief review of the funding implications. In the early 1980s regulatory environment in Australia and New Zealand, the companies had little choice but to obtain money domestically through debenture or share issues. The freeing of foreign exchange restric-

Table 5.5 Activity profile of Goodman Fielder Wattie Ltd, 1988

Groups	% of company activity				% by company region		
	Sales	Employment	Profit		Sales	Employment	Profit
Consumer foods	38.0	32.1	33.6	A	24.6	14.9	22.5
				NZ	13.5	17.1	11.2
Milling and poultry	23.8	19.3	27.6	A	17.4	9.7	19.4
				NZ	6.3	9.5	8.3
Bakeries	20.9	27.7	11.7	A	14.7	21.2	3.9
				NZ	6.2	6.5	7.8
Gelatine	8.2	8.5	7.6	A	8.2	8.5	7.6
				NZ	—	—	—
Textiles	8.8	12.1	10.0	A	—	—	—
				NZ	8.8	12.1	10.1
Total sales ($m.)	2,158.0			A	1,403.4		
				NZ	754.9		
Total employment		16,845		A		9,210	
				NZ		7,635	
Total profits ($m.)			235.0	A			143.2
				NZ			92.1

Source: Calculated from Goodman Fielder Wattie Ltd (1988)

113

Richard Le Heron

Table 5.6   Sales per employee, Goodman Fielder Wattie, 1988 ($000s per employee)

Group	Australia	New Zealand
Consumer foods	210	100
Milling and poultry	220	80
Bakeries	80	120

Source: Calculated from Goodman Fielder Wattie Ltd (1988)

Table 5.7   Long-term liabilities in foreign currencies ($m.)

	Wattie Industries Ltd ($NZ)		Goodman Group Ltd ($A)				
	NZ	Overseas	NZ	A	US	UK	Dutch
1980							
1981							
1982	50	13	11	—	11	—	—
1983	64	15	24	—	—	—	—
1984	77	20	64	29	—	—	—
1985	142	59	210	123	—	—	—
			Goodman Fielder Ltd				
1986	76	56	55	217	38	—	—
1987	116	158	40	89	22	241	—
			Goodman Fielder Wattie Ltd				
1988			138	70	253	273	56

Source: Company annual reports

tions, as part of government deregulation, opened up United States and European sources. These were not exercised often, until the funding needs of mergers and investments (e.g. GF, GFW) outstripped what could be absorbed locally. The foreign currency liabilities shown in Table 5.7 indicate relatively late use of the world money markets. One significant effect of raising money in another currency is exchange risk, and for sizeable long-term loans and so on the impact of currency fluctuations is potentially enormous. To avert the risk, companies often invest in the denominating country. As Table 5.7 indicates, Britain and North America had an attraction.

Undoubtedly GFW saw itself as a global player when in 1985 the directors were pictured in front of a world map. The first step made was a 14.6 per cent (later increased to 29.2 per cent) in RHM, a major European food marketer with a growing presence in North America. The investment was in line with the company's policy of taking strategic holdings in companies performing well in broadly similar fields. RHM was the largest food marketer in its main market (about a third), headed a major bakery chain (accounting for a quarter of the market), was prominent in cake manufacture, and also a large manufacturer and marketer of grocery items with strong brand names. Whether the initial RHM move was part of a fully European concept or merely a British-directed investment is unclear. However the move was soon bolstered with a 98 per cent acquisition of Meneba NV (Netherlands) which gave a bridgehead for GFW in Europe. Meneba has a similar core to GFW, a turnover of $A550m., including 20 per cent exports. C. Lyon, GFW London-based director said at a press interview that the decision was taken after consultants had advised GFW that 'pan European concentration in the flour and flour related areas has yet to begin seriously' (Anon 1988:14). The consultants had favoured Holland as a country from which free trade access to 44 per cent of the European Community population could be secured. Lyon added, 'We don't see tremendous opportunity from 1992 for Meneba itself, but we want to get a base there and with other acquisitions, we will then have a presence where we can start to move products across boundaries.'

The uproar over the RHM take-over bid (lodged in July 1988) revealed the dilemma the company was in over its expansion strategy (Howie 1988; Stokes 1988; Verdon 1988; Wisniewski 1988). Suggestions had been made that the company was having trouble finding suitable acquisition targets for the first phase of its proposed global expansion. In this light, RHM was probably a logical choice, despite opposition to GFW input in RHM. RHM institutional ownership was perhaps thought to aid the chance of success. A take-over of RHM however was a complex financial and political proposition. The bid was to be underwritten by the Banque Nationale de Paris and Warburgs, Samuel Montague. A three-part deal consisted of a rights issue of new GFW ordinary shares ($362m.), a European convertible securities issue (£100m.) and a seven-year loan facility ($5.28b.) involving eight banks (among others Amsterdam Rotterdam Bank NV, Banque Nationale de Paris, Canadian Imperial Bank of Commerce, the Hong Kong and Shanghai Banking Corporation, the Industrial Bank of Japan, and the Westpac Banking Corporation). Half the loan facility was to refinance the working capital of the enlarged group. The referral to the United Kingdom Merger and Monopolies Commission after sustained nationalist reaction prompted GFW to withdraw the bid but subsequently either a lack of buyers or a genuine interest in the purchase of RHM has seen GFW retain its interest.

Undue attention on GFW's European expansion could easily cloud the significance of substantial investments in South America via the gelatine arm, the strong pressure through Wattie in the New Zealand meat and fishing industries and the South East Asian interests, again Wattie-oriented. GFW is much more than a giant bakery, as might be inferred from reportage of the European scene. The company is more accurately a food conglomerate with a number of 'footholds' in major markets around the globe.

Concluding comments

This study of the geography of growth of GFW out of New Zealand contains many insights about the imperative for national food companies to internationalize and the complex mix of structural, competitive, corporate, and local factors that must be considered when interpreting the geography of particular enterprises.

The focus on internationalization represents an important extension to the past analytic practice in the field of enterprise geography. The GFW development was interpreted by establishing the structural context before proceeding to explore the competitive, corporate, and local relations of importance to the company's evolution. Deregulation of the New Zealand economy was a precondition unlocking the companies, but the limited growth prospects in the economy also forced offshore expansion. Without the critical shift in economic management by the New Zealand government, the possibility of a GFW being eventually formed could not have been seriously entertained. However, once the companies were exposed to potentially all aspects of the international economy, the company focus and therefore the primary analytical focus had to shift to competitive issues in Australasia and elsewhere and matters of corporate strategy.

Three dimensions of the evolving GFW entity were examined in order to arrive at how far the emerging organizations had internationalized operations. Market dependence and orientation, location of production facilities either wholly owned or of associate companies, and the sources of funds used for expansion became progressively more global in character and geography. After each round in merger activity it was noticeable that the new corporate entity was able or had to rearticulate key relationships to survive and grow. GFW maintained momentum by building on its food manufacturing base. The 1988 GFW was a company with all groups more internationalized and with widening spatial spheres of operation. In character and scope GFW was global.

A counter take-over bid by RHM for GFW in 1989 illustrates a general feature of capitalist production: enterprise ownership may change suddenly and dramatically. Whether different ownership would be a material factor in the integration, co-ordination, and control of Australian and New Zealand food production in the world economy cannot be predicted. What can be identified from this study however is that any geography of enterprise perspective used to analyse such developments must explicitly incorporate the internationalization and regulation of capital, in their diverse forms.

The GFW case exemplifies the desirability of achieving a view of enterprises that brings into focus the different causal powers of organizations as they evolve. Significantly the industrial geography literature places little emphasis on the definition of the main relationships that define entities. To achieve this explanatory objective, however, at least three methodological points must be recognized. First, attention has to focus not only on what new causal powers are available but also how they are the product of human agency in organizations. Second, the discovery of new spatial patterns does not necessarily imply the existence of new causal powers. The causal mechanisms connecting outcomes to processes need to be carefully specified. Third, treatment of enterprises in isolation from their structural context should be avoided. Much geography of enterprise work has overlooked or under-emphasized these concerns. Two questions help sharpen the approach explored in the chapter. What growth options are open to organizations at different levels of causal development? And what constraints in various contexts bear upon the exercise of options by organizations? These questions and their answers should greatly assist in developing the geography of enterprise field.

The internationalization thesis suggests that, in a world economy featuring open and deregulated national economies, fewer obstacles will block global expansion of growing enterprises. The reality of course is that only a relatively small number of companies are in a position to operationalize such strategy. Those that can and do may quickly emerge as significant global companies. GFW is one such company. Its significance, however, lies less in its success which is considerable or its example which is illustrative. Rather GFW is contributing to the growing concentration in world food manufacturing. This implies a new structural reality. The challenge

Richard Le Heron

to manage the provision of Good Food World-wide socially will be
one of the central economic and political tasks of the era.

Note

The study forms part of the 'Transformations of Land-based Production in
New Zealand' research programme in the Department of Geography,
Massey University. Funding support from the Social Sciences Research
Fund Committee is gratefully acknowledged. Mike Roche and Judy Le
Heron provided thoughtful comments on a draft and Anneke Visser
graciously typed the manuscript.

References

Anon. (1981) 'Investment in dynamic group', *Wattie Group News* 24:2.
Anon. (1986) 'Business Unit Restructures', *Wattie News* 40:3.
Anon. (1988) 'More moves by GFW giant', *The Dominion*, 7 May.
Bryan, R. (1987) 'The State and internationalisation of capital: an
    approach to analysis', *Journal of Contemporary Asia*, 17, 3: 253–75.
Cave, S. (1987) 'Gobbling up the food industry', *NZ Listener*, 4 April, 13–
    15.
Fagan, R. H. (1988) 'Australia in the global economy', paper delivered to
    IGU Commission on Industrial Change, Rutherglen, Tasmania, August.
Gooding, B. (1987) 'Food giant still holds all the cards', *New Zealand
    Farmer*, 13 January.
Goodman Fielder Ltd (1986–7) annual reports.
Goodman Fielder Wattie Ltd (1988) annual report.
Goodman Group Ltd (1980–5) annual reports.
Hayter, R. and Watts, D. (1983) 'The geography of enterprise: a re-
    appraisal', *Progress in Human Geography* 7: 154–81.
Howie, C. (1988) 'British MPs condemn GFW bid', *The Dominion*, 23
    July.
Krumme, G. (1969) 'Towards a geography of enterprise', *Economic
    Geography* 45: 30–40.
Le Heron, R. B. (1980a) 'The diversified corporation and development
    strategy – New Zealand's experience', *Regional Studies* 14, 3: 201–18.
Le Heron, R. B. (1980b) 'Exports and linkage development in manufactur-
    ing firms: the example of export promotion in New Zealand', *Economic
    Geography* 56, 4: 281–99.
Le Heron, R. B. (1988a) 'State, economy and crisis in New Zealand in the
    1980s: Implications for land-based production of a new mode of
    regulation', *Applied Geography* 8, 4: 273–90.
Le Heron, R. B. (1988b) 'The question of production: manufacturing and
    other issues', paper presented at IGU Symposium on 'The Pacific
    Century', IGU Sydney, August.
Le Heron, R. B. and Roche, M. M. (1988c) 'Reglobalisation of the New

Zealand food and fibre system: an organisational perspective', paper presented at IGU Commission on Rural Systems, Auckland, August.

Le Heron, R. B. and Warr, E. C. R. (1976) 'Corporate organisation, corporate strategy and agribusiness development in New Zealand: an introductory study with particular reference to the fruit and vegetable processing industry', *New Zealand Geographer*, 32:1, 1–16.

McDermott, P. J. and Taylor, M. J. (1982) *Industrial Organisation and Location*, Cambridge: Cambridge University Press.

McNee, R. B. (1958) 'Functional geography of the firm, with an illustrative case study for the petroleum industry', *Economic Geography* 34: 321–37.

Massey, D. and Meegan, R. (1985) *Politics and Method*, London: Methuen.

New Zealand Commerce Commission (1987) Decision No 201A Merger Proposal Involving Goodman Fielder Ltd and Wattie Industries Ltd.

Ryan, D. (1987) 'Goodman outlines major plans for new group', *National Business Review*, 30 November.

Steel, S. (1987) 'New food company will look overseas', *National Business Review*, 29 October:5.

Stokes, A. (1988) 'Repelling invaders. 'We will fight on the beaches' stuff from Ranks', *Sunday Star*, 24 July.

Taylor, M. J. (ed.) (1984) *The Geography of Australian Corporate Power*, Sydney: Croom Helm.

Taylor, M. J. and Thrift, N. J. (eds) (1982) *The Geography of Multinationals*, London: Croom Helm.

Taylor, M. J. and Thrift, N. J. (eds) (1985) *Multinationals and the Restructuring of the World Economy*, London: Croom Helm.

Thomas, M. D. (1980) 'Explaining frameworks for growth and change in multiregional firms', *Economic Geography* 56, 1: 1–17.

Torrance, F. (1986) 'Wattie makes move to expand off-shore', *New Zealand Times*, 18 May.

Tuxford, L. (1988) 'Where one-market concept leads', *The Dominion Sunday Times*, 13 March.

Verdon, L. (1988) 'Goodman's RHM plan "mean but not outrageous" ', *Evening Post*, 15 July.

Wattie, J. (1971) 'Chairman and Managing Director's Report', J. Watties canneries prospectus, May.

Wattie Industries Ltd (1977, 1980–7) annual reports.

Watts, H. D. (1980) *The Large Industrial Enterprise: Some Spatial Perspectives*. London: Croom Helm.

Weir, J. (1987) 'Bitter pill made sweeter for GFL and Wattie', *National Business Review*, 12 August.

Wisniewski, H. (1988) 'RHM hits back in bid row', *The Dominion*, 20 July.

Chapter six

ccFriesland
Spatial dynamics within a dynamic company

Egbert Wever

Introduction

There are major differences in the growth trajectory of firms (Taylor and Thrift 1982). In this chapter some ideas and models from the literature on industrial geography and business administration will be confronted with the reality of a large Dutch dairy company, ccFriesland. Some of this company's decisions to realize growth or guarantee continuity have had clear consequences for its spatial configuration. Other strategic decisions have not influenced this configuration, although they imply basic changes in the number and kind of activities performed. Hence: spatial dynamics within a dynamic firm.

Before dealing with ccFriesland itself, we present a theoretical framework, which we then use to confront opinions expounded in the literature with the reality of ccFriesland.

The growth of companies: theoretical notions

There are many reasons why companies grow (Hakanson 1979; Lloyd and Dicken 1977). Large companies are assumed to be in a favourable competitive position compared to small ones. They can create economies of scale, they can avoid underutilization of machinery, they have more options to reduce uncertainty and risk in their environment, they can offer their employees better conditions (salaries, promotion), etc. However, in order to grow, a company has to be competitive: it should obtain better access to the market, introduce new or better products, produce at lower costs, be able to find niches, etc. These conditions are in fact often the reason for starting a firm (Keeble and Wever 1986).

The competitiveness of a firm can be based on firm-internal (innovation, marketing abilities) or firm-external (low-cost location) aspects. As long as the firm can maintain its advantage over competitors, it can grow. Generally it will start to sell on a regional or national market (Thomas 1980). A critical moment arrives when the firm decides to go abroad (Fröhlich 1976). The most simple approach to international markets is to export from the home country. This strategy is attractive when the importing countries do not restrict imports and the price of the product, including transport costs from the home country, is competitive. But there are often restrictions, intended to protect the importing country's own industries.

If restrictions prohibit exports, the company has a choice between direct investment and portfolio investment. By direct investment, a company takes over an existing plant or it builds a new plant, alone or with others (joint venture). In either case the company wants to control the activities involved. Portfolio investments are financial investments, mostly made by buying shares on the stock market; there is no intention to control the activities of the companies involved.

For a long time, portfolio investments were considered 'atypical' for manufacturing companies (Fröhlich 1976). This is definitely less true nowadays. Moreover, there is no big difference between portfolio investment and the acquisition of minority shares in several companies. This chapter deals mainly with exports and direct investments, as ccFriesland is not active in portfolio investment.

A company can choose between various ways to grow (Ansoff 1968): by market penetration, market development, product development or diversification (Figure 6.1). Within each category a strategy of internal (extension of existing plants or building of branch plants) or external growth (acquisition of existing plants) can be followed. Also relevant in this respect are the constraints on growth (Hakanson 1979):

- demand restraint: a strategy of 'more of the same' will in the end, in line with the idea of the product life cycle, lead to market saturation;
- managerial restraint: some firms are more able to overcome the demand constraints than others as their management sees new market possibilities, where others do not (Penrose 1959);
- financial restraint: utilizing market possibilities presupposes adequate financial resources;
- locational restraints: sometimes growth at existing locations becomes unfeasible or impossible, e.g. because of input access restraints, or market access restraints.

	PRODUCT	
	EXISTING	NEW
MARKET — EXISTING	MARKET PENETRATION	PRODUCT DEVELOPMENT
MARKET — NEW	MARKET DEVELOPMENT	DIVERSIFICATION

Figure 6.1   The strategy matrix of Ansoff
Source: Ansoff 1968:99

As a consequence a firm normally shows an irregular growth path.

Spatial growth models

Partly based on the Ansoff matrix, Hakanson (1979) formulated a spatial growth model with five stages (Figure 6.2). It is a model for the internal growth of a single-product company with an emphasis on market penetration and market development. Although Hakanson (1979:135) agrees that 'Continued growth without diversification is impossible', this does not influence his model: 'diversification adds complexity, but the overall pattern remains the same' (Hakanson 1979:131).

Other models have much in common with the Hakanson model. Taylor (1975) distinguishes three separate stages within Hakanson's stage two. Wertheimer (Taylor and Thrift 1982) does the same for Hakanson's stage four. More relevant for this contribution is the addition made by Dicken (1986). He differentiates between internal (branches) and external (acquisitions) growth, and he includes reorganization processes (Figure 6.3).

Taylor and Thrift (1982) have criticized the Hakanson model, because it regards multinationals as the end product of a growth continuum that starts with the privately owned single-plant firm. They see at least four different sequences, each one appropriate for one category of firm. The multinational firm is one of these four categories. Moreover, they add that nowadays 'the smaller firm's

ccFriesland

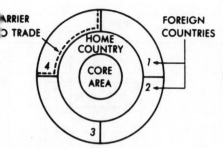

The action space of the corporation

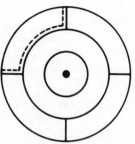

Stage 1 The single-plant firm

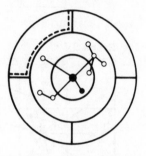

Stage 2 The penetration of the national market

Stage 3 The adoption of overseas sales agents

Stage 4 The establishment of foreign subsidiaries

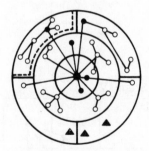

Stage 5 The multinational industrial corporation

● Mother plant and head office   ○ Sales office

● Production plant   ▲ Sales agent

Figure 6.2 The Hakanson model

Source: Hakanson 1979:131–5

Stage I

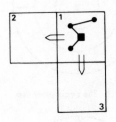

Stage II

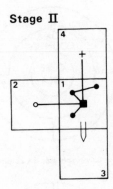

Stage III

Stage IV

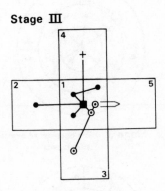
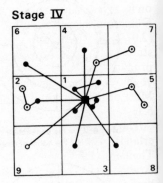

Stage V

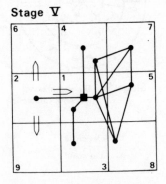

■ Headquarters
● Production plant
○ Sales subsidiary
+ Licensing arrangement
⊙ Acquisition
⊂ Exports

Figure 6.3 The Dicken model
Source: Dicken 1986:215

chances of becoming a large business organization rapidly diminish'
(Taylor and Thrift 1982:23).

The remarks of Taylor and Thrift concerning the Hakanson
model, and indirectly the Dicken model, are certainly correct.
Nevertheless, this chapter proceeds from the Dicken model,
because at first sight that fits best the growth path followed by
ccFriesland.

The reality of ccFriesland

The company

ccFriesland is one of the five large Dutch dairy companies. In 1987,
on its seventy-fifth anniversary, it realized a turnover of 1.6 milliard
Dutch guilders. It employed 4,936 persons, less than 50 per cent
(2,074) of whom were working in the Netherlands. ccFriesland
started with the production of condensed milk. This is still the main
product, but now the mix includes milk powder, baby foods,
yoghurts, ice-cream, and chocolate milk and lactose (Figure 6.4).
Most of these products are sold in many parts of the world (Table
6.1).

The company participates in production units outside the Neth-
erlands: Guam (USA), Okinawa (Japan), Indonesia, Malaysia,
Thailand, Taiwan, West Germany, Nigeria, North Yemen, Saudi
Arabia, and Pakistan. Production with licenses for ccFriesland
brand names takes place in the United States ('Longevity') and in
Australia, Korea, Guatemala, and El Salvador (all 'Foremost'
brand). Moreover there are sales agencies in Singapore, Hong
Kong, Paris, Guangzhou, Brussels, and Athens.

This chapter deals with the way ccFriesland has grown since it
was established in 1913 in Leeuwarden, the capital of the province
of Friesland. Three topics will be dealt with in more detail: in the
first place the contribution of the various product–market combinations (PMCs) to this growth; in the second place the strategies
pursued; and in the third place the resulting spatial pattern.

During its seventy-five years of existence, ccFriesland has
introduced several new products and entered many new markets.
Not all attempts turned out to be a success. Some products were not
accepted by the consumers, some markets were lost to competitors.
Every product–market combination has its own story. It is, of
course, impossible to deal with them all in this contribution. Only
the main characteristics of the process, illustrated by specific cases,
can be given. More detailed information can be found elsewhere
(Wever 1989; Tjepkema 1963).

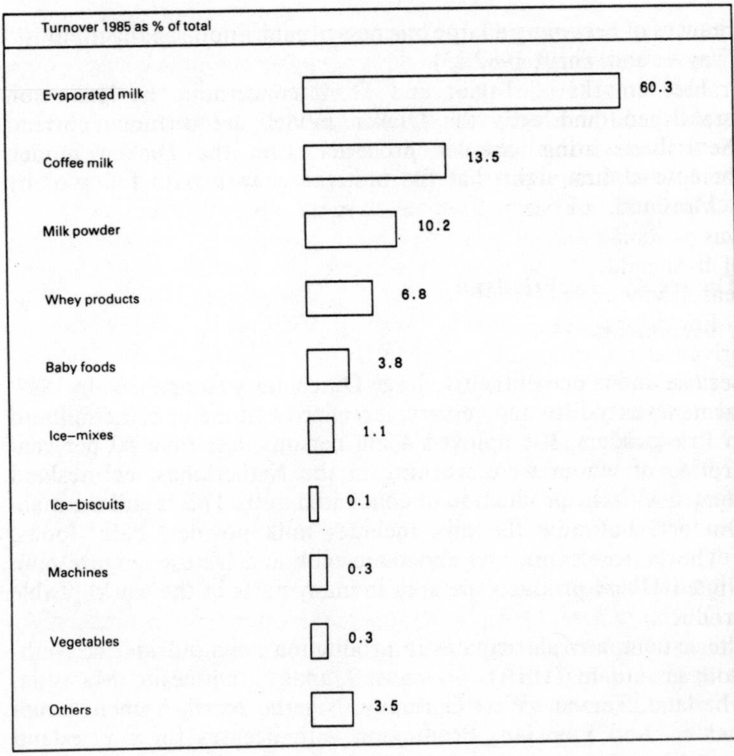

Turnover 1985 as % of total

Product	%
Evaporated milk	60.3
Coffee milk	13.5
Milk powder	10.2
Whey products	6.8
Baby foods	3.8
Ice–mixes	1.1
Ice–biscuits	0.1
Machines	0.3
Vegetables	0.3
Others	3.5

Figure 6.4 The contribution of various products to ccFriesland's turnover, 1985

Source: ccFriesland

Table 6.1 Geographical pattern of company turnover, 1987

	% of total
The Netherlands	18
Europe	29
Africa	15
Asia	35
America	3

Source: ccFriesland

Goals and constraints

To understand the growth path of ccFriesland, it is important to know why it was founded. That had nothing to do with an innovative Schumpeterian entrepreneur starting a new activity or discovering a market niche. The first condensed milk patents were granted in 1856 in the US. In 1913, when ccFriesland was established, there were twenty plants operating in the Netherlands, the first one dating back to 1882. Even in the province of Friesland there were already three condensed milk producers.

Moreover, ccFriesland started to make a product for which there was no demand at all in the Netherlands, because of the availability of fresh milk. As in those days overproduction did not exist, the reason why ccFriesland was founded is not self-evident.

For a long time the Dutch dairy industry was dominated by private firms, with milk-producing farmers in a dependent position, because of the perishability of milk. To counter this dependency the farmers established co-operative dairy plants, the first one in Warga in Friesland in 1886. Gradually these co-operatives took over the production of butter and cheese. As a consequence the private companies had to look for other product–market combinations. One of the alternatives was condensed milk.

The biggest market for condensed milk at that time was the United Kingdom (also the biggest market for other Dutch dairy products) where it was used as a less perishable and cheap alternative for fresh milk in the big agglomerations. So far so good. Both groups had their own product and market. Problems arose when the demand for condensed milk increased. The private firms had to buy more milk from individual farmers or from co-operatives. They were ready and able to pay a high price for milk, higher than the co-operatives did. This created a problem for the farmers of the co-operatives. They knew from experience that dependency on the private sector was dangerous. On the other hand, the high milk price could not be overlooked. This conflict between co-operative ideal and individual business was solved by the decision of thirty Frisian co-operatives jointly to start a condensed milk firm: ccFriesland.

ccFriesland was the result of a defensive strategy of the Frisian co-operative movement, i.e. to fight the private firms. Although ccFriesland should help to optimize the income of the dairy farmers, expectations were very modest. For that reason attempts to interest co-operatives in the neighbouring province of Drenthe failed, mainly because these co-operatives were not in a situation where private condensed milk firms were looking for their milk. But even in Friesland condensed milk was a product of secondary importance. At the start in 1913 it was decided that all participating co-operatives were obliged to deliver maximally 5 per cent of their milk to ccFriesland. They could use at least 95 per cent themselves for milk, yoghurts, cream, cheese, butter, etc. Later, when the activities of ccFriesland became a substantial element in the dairy farmer's income, this delivering percentage was raised, but even now it is only 30 per cent. Because of market conditions ccFriesland does not always claim for 30 per cent. In 1988, in fact, it asked for less than 50 per cent of its maximal claim.

Important too is the fact that ccFriesland is a top-cooperative. In 1913 it started as an activity of thirty dairy co-operatives; in 1938, sixty-nine co-operatives participated and in 1988 only five. This reduction had nothing to do with a decreasing interest of the dairy farmers in ccFriesland. It is the result of a concentration process that took place after 1955 everywhere in the Netherlands (Van den Bremen 1977).

The dairy co-operatives, the owners of ccFriesland, use most of their milk to produce dairy products (mostly cheese). Of course they did not allow ccFriesland to become a competitor. ccFriesland had to keep its hands off a number of product-market combinations. For example, for a long time ccFriesland was not allowed to sell chocolate milk on the Dutch market. There was no restriction on exports, as that would not trespass on the terrain of the co-operatives. It explains why sales on the Dutch market until 1950 were negligible. Then condensed milk was successfully introduced as coffee milk (market development).

Condensed milk: market penetration

Market position

In 1913 ccFriesland started a strategy of market penetration based on export, as there was no market in the Netherlands. Up till 1940 the United Kingdom was the most important market for all big US, Swiss, and Dutch condensed milk producers (especially skimmed sweetened condensed milk). When ccFriesland entered this market, it had only two firm-specific advantages: large quantities of milk and traditionally good contacts with the UK dairy market.

Although the first results were not impressive, over time ccFriesland succeeded in gaining a permanent place among the Dutch exporters: in 1938 its share was 15 per cent. During the 1920s the market in Indonesia (a Dutch colony at that time) was penetrated. This market was nearly monopolized by the Swiss company Nestlé (Den Hartog 1986). Other markets in Asia and Africa followed (Table 6.2). The most important ccFriesland markets now are Greece, Ivory Coast, Nigeria, and the Arab

Table 6.2 Condensed milk export pattern (vol. %) of ccFriesland

	1929	1950	1980	1987
Sweetened				
Europe	82.5	6.8	10.0	7.7
Asia	14.5	63.4	13.0	22.6
Africa	1.2	21.0	70.3	60.8
America	2.7	8.6	6.8	9.7
Evaporated milk				
Europe	90.2	46.4	30.1	50.1
Asia	4.5	31.3	24.8	24.8
Africa	2.6	12.9	43.7	24.4
America	2.7	9.4	1.3	2.7

Source: ccFriesland

Emirates. Over time well-known brand names were developed like 'Dutch Lady', 'Peak' and 'Noy Noy'.

For sweetened condensed milk the European (=UK) phase was followed by an Asian phase and then by an African phase. Over time the importance of Europe and Asia declined in a relative as well as an absolute sense. In absolute numbers this sweetened condensed milk was the most important type until 1950. Condensed milk without sugar (evaporated milk) nowadays accounts for more than 80 per cent of all ccFriesland's condensed milk exports. Here the same tendency can be noticed apart from the revival of the European market (mainly Greece).

In a sense the data for Asia and Africa in Table 6.2 reflect Vernon's (1966) original theory of the product life cycle. After a period of growing exports a phase of stagnating and even decreasing exports sets in. The reason is that condensed milk is replaced by a substitute. In the last phase a number of the former importing countries export this substitute ('recombined' or 'filled' milk). Until recently export from these former importing countries has not thrown a wrench in ccFriesland's export works. But now they are allowed to enter all ccFriesland markets. Is this the first step of ccFriesland on its way to becoming a global company? Of course, in this case there is no export to the Netherlands as there is no condensed milk market in the Netherlands, apart from coffee milk. This export is oriented towards countries originally importing from the Netherlands. In the long run this may lead to a decrease of production in Leeuwarden, in accordance with the model of Vernon.

Spatial aspects

For penetrating new markets ccFriesland consequently used sales agencies, as described by Hakanson (1979) and Dicken (1986): in the UK MacPherson Train & Co., in Indonesia the Dutch trading company Internatio, in the Philippines Wise & Co. There was no pressure to establish sales offices of its own. The first ccFriesland office in Hong Kong came quite unexpectedly. In fact, an office in the Dutch colony Indonesia, a much bigger market, would have been a more natural development.

In Hong Kong the Central Trading Company acted as ccFriesland's agent. It did its job well, but ran into financial trouble in 1936. This might have had negative consequences for ccFriesland. So one of the directors was sent out on inspection. He reported that the company had got into trouble by coincidence, but the management qualities of the company owner were excellent and his loyalty to ccFriesland indisputable. He advised creating a ccFriesland sales office in Hong Kong with the former agent as the director. If the Central Trading Company had not been in trouble, and if ccFriesland had not analysed the reasons, it would have been quite unlikely that the first sales office would be located in Hong Kong.

The same procedure was followed by ccFriesland elsewhere. Well-performing agencies were taken over. In 1960 ccFriesland participated in Pierson in Paris, its former agency for French Africa. In Greece it took over its former agency Genka in Athens. Although some Dutch employees were added to the management of these newly acquired agencies, most of the work was done by the 'old' experienced staff, implying only minor changes and a strong reliance on their regional know-how of the market. Of course, the acquisition of a former agency was not always a success. In 1962 ccFriesland took over an agency in West Germany ('Karl Krings Friso Import und Grosshandelsgesellschaft' located in Diepholz). When this sales office did not perform well it was closed in 1983. From that date 'independent' agencies were used again. By the way, ccFriesland not only uses agents, it is an agent itself too. On Guam it is a bottler and sales agency for Coca Cola. In Thailand it acts as a sales agency for Wander, a daughter of Sandoz, for Ovomaltine.

In the Dicken model the next phase is the establishment of production facilities elsewhere. In the 1950s, after more than forty years, ccFriesland realized its first acquisitions. In 1955 several small dairy plants located within Friesland were acquired from a private company (Lijempf). The only reason was that ccFriesland was interested in the milk to which these plants had access. After the take-over, the plants were closed or used for other purposes: an example of (backward) vertical integration in order to safeguard the demand for milk inputs. In 1956 'De Ommelanden', a dairy co-operative in the neighbouring province of Groningen, was acquired, together with another top-cooperative. The reason in this case was that the company was interested in the milk and the production capacity for condensed milk. There were another two strategic elements in this acquisition. Firstly, a private competitor so close by was considered very unpleasant. Secondly, the top-cooperative in the neighbouring province of Drenthe (DOMO) was considering starting the production of condensed milk. ccFriesland would not be able to stop DOMO, as this top-cooperative had milk itself. So ccFriesland offered DOMO participation in 'De Ommelanden'. That offer was accepted. A potential competitor had become a partner. Much later, in 1977 Wöhrmann, located in Appeldorn in West Germany, was acquired. Here again expansion of production capacity was the argument for taking over Wöhrmann. Wöhrmann was not unknown to ccFriesland. In periods when ccFriesland could not meet the demand for condensed milk it bought additional quantities from Wöhrmann (jobber function).

Unlike the Dicken model these three acquisitions had hardly anything to do with a strategy of market penetration. Only in the acquisition of Wöhrmann did an element of market penetration play a role. However, this was not the case for condensed milk, but for the fresh milk sector of this firm, mainly sold in the nearby Ruhr area. The acquired Lijempf plants in the province of Friesland were all active in the Dutch fresh milk sector, a sector ccFriesland was not allowed to enter. 'De Ommelanden' was producing condensed milk, but only for export markets (like Wöhrmann and ccFriesland itself). So the argument for these three acquisitions was primarily ccFriesland's lack of milk, the result of a growing demand for condensed milk. There was an alternative: expansion at Leeuwarden. But in that case the participating co-operatives should deliver more milk to ccFriesland. However, this was not a realistic option.

It is not surprising that ccFriesland did not consider direct investments abroad, apart from investments in sales offices, for a long time. By investing in condensed milk plants abroad it would be impossible to use the milk of the Frisian co-operatives, as milk is perishable and expensive to transport. Investing abroad would imply fewer exports from Friesland and fewer sales possibilities for Frisian milk.

However, in the middle of the 1950s the first signs of a new development were noticed. New competitors were penetrating some export markets with a cheap alternative: 'recombined milk' and 'filled milk'. They used milk powder and butter fat, the ingredients of condensed milk, and 'recombined' them again. For 'filled milk' vegetable oils were used. By buying the ingredients on the world market or by using local vegetable oils both alternatives were much cheaper than imported condensed milk. Moreover, the alternatives were welcomed by the governments of the importing countries. It created new jobs, used local resources ('filled milk'), saved foreign currencies, and reduced external control: the well-known advantages of import substitution.

The private condensed milk companies like Nestlé quickly responded to this trend, but ccFriesland played a waiting game. They expected that the low price of the alternatives would not be a problem, as the ccFriesland products were of high quality and well known. This expectation proved to be correct. But the situation changed when some countries started to restrict the import of condensed milk in order to stimulate their own production of alternatives: a direct consequence of the import substitution policy.

For ccFriesland there was no choice. If they would invest abroad they would lose an outlet for the milk of their associated dairy farmers. If they would not, they would lose markets too, entailing decreasing possibilities for selling Frisian milk. So it was decided to enter the 'recombined' and 'filled milk' market, although the export from Leeuwarden would be continued as long as possible and the establishment of ccFriesland recombined or filled milk plants abroad would be postponed as long as possible. In 1958 a cautious first attempt was made. A Philippine recombined milk producer was allowed to use ccFriesland brand names. The royalties compensated slightly for the decreasing export. The first participation in a recombined milk plant dates back to 1964 (Malaysia). Up to 1974 ccFriesland participated in plants in Singapore, Mozambique, Vietnam, Thailand, Indonesia, and Nigeria. The first three were later closed or sold again, partly due to political disturbances (Mozambique and Vietnam).

Here again ccFriesland followed a strategy of participation in existing firms. The fact that in many countries joint ventures were obligatory was therefore not a handicap. Where new activities were started was more a matter of chance than systematic search. For example, in Vietnam the ccFriesland agent wanted to start a recombined milk plant of its own. That would negatively influence ccFriesland's sales. So when this agent had difficulty financing his idea, ccFriesland was ready to lend him money on the condition that they would get a 50 per cent share in the new company (Cosuvina). The plant, started in 1970, was closed in 1975 because of the troubles in Vietnam at that time.

As a second example, in 1976 ccFriesland was informed by its former partner in Cosuvina that the American Foremost McKesson Company wanted to get rid of its poorly performing filled milk plant in Jakarta, Indonesia. At that time ccFriesland and its Indonesian partner Mantrust had a recombined milk plant in Jakarta: PT Friesche Vlag. A lack of capacity made both partners start negotiations with the Americans, leading to the take-over of PT Foremost Indonesia.

For a long time ccFriesland's investments in the recombined milk sector were defensive. Only when there was danger of losing the market was it decided to become active. Sometimes they waited too long and a market was lost, as was the case in Ghana. Nevertheless, in a financial sense this strategy turned out to be advantageous. Although the export from Leeuwarden decreased or stopped, ccFriesland was paid for technical assistance and for the use of its brand names. And of course it took its share of the profits. As an illustration, in 1986 ccFriesland made a disappointing profit of 7.9m. Dutch guilders (some $US4m.). The contribution of the participations in South East Asia to this profit was more than 50 per cent, exclusive of an even bigger amount paid for technical assistance and royalties. It opened the way for the board of directors to respond to opportunities in a more offensive way. It resulted in the acquisition of PT Foremost Indonesia, of Alaska in Thailand, and the biggest success until now, the acquisition of all dairy activities of the Foremost McKesson company outside the US. With this acquisition, including the name 'Foremost' ccFriesland obtained a strong market position in countries like Nigeria, Saudi Arabia, Thailand, Taiwan, and on the islands of Guam and Okinawa. Moreover, with this take-over ccFriesland could enter new markets: soft ice, drink milks, milk shakes and yoghurts.

Compared to the Dicken model, the establishment abroad of recombined milk plants was not ccFriesland's preferred option. But there was clearly no choice. As in the model there is a relation between participation and headquarters. This relation differs from that characterizing the acquisitions made to safeguard the milk base. 'De Ommelanden' as well as 'Wöhrmann' can be considered to a high degree pure branch plants for production. The marketing of the condensed milk is done by ccFriesland from Leeuwarden. 'Wöhrmann', however, does the marketing of the fresh milk sector for the Ruhr area itself. For the recombined plants, many of which are participations, ccFriesland generally tries to control the management. Fees are paid for technical assistance and royalties for the use of ccFriesland brand names. Sometimes the production capacity of the recombined milk plants is used to meet a sudden demand in another country. However, there is no flow of material goods between Leeuwarden and the plants abroad, although in the early 1960s there was some hope that Frisian milk powder could be used for the production of recombined and filled milk. But even the substantial EC subsidies did not make that a feasible option.

In general the recombined milk participations have a much more autonomous position than 'De Ommelanden' or 'Wöhrmann'. This is partly related to the fact that they could enter markets that ccFriesland was not allowed to enter in the Netherlands. Especially the fast-growing fresh milk sector (ice-cream, milk shakes, yoghurts etc.) turned out to be an attractive market. For these products the marketing and the R&D are mostly done by the participations themselves, for in spite of a tendency towards more uniform consumer preferences, there are still national differences. In South East Asia sweetened drinking milks and yoghurts are popular products for which there does not seem to be a market in the Netherlands. For such reasons, the relation between headquarter in Leeuwarden and participation abroad concentrates on technical and management assistance, and on the use of ccFriesland's brand names.

Product development and market development

A single-product exporting company runs high risks. To reduce these risks ccFriesland made many attempts to broaden its product mix and to find new markets. Initially these attempts concentrated on familiar milk or milk-related products. Yet there were many failures. For example, in the 1930s chocolate milk was introduced into the Indonesian market without any success. Two of the biggest successes of this product development and market development strategy are milk powder and coffee milk.

Milk powder

ccFriesland tried to include milk powder in its product-mix several times. Milk powder is a cheap alternative for condensed milk, so it could be sold in the same countries to which ccFriesland was exporting. Moreover, milk powder could easily be included in the activities of the sales offices and agencies for condensed milk. However, as some of the participating co-operatives, organized in another top-cooperative Frico, produced milk powder themselves, these attempts were opposed. In general Frico did not sell to individual households, it sold in bulk. Moreover, it was not very active in those countries where ccFriesland operated. Nevertheless, it would be unattractive for Frico to lose a potential outlet, even when this potential market would be lost to another Frisian company. But at last in 1953 ccFriesland was allowed to produce milk powder for its export markets, but only for use in households. The bulk market was reserved for Frico. However, the impact of this decision was restricted as the total quantity of milk ccFriesland could process did not increase. The increase of the powder production implied a decrease in the production of condensed milk.

Since then production and export have increased sharply. In 1963 it was 1.8 m. kg, in 1987 13.1 m. kg. Additionally ccFriesland buys powder from other companies (jobbers) regularly, packages it at Leeuwarden, and exports it with its own labels. The most important jobber is Wöhrmann. Powder is also bought by DOMO. This participant in ccFriesland is by far the biggest producer of milk powder in the northern part of the Netherlands. The reason for ccFriesland to buy additional powder is the limited quantity of milk available to ccFriesland itself. Even including these additional purchases ccFriesland is, within the Dutch context, a small producer. Its share in the Dutch export is only some 13 per cent. The most important markets are South Yemen and Nigeria.

For milk powder there was not any pressure to establish plants abroad: ccFriesland never left stage two in the Dicken model. Yet it was important for the company; when demand for condensed milk decreased there was at least an alternative.

Coffee milk

For a long time ccFriesland was hardly active on the Dutch market as there was no interest in condensed milk. In the 1930s it tried to introduce evaporated milk as a substitute for coffee cream. It is said that this idea was launched by an employee of ccFriesland. When sailing or camping he used to take condensed milk for his coffee as a substitute for cream, which is much more perishable. When ccFriesland accepted this idea, the market was tested. All coffee houses, restaurants, milkmen, and grocery shops in the city of Leeuwarden were given some free tins of evaporated milk to try. The result was disappointing. A trial in the city of Groningen had the same result. So in 1935 it was decided to stop the expensive campaign. Apparently, there was no market.

Although there was an increase in the demand for coffee milk in the years after, ccFriesland did not see much perspective for the product. But the situation changed when, just before and during the Second World War, the long shelf life of condensed milk was discovered. Although production during the war had been

temporarily stopped, Frisian Flag coffee milk was well known aft
the war, and ccFriesland became the market leader in tl
Netherlands.

The case of ccFriesland illustrates the fact that firms are ofte
confronted with unpredictable turbulence in their environment
When ccFriesland had the idea it could make a profit on coff
milk, the Korean War started. In February 1951 the Dutc
authorities prohibited the use of tins. At that time all coffee mil
producers in the Netherlands used tins, except one (Nutricia), tha
used bottles. It took ccFriesland three months before it was able t
sell its Frisian Flag in bottles. For three months the consumers ha
to use other brands. It took ccFriesland another year to recaptui
its leading position.

Now ccFriesland is the market leader for coffee milk in tl
Netherlands. In 1987 more than 50 m. kg was produced. Its shar
in the Dutch market for full milk is nearly 70 per cent. In order t
safeguard its position, ccFriesland participated in a dairy wholesa
ing company. It also introduced coffee milk with less fat conter
and it built a distribution centre in Vianen in the middle of th
country to deliver to small clients located in the western or souther
part of the country (big clients are supplied from Leeuwarden).

From a spatial point of view, apart from the distribution centr
no other locations are involved. As there is hardly any export, thi
product does not even reach the first stage in the Dicken model.

Diversification

Milk powder and coffee milk helped to reduce the risks tha
characterize a one-product company. For ccFriesland, milk powde
was a new product to be introduced in existing export market
according to a market penetration strategy. Coffee milk, an 'olc
product (condensed milk), was introduced into a new market. In it
attempts to broaden its product mix ccFriesland was also active ii
bringing new products onto new markets, in its strategy of diversifi
cation. Yet diversification was not given high priority for a lon,
time. Quality control, to support the brand names, was considere
to be more important, although eventually quality contrc
developed into R&D activities. However, because of the origin an
the modest size of ccFriesland, these R&D activities are closel
related to the 'milk line'. Therefore two lines will be distinguishe
within the diversification strategy: one based on milk, the other on
having no relation at all with milk. Some examples will be giver
from both sectors.

The 'milk line': lactose or milk sugar

ccFriesland has always been interested in whey. Whey is a by-product of cheese-making. As the participating co-operatives produced cheese, they had plenty of whey. It was mainly used to feed the cattle. The co-operatives supported research looking for higher valued uses. It resulted in the production of lactose or milk sugar. Since 1948 two varieties have been made: edible lactose, used for instance in baby food and chocolate, and pharmaceutical lactose, used in medicine. Lactose is not a consumer product, but a bulk product.

In 1987 ccFriesland produced more than 15 m. kg edible and nearly 5 m. kg pharmaceutical lactose (1960: 1.9 resp. 2.0 m. kg). It is the third producer in the Netherlands, with more than 20 per cent of the total output. The strong increase in production implies that since the 1960s whey has far surpassed milk in quantities as a raw material: in 1987 ccFriesland processed more than 500 m. kg, as compared to some 300 m. kg milk and less than 100 m. kg skimmed milk.

Although lactose is a small product compared to condensed milk in volume as well as in annual turnover, ccFriesland considers it an important product. It has slightly reduced the extreme dominance (and risks) of condensed milk. It has created a new and abundant resource base.

Of the lactose produced in Leeuwarden, some 80 per cent of the pharmaceutical product and 90 per cent of the edible product is exported. Here too, ccFriesland had to follow a market penetration strategy, with the help of sales agencies. As lactose is a raw material for the manufacturing sector, the sales agencies for milk powder or condensed milk are not involved. Moreover, most of the export goes to countries other than the destination of condensed milk or milk powder. The main export recipients are Japan and West Germany.

For lactose there has never been any pressure to proceed to stage two in the Dicken model. There is no lack of whey, as cheese is the main product of the participating dairy co-operatives, and there are no specific regional markets (lactose is a global product), and hardly any import restrictions. Recently the board of directors has decided to end all whey activities. Modern ultrafiltration techniques make it more efficient to process the whey where it is produced, in the cheese factory.

The 'milk line': some other products

Many more products based on milk as raw material have been introduced. Some of these are really product innovations of ccFriesland. It was well known that a synthetic fibre could be made from milk. Courtaulds was one of the producers, selling it as 'fibrolane'. In 1940 ccFriesland started the production of this milk yarn. In 1943 a top-production of 4,000 kg/week was realized After a short intermezzo because of a shortage of milk during the war the plant was re-activated in 1945. However, consumers considered the milk yarn as a wartime substitute. When the war was over they wanted to have real honey, real wool, etc. Because of a lack of demand the plant was closed in 1951.

In 1957 ccFriesland together with other companies started the production of milk for feeding calves and other uses. This calf feed is based on milk powder. It is still produced in Sloten in an old dairy plant that was taken over in 1955. Less successful was the introduction in 1976 of artificial meat, a real ccFriesland innovation, based on a mixture of fibres from milk albumen and meat. However, the meat processing companies were not convinced of the qualities of this artificial meat. As a consequence the activities were stopped in 1977.

Although the R&D activities of ccFriesland were concentrated on 'milk', the firm's scope for expansion was limited. As was said before, it was not allowed to enter markets in which the participating co-operatives were active. As these co-operatives had their own milk-oriented R&D activities, the options for ccFriesland were restricted to small niches. For example, ccFriesland is not allowed to be active in the Dutch soft ice market, although it is one of the market leaders in East Asia.

Real diversification

'Long run growth requires either a steady geographical expansion of the market area or the continuous innovation of new products. In the long run only product innovation can avoid the constraint imposed by the size of the world market for a given product' (Casson 1983:24). Although ccFriesland always considered new products within the 'milk line' as diversification, it has also tried products outside this 'milk line'. Many of these attempts can be characterized as opportunistic. They mainly took place in the period when the financial performance of the firm was extremely good. In that situation evidently less emphasis was placed on a careful analysis of the possibilities.

As a first example, in 1964 ccFriesland bought Bijlenga Engineering in Leeuwarden, a firm with an outstanding tradition in the Frisian dairy industry, producing machines for cheese manufacturing. One of the managers of ccFriesland was the chairman of its board of directors. When the owner-president of Bijlenga died, this board was asked by the heirs what to do with the firm. Since no other candidates for a take-over could be found, ccFriesland did, arguing that this would be a positive contribution to the Frisian dairy industry as a whole. In 1972 ccFriesland sold Bijlenga Engineering to the Swedish company Alfa-Laval because it was considered to be too far removed from the core activities.

As a second example, in 1966 ccFriesland was asked to participate with other co-operatives in the northern part of the Netherlands in a plant for the manufacture of potato chips. Although there had been a market survey it turned out that the chips they made (Crespa chips) could not compete with the market leaders, Golden Wonder and Smith's Chips. The small participants immediately withdrew. The two remaining co-operatives, including ccFriesland, went on for some time without any success. In 1970 the plant was closed since attempts to sell it had failed.

Potato chips were part of the product mix of ccFriesland for only four years. Some soft drinks disappeared even faster: Cockta after three years, Simandra after two years and Sprento after only one year (just like artificial meat). The production of vending machines for drink milk for canteens was also stopped after one year as was a chocolate milk powder.

Notwithstanding these attempts there was also some countervailing force within ccFriesland to prevent extreme diversification. ccFriesland is owned by dairy co-operatives. The supervisory board consists of representatives of these co-operatives. Many of them originate in the dairy farming sector, some run a farm themselves. Traditionally these members of the board look at diversification attempts from the point of view of their contribution to ccFriesland's ultimate goal: selling the milk of its farmers at the best possible price. This sometimes limited the options of the board of directors.

For example, in 1957 ccFriesland started the production of a soft drink called Rivella, introduced some years before by a Swiss company on the Swiss market. The management was informed about Rivella by chance. The head of the sales department, who happened to be on holiday in Switzerland, was ordered to contact the Swiss company immediately. The first impressions were positive, so the board of directors made a proposal to the supervisory board to start production on a licence base, as the financial prospects looked fine. The project was indeed started, but it was difficult to convince the supervisory board of its viability. Its members had serious objections to the proposal because the product had hardly any relation with milk. The argument that the project looked profitable was not enough. According to one of the members: 'If we are going to make Rivella we may as well produce bicycles.' In other words: ccFriedland should stay out of non-milk activities.

This restriction may have been annoying for the board of directors, but it implied that real diversifications were looked at very critically. That may have reduced the pressure on the board of directors to start real diversification on a large scale. There was a built-in 'back-to-basics' tendency which counterbalanced the popular strategy of diversification. This trend made good business sense. After all many diversifications of ccFriesland that were unrelated to milk were certainly not big successes. Some, in fact, were real failures. This is not surprising, as diversification is a strategy that is often propounded, but very difficult to perform.

The attempts to diversify and to develop new products have two locational characteristics. First, nearly all were oriented towards the province of Friesland. Secondly, there were hardly any locational choices involved. For acquisitions, like Bijlenga and Lijempf, this is quite understandable. But even when new products were introduced no alternatives were explored regarding the location of the plants. The production of milk yarn took place at Leeuwarden near the R&D department in one of the existing buildings. In the R&D department artificial meat was produced (for a short time). Leeuwarden was also the preferred location for the production of calf feed. However, this was prohibited for hygienic reasons. It was therefore decided to operate in Sloten, where ccFriesland still owned an abandoned dairy plant (taken over from Lijempf). Another old, unused Lijempf plant (in Wolvega) accommodated the production of Rivella and other soft drinks. The old Lijempf plant at Berlicum, near Leeuwarden, underwent several changes in its function within the ccFriesland organization. After the acquisition in 1955 it became a regional collecting centre for milk for a number of years. Later on and after some years of disuse, Sweden Freezer ice machines were assembled there, followed for a short period by complete production of these ice machines. Still later Berlicum became the location where ice wafers were made, which employed a different labour force (women) than had been used in the production of ice machines. Some years ago the Berlicum site was closed for good.

Expansion and restructuring

Notwithstanding the counter-balancing forces, there were many small-scale ad hoc diversification moves. This resulted in a very diffuse product mix, consisting of a small number of 'big' products and many 'small' products. As long as the company as a whole performed well, this did not constitute a real financial problem. But in periods of poor performance, the board of directors realized that the diversification strategy did not result in the predicted synergetic effects. On the contrary, they had to invest a lot of time in problematic small activities. But when the problems involved the big products, it was hardly worthwhile to expend energy on the small ones. Therefore in 1980, when profits were still huge, it was decided to re-evaluate the mix of small products.

All small products (consumer goods) were put into one portfolio matrix. Expectations for market growth and about the competitive strength of the company were used to evaluate the different products. Actually, in reality this is a difficult exercise. It assumes that all overhead costs are correctly split over the various products. The result for ccFriesland is given in Figure 6.5. The total picture was disappointing. It culminated in the decision to sell a number of products to other firms or to liquidate them. For the products with enough prospects a profit centre was established, deliberately located outside Leeuwarden in order to avoid anti-synergetic effects. For two products the decision whether to 'make or buy' resulted in the decision to stop production.

From a spatial point of view the diversification strategy had a simple scenario. Nearly all attempts were oriented towards the Dutch market. Production was concentrated in Friesland, in plants already owned by ccFriesland. For distribution purposes the centre in Vianen was used. The evaluation of the small products resulted in the establishment of a new profit nucleus dealing with mostly 'small' products. The head office of this profit nucleus, as well as part of the production, is located in Hoofddorp, near Amsterdam. These 'small' products never left stage one of the Dicken model.

On a higher level, restructuring within ccFriesland will continue. The situation in the co-operative movement in the northern part of the Netherlands is not ideal. Several co-operatives have their own interests. And although some top-cooperatives have already integrated even on that level there are clear particular and clear general interests, for even in the co-operative movement solidarity has its price. Thus, it is quite understandable that for decades attempts have been made to integrate all activities. At present these attempts have reached a new phase. Even if overall consolidation, which would forge the biggest dairy company in the Netherlands, may not be feasible, integration will definitely take place. It will certainly have consequences for ccFriesland, if the company continues to exist under that name.

Theory and ccFriesland's reality

Our findings may be summarized in the following conclusions.

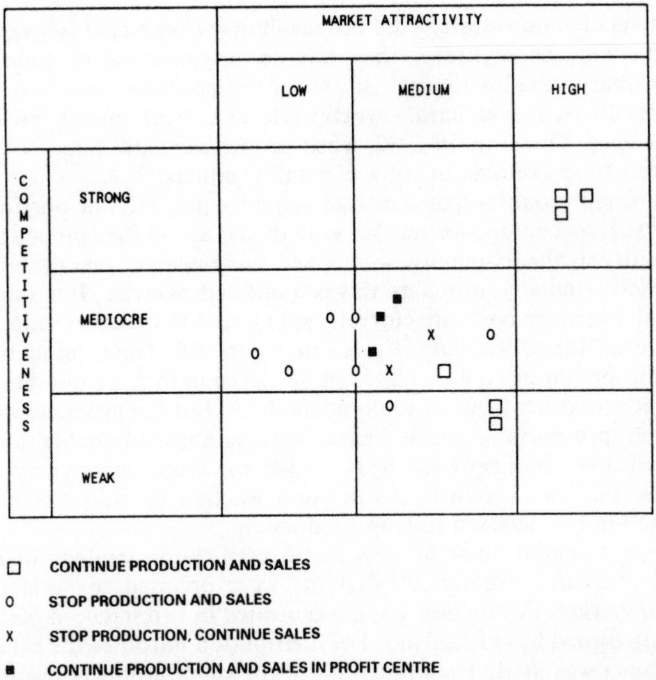

		MARKET ATTRACTIVITY		
		LOW	MEDIUM	HIGH
C O M P E T I T I V E N E S S	STRONG			□ □ □
	MEDIOCRE	O O O O	■ ■ X O O ■ X □	
	WEAK		O □ □	

□   CONTINUE PRODUCTION AND SALES

O   STOP PRODUCTION AND SALES

X   STOP PRODUCTION, CONTINUE SALES

■   CONTINUE PRODUCTION AND SALES IN PROFIT CENTRE

Figure 6.5   The ccFriesland portfolio for the small product segment

Source: ccFriesland

1 It is difficult to categorize multi-product firms on the basis of models like those of Hakanson and Dicken. Some products will be in quite a different stage than other ones. Looking at the number of its products, ccFriesland could be categorized as a stage-one firm. Looking at the most important product in terms of annual turnover (condensed milk), ccFriesland corresponds well to the sequence of the Dicken model.

2 For a company producing consumer goods, the construction of greenfield plants is hardly worthwhile. Success is dependent on market power. Nearly all ccFriesland activities abroad are related to acquisitions and participations.

3 Even growing companies are restructuring all the time. ccFriesland closed or sold many plants, partly because of developments in its environment, partly because of their poor financial performance.

4 The continuous process of restructuring suggests much more dynamics than can be seen from the locational pattern. Several

diversification attempts of ccFriesland took place in plants that had lost their former function. In the acquired dairy plant at Berlicum, a sequence of highly divergent products were made before it was closed definitely.

5 To understand the character of the growth process of an individual company, the history of that company has to be consulted. The defensive strategy of ccFriesland concerning condensed milk and the diversification in the 'milk line' are clearly related to its position within the co-operative dairy movement in the province of Friesland.

References

Ansoff, H. J. (1968) *Corporate Strategy, an Analytical Approach to Business Policy for Growth and Expansion*, Harmondsworth: Penguin.

Bremen, J. W. van den (1977) 'Verandering en Continuïteit. Een studie over de dynamiek in en van de ruimtelijke organisatie van de bedrijvigheid met speciale aandacht voor het stelsel van melkverwerking in het ruraal-urbaan spanningsveld in Nederland', Ph.D., University of Groningen.

Casson, M. (1983) *The Growth of International Business*, London: Allen & Unwin.

Dicken, P. (1986) *Global Shift. Industrial Change in a Turbulent World*, London: Harper & Row.

Fröhlich, F. W. (1976) *Multinationale Ondernemingen: Ontstaan, Organisatie en Management*, Utrecht/Antwerpen: Spectrum.

Hakanson, L. (1979) 'Towards a theory of location and corporate growth', in F. E. I. Hamilton and G. J. R. Linge (eds) *Spatial Analysis, Industry and Industrial Environment*, vol. 1, *Industrial Systems*, Chichester: John Wiley, 115-39.

Hartog, A. P. Den (1986) 'Diffusion of milk as a new food to tropical regions: the example of Indonesia 1880-1942, Ph.D., University of Wageningen.

Keeble, D. and Wever, E. (1986) (eds) *New Firms and Regional Development in Europe*, London: Croom Helm.

Lloyd, P. E. and Dicken, P. (1977) *Location in Space; a Theoretical Approach to Economic Geography*, London: Harper & Row.

Penrose, E. T. (1959) *The Story of the Growth of the Firm*, New York: John Wiley.

Taylor, M. (1975) 'Organizational growth, spatial interaction and location decision-making', *Regional Studies* 9:313-23.

Taylor, M. and Thrift, N. (1982) (eds) *The Geography of Multinationals*, London: Croom Helm.

Thomas, M. D. (1980) 'Explanatory frameworks for growth and change in multiregional firms', *Economic Geography*, 1-18.

Tjepkema, K. (1963) *Dat is 't Kondensfabryk. Een halve eeuw coöperatieve condensindustrie in Friesland. Uitgegeven ter gelegenheid van het 50-jarig bestaan van de ccFriesland*, Leeuwarden.

Egbert Wever

Vernon, R. (1966) 'International investment and international trade in the product cycle', *Quarterly Journal of Economics*, 80:190–207.

Wever, E. (1989) *Afzender: ccFriesland*, published on the 75th anniversary of ccFriesland, Leeuwarden.

Wissema, J. G. (1986) *De kunst van strategisch management: invoering, toepassing, trends*, Deventer: Kluwer Nive/VSB.

Chapter seven

MacMillan Bloedel
Corporate restructuring
and employment change

Trevor Barnes, Roger Hayter and Eric Grass

Introduction

In North America, patterns of labour vulnerability within broadly
differentiated labour markets were well established during the
recessionary periods of the 'long boom' of the 1950s and 1960s. At
least the relevant literature stated as much. It was argued, to use the
vernacular, that the 'white-collar jobs' of senior management,
scientists and engineers ('primary independent labour markets')
were rarely scathed while lay-offs of 'blue-collar' workers among
unionized industries ('primary subordinate labour markets') were
carried out on the basis of seniority. With economic recovery, the
laid-off employees were then re-hired based on an order determined
by a formal agreement between unions and management. In the
non- or weakly-unionized industries, managerial discretion over
lay-offs and re-hiring of workers ('independent labour markets')
was greater.

This seemingly regular and enduring pattern ended in Canada
around 1981 when the country, as elsewhere, entered an abrupt,
severe, and sustained recessionary period (Norcliffe 1987). National
unemployment rates jumped a full 6 per cent from late 1981 to late
1982. Furthermore, the effects of the recession were geographically
uneven. The resource-dependent peripheral regions of Canada,
including the focus of our study, British Columbia, were particularly badly hit. The legacy of that crisis continues to be evident in
these hinterland regions.

In addition, it also became evident that the recessionary conditions of the early 1980s heralded profound changes in the
organization, location, and methods of production in advanced
capitalist countries ('economic restructuring'). Whether these
changes were a precipitate of crisis, or whether crisis was their
precipitate, the combination of recession and restructuring during
the 1980s had a deep-seated effect on employment levels, relations,

structure, and location. The facet of employment change addressed in this chapter is the effect of a sustained period of recession and restructuring on labour vulnerability, with particular reference to MacMillan Bloedel, a large British Columbian-based forest product corporation, and, until the 1980s, Canada's leading forest enterprise. Empirically, we examine the employment changes implemented by MacMillan Bloedel at its various manufacturing operations and head office within British Columbia between 1980 and 1988. We analyse in particular detail the nature of employment changes during this period at two large plants in order to reveal the internal workings of a given labour market segment and the way in which labour vulnerability within that segment is defined.

Within the geography of enterprise tradition our chapter builds on the theme of *in-situ* employment change and locational adjustment by firms over time (Hayter and Watts 1983: 166–8; Krumme 1971; Steed 1968) by incorporating labour market, and more specifically, labour segmentation theory. While this theory has been used to help explain shifting patterns of employment change (Clark 1981; Danson 1982; Massey 1984) we suggest that our firm-level study of employment change in the resource sector during a period of recession and restructuring contributes to the literature in at least two respects. First, most studies of employment change examine a limited range of secondary manufacturing sectors, sectors characterized by relatively high capital mobility. Within this limited domain, industrial geographers have then emphasized the corporate strategy of geographical relocation as a means of dealing with labour, and thereby defining patterns of labour vulnerability. The resource industries, in contrast, are severely, albeit not absolutely, constrained in terms of location precisely because they are resource industries. *In situ* employment changes are the norm. Resource firms, therefore, must employ a different set of strategies, at least until very recently, not discussed in the literature because of the emphasis on 'the geographical solution'. Explicating such strategies, however, is essential if we are to understand both the mechanisms of employment change in general, and the changing pattern of labour vulnerability in particular.

Second, because industrial geographers have emphasized the geographical solution, they have not always unpacked the internal dynamics of particular segments of local labour markets in a given place and time. By asserting that through relocation firms switch from say, the primary subordinate labour market in one place, to a secondary labour market in another, researchers have not had to examine the internal complexities of each labour market; for the important issue is only the relationship between labour markets, not the relationships that subsist within them (a notable exception is Clark 1986; see also Morris 1988 for a preliminary discussion of 'core' and 'periphery' components of given labour market segments). In contrast, when dealing with *in situ* change, the focus is necessarily on the internal dynamics within the same labour market. A case study of the resource sector, therefore, necessarily pushes the inquiry into a discussion of the internal differences and dynamics within particular segments of the labour market at specific times and places.

This chapter is divided into three sections. First, we review and explore aspects of the relationships between firms and labour markets in times of recession. In particular, we try to substantiate our claim that in many ways the resource sector falls outside the current parameters of theoretical discussion with respect to restructuring and recession. Second, from the onset of recession in the early 1980s we note changes in MacMillan Bloedel's strategy and structure world-wide and identify the specific employment level changes in the firm's British Columbian facilities. In this regard, our case study of MacMillan Bloedel also illustrates how the leading companies of 'peripheral' regions frequently come under the control of more powerful and centrally based corporations. Third, we detail the employment changes at two of the firm's largest and long-established sawmills. It is here that we see the internal workings of a given labour market segment, and also the way in which labour vulnerability within that segment is defined.

Firms, labour markets and recession

Over the last decade there has been an increasing amount of research on the effect of recession on corporate plans (Massey and Meegan, 1982; Townsend 1983; Hayter 1985, 1986; Clark 1986). Frederickson and Lindmark (1979:179), for example, argue that the immediate impact of recession is to encourage 'cost hunt' by reducing, at least temporarily, variable costs. Clearly, a key variable cost is labour. The result has been a number of studies documenting the change in the employment relation as capital seeks to erode the strength of labour. The special contribution made by geographers to such discussion is the emphasis placed on a changing spatial division of labour. Precisely because place matters, firms are able to 'cost hunt' by relocating and tapping into less costly and/or more pliant 'greenfield' local labour markets. Although not always explicitly recognized, the spatial divisions of labour thesis bring together two different kinds of literature.

The first, and best known, is the geographical theory of plant location. Although not couched in terms of the neo-classical theory of the firm, work, such as Doreen Massey's (1984), still rests on the premise that firms maximize profits and/or minimize costs. Furthermore, the central cost to minimize is labour. Firms then rationally stalk the regions looking for the least cost and most conducive labour markets. In this sense, as Clark (1986) notes, Massey's work is really a theory of relative advantage. As such, it is best viewed as a sophisticated explanation of labour market variation across space, but not an alternative explanation of plant relocation.

The second literature is that on labour market segmentation. Although the historical antecedents of the labour market segmentation thesis include Alfred Marshall and even Adam Smith, it was first systematically discussed by Kerr (1954) in the 1950s, using the feudal metaphors of guild, manorial, and free agency to label each of the labour market segments (Loveridge and Mok 1979). Gordon (1973) subsequently reduced the categories to two in his 'dual labour market' theory proposed in the early 1970s, while Doeringer and Piore (1971) at around the same time in effect re-labelled Kerr's original categories respectively as, primary independent, primary subordinate, and secondary. More recently, Loveridge and Mok (1979) advocate the addition of a fourth labour market segment to Doeringer and Piore's original trichotomous scheme by subdividing the secondary segment into independent and subordinate components. The argument for each one of these different typologies is in effect the same: the labour market is not perfectly competitive but is divided into non-competing segments. Each segment, however, provides a quite different set of employment relations. Crudely, the primary segment is characterized by 'high wages, good working conditions, employment stability, chances of advancement, equity, and due process in the administration of work rules', while jobs in the secondary labour market tend to have 'low wages and fringe benefits, poor working conditions, high labour turnover, little chance of advancement, and often arbitrary and capricious supervision' (Doeringer and Piore 1971:165).

Because of the differences between the two labour markets, it is generally believed that lay-off decisions by firms discriminate between labour market segments. In particular, it is argued that because firms have made considerable 'fixed' investment in terms of recruitment and firm-specific training within the primary labour market (firms create an internal labour market), they are reluctant to shed this labour segment. In contrast, the secondary labour market consists of workers who either have general skills or very few skills, and are therefore extremely vulnerable to lay-offs (firms easily hire and fire because of an external labour market).

Although the labour market segmentation thesis was conceived in a-spatial terms, it was readily apparent that it had a direct spatial application. Indeed, primary and secondary labour markets are, to use Cooke's (1983) term, 'spatially discontinuous' (see also Danson 1982). It is here that the link is forged with the literature on plant location. With a given technology, firms relocate to tap into the appropriate spatially-circumscribed labour market segment.

For our purposes, the interesting theoretical conclusion that emerged from the melding of the two literatures is a different view of a firm's discriminatory labour market practices during a recession. It was increasingly recognized that through the restructuring of organization, technology, and sub-contracting links, firms could find it more profitable to lay off primary workers, especially primary subordinate workers, and substitute for them secondary labour market workers in very different locations. In such instances, traditional notions of labour vulnerability are clearly turned upside down. For example, in Massey's (1984) work on the location of micro-electronic assembly plants in south Wales, the relocation of the production plants of electronic firms from the central cities of London and Manchester to south Wales represents an attempt to switch between two different labour market segments from primary subordinate to secondary. In discussing issues of patriarchy, the existence of close-knit communities, and the history of past industrial investment in the south Wales region, Massey is explaining why there exists within that region a secondary labour market composed mainly of female workers, and thereby one that is seductive to the electronic firms moving there.

The spatial divisions of labour argument, and its associated thesis about labour vulnerability, is both powerful and impressive. Its potential shortcomings are also clear, however. First, the idea that firms locate and invest so as to maximize profits and minimize costs has been attacked empirically. Webber (1988), for example, shows that for the Canadian manufacturing sector, at least, there is no relationship between investment flows and profit rates (see also Webber 1989 and Massey's 1989 response). And theoretically there is a huge literature on satisficing and institutional theories of the firm that dispenses with any kind of maximizing framework (Rozen 1985). Second, although economic geographers have not been very critical of the segmented labour market thesis, economists have. The principal criticism is the lack of empirical evidence to support such a thesis. Thus, it is argued that in those empirical studies completed there is little correspondence between the categories of information collected and the categories that such data is supposed to test. More broadly, researchers testing for segmentation have employed macro-level statistics to verify a micro-level phenomenon. In a severe critique Cain (1976:41) has gone further and argued that the segmented labour market thesis has no thesis to test. It is merely a taxonomy, because it provides 'no rule . . . to designate which jobs go into one or the other sector'.

Our approach to this issue is more circumspect. While recognizing these criticisms, we think they are not definitive. To argue that labour segmentation has not been properly empirically tested to date, for example, does not rule out correct testing in the future. Furthermore, the argument that labour segmentation has not yet been correctly tested is not itself a valid reason to dismiss it, as its critics urge. Our concern with the spatial divisions of labour argument, and its corollary views about labour vulnerability, is that it logically only applies to those manufacturing firms that are able to relocate. There are, however, a number of industries where this is not an option, for example, the resource sector. In this case the spatial divisions of labour argument breaks down in a number of respects. First, it does not make sense to speak of plants relocating to maximize profits/minimize costs. Any changes have to be *in situ*. Second, it also does not make sense to speak of switching between labour market segments. A resource firm must carry out changes with the existing labour market segment in that place. And third, the spatial divisions of labour argument is of no help in understanding labour vulnerability in a sustained recession within the resource sector because such a thesis is not concerned with the internal dynamics of a given labour market segment. Rather, its focus is only the relationship between segments.

To examine what does happen to employment during a prolonged and deep recessionary period within the resource sector we turn to our case study, MacMillan Bloedel which, since the early decades of this century, has been an important force in the forest product industries of British Columbia.

MacMillan Bloedel

The origins of MacMillan Bloedel, its expansion and impacts within British Columbia and then elsewhere, and subsequent adjustments to its corporate system until the early 1980s have been well documented (Hayter 1976; MacKay 1982; Schwindt 1976). In brief, the British Columbian origins of MacMillan Bloedel can be traced to the MacMillan Export Company; Bloedel, Stewart, and Welch; and the Powell River Company which were respectively incorporated in the province in 1919, 1911 and 1910. The first two companies merged in 1951 and the resulting company then merged with the Powell River Company in 1959. In 1965 the company became known as MacMillan Bloedel.

All three founder companies had expanded operations and achieved a limited degree of integration by the 1940s. After 1945, as a result of the mergers, large-scale investments and joint ventures, the firm grew rapidly in pursuit of horizontal and vertical integration strategies. By 1976 McMillan Bloedel had become the leading Canadian producer of lumber and newsprint, the second largest producer of plywood, and an important producer of market kraft pulp, paperboard, fine papers, and converted paper products especially corrugated containers, and a number of wood-based products such as shingles and particleboard. MacMillan Bloedel concentrated its expansion in the south-western littoral British Columbia until the 1960s, after which the firm rapidly expanded to Europe, the United States, eastern Canada and to some extent to South East Asia. MacMillan Bloedel also invested in major R&D programmes which were principally located near its Vancouver head office, British Columbia. As an autonomous and publically traded multinational and the largest forest product company in Canada, by the mid 1960s MacMillan Bloedel had reached the peak of corporate power in the province.

During the 1970s, MacMillan Bloedel remained the leading forest product (and industrial) company in British Columbia. At the same time, the more volatile economic conditions of this period were reflected in MacMillan Bloedel's performance. In fact, in the recessionary year of 1975 the firm recorded its first loss as a publicly owned company of $18.9m. This loss, which directly stemmed from the firm's shipping subsidiary, which had negotiated long-term charters at peak rates and had ordered new ships to be built just before a precipitous decline in demand for shipping, resulted in resignations by the two senior executive officers and various cost cutting measures (MacKay 1982: 296–315). It also signalled a shift in corporate strategy. In particular, plans to diversify away from the forest industries were withdrawn and the few, relatively small-scale diversification ventures were divested. In addition, MacMillan Bloedel decided not to expand the international scope of its operations further geographically. Rather, the firm became primarily concerned with expanding, modernizing, and integrating its existing global network. Doubtless, growing global uncertainties and escalating capital costs were important factors underlying this strategy.

As events transpired, as part of an industry-wide trend in North

America, MacMillan Bloedel enjoyed record high earnings and record high production levels in 1979 and earnings and production remained very strong in 1980. Stimulated by this performance, MacMillan Bloedel, once again as part of an industry-wide trend, embarked upon a major capital investment programme in 1979–80. Indeed during the 1979–82 period MacMillan Bloedel spent over $1.1bn on its facilities, particularly those in the southern US and British Columbia. Unfortunately, these capital expenditures started to come on stream as the worst recession in fifty years to hit the forest industries, and the economy, began. Moreover, in early 1981, MacMillan Bloedel was acquired by the Toronto-based Noranda Corporation.

The size of MacMillan Bloedel, its earnings performance, the value of its human capital and timber assets, which included some of the highest yielding privately owned land in Canada, along with the fact that MacMillan Bloedel was a relatively widely held publicly traded company, made the company an attractive, if expensive, take-over target. In fact, in 1979, an attempt to acquire MacMillan Bloedel by Canadian Pacific, a Montreal-based conglomerate, was rebuffed by the provincial government of British Columbia, the major forest land-owner in the province. At the time, the government argued that 'BC resources were not for sale'. Ironically, the provincial government was at least partially responsible for a successful take-over of MacMillan Bloedel by another eastern Canadian firm, Noranda of Toronto. Thus, the British Columbia Resources Investment Corporation, set up by the provincial government in 1979, initiated a take-over bid of MacMillan Bloedel in early 1981. As a consequence, MacMillan Bloedel became a legitimate take-over target and in another hostile bid, in May 1981, Noranda obtained a 49 per cent controlling interest in MacMillan Bloedel.

Within the decision-making parameters now set by a parent company, MacMillan Bloedel became overwhelmingly concerned with coping and surviving the recession and in a relatively short period of time the firm was significantly restructured. The remainder of this chapter focuses particularly on the employment implications of this restructuring in British Columbia. Information is drawn from interviews with corporate and plant management, union representatives and from secondary sources such as MacMillan Bloedel's annual reports, newspaper cuttings, and trade directories.

MacMillan Bloedel: employment corporate restructuring and change in British Columbia 1981–8

The effects of the recent recession in the forest product industries within British Columbia were harsh. In 1981, for example, the forest industries incurred a massive $500m. loss and generated a return on capital of just 0.6 per cent. In 1979, in contrast, the industries had generated a $500m. profit and a return on capital of 8.9 per cent (Farris 1983:49). Every important company which publicly reported its financial performance incurred losses in the early 1980s, and in several instances losses were recorded in three consecutive years. Debt-equity ratios also increased dramatically, and production of key commodities in 1981 and 1982 dropped well below the record 1979 levels. In addition, as might be expected, job losses were substantial and rapid. Indeed, between 1979 and 1982 job losses in the provincial forest product industries amounted to at least 23,000. Moreover this reduction in employment, which was concentrated in the coastal region and in the sawmilling and plywood industries, has proved to be largely permanent although production and profit levels have recovered (Grass and Hayter 1989). With its British Columbia facilities entirely within the coastal region, MacMillan Bloedel was a central actor in the restructuring of the forest industries of the province at this time.

Corporate restructuring

The effects of the recession of the early 1980s on MacMillan Bloedel's financial performance were substantial and serious (Table 7.1). Thus, following the record sales of $2.46bn in 1980 sales dropped to $2.21bn in 1981 and $1.84bn in 1982, while the 1980 level was not surpassed again, even in nominal terms, until 1986. Earnings also declined and in 1981 and 1982 MacMillan Bloedel experienced significant operating losses, a large net loss in 1982, and relatively small earnings of surpluses in 1983 and 1984. The high level of capital investment of the 1979–82 period, which the firm had no option but to complete, also contributed to MacMillan Bloedel's immediate financial problems by adding capacity as demand declined and by helping to raise the firm's debt-equity ratio. Bearing in mind the spiralling interest rates of the time, MacMillan Bloedel's debt–enquiry ratio increased markedly between 1979 and 1982.

To cope with its financial problems, and within the context of its new reality as a subsidiary company, MacMillan Bloedel embarked upon various cost-cutting, extraordinary revenue-generating, and

Table 7.1 MacMillan Bloedel: selected financial statistics 1979–87

	1979	*1980*	*1981*	*1982*	*1983*	*1984*	*1985*	*1986*	*1987*
Sales $bn.	2.20	2.46	2.21	1.84	2.04	2.13	2.34	2.51	3.13
Investment $m.[a]	280.4	327.7	307.9	206.8	103.6	137.7	96.6	100.0	256.6
Earnings $m.[b]	154.9	113.2	(26.7)	(93.3)	2.8	19.3	42.9	133.3	280.6

Source: Financial Post-Card Corporation Service

Notes: a. Refers to capital investments.
b. Refers to operating earnings (losses) after taxes excluding extraordinary items.

some product–development measures. Thus by the end of 1984 MacMillan Bloedel had reduced its work-force, world-wide, by about 35 per cent mainly via lay-offs and attrition but also through sale of assets to other firms to generate badly needed cash. In particular, MacMillan Bloedel sold a newsprint manufacturing facility in New Brunswick in July 1981 for $145m., a 50 per cent interest in a fine paper making facility in the Vancouver area in February 1983, a 50 per cent interest in its various corrugated container operations across Canada in June 1983 for about $26m. and in the same year MacMillan Bloedel reduced its interest in a Dutch fine paper producer for $88m. (and a net gain of $45m.). In addition, in 1981 MacMillan Bloedel sold its head-office building in downtown Vancouver, a paper bag plant in 1984, and in 1983 it merged its (eight) corrugated container facilities in the UK with those of a British firm. MacMillan Bloedel also generated cash in this period by new share issues and by sales of future tax benefits in the US which in 1982 alone realized extraordinary gains of $36m.

Within British Columbia, MacMillan Bloedel introduced a new organizational structure in 1982 which ostensibly represented a 'decentralization' of decision-making from the Vancouver head office to three regional spheres of operation based on the integrated forest product complexes at Powell River, Port Alberni, and Harmac. In reality, decentralization implied two distinct motives. First, decentralization clearly represented an attempt to establish explicit accounting responsibility at sub-regional levels within coastal British Columbia to reinforce enthusiasm for productivity improvements and profitability in all operations among managers and employees. Second, decentralization appears to have provided a euphemism for the downsizing of MacMillan Bloedel's Vancouver head office which in turn reflected MacMillan Bloedel's reduced size and complexity and its subsidiary status.

MacMillan Bloedel obviously needed to reduce its costs

drastically and obtain cash injections in the early 1980s to offset operating losses. In this regard, it should be noted that plant closures and lay-offs are themselves not 'costless'. During 1982, for example, MacMillan Bloedel booked $65.7m. for severance, closure and related costs.

The firm also needed to maintain a capital investment programme, albeit at a reduced level. To some extent, MacMillan Bloedel's investments have been 'non-discretionary' and related, for example, to equipment repair and maintenance and logging and construction. In addition, the firm has invested in new technology to increase efficiency and to add value to its product mix. MacMillan Bloedel, for example, recently innovated a new high strength wood beam product, 'Parallam', which it had researched and developed over a twenty-year period and at a cost of $50m. In fact, the recession of the 1980s reinforced MacMillan Bloedel's concern for a more value-added product-mix. The general thrust of MacMillan Bloedel's capital investments, however, has been labour-saving.

Employment change in British Columbia

With few exceptions, job losses among MacMillan Bloedel's facilities within British Columbia have involved permanent lay-offs and early retirements (Table 7.2). Moreover, all of these workers may be classified as primary workers. Production workers at MacMillan Bloedel's mills, pulp and paper plants, and plywood factories are clearly part of the primary subordinate segment as defined by Doeringer and Piore (1971). Such workers are represented by strong unions, notably the International Woodworkers of America (IWA) and the Canadian Paperworkers Union (CPU), earn relatively good wages (1988 wage rates are between approximately $16 and $21 an hour plus benefits), and have relatively good work conditions. Furthermore, up until the early 1980s there was a well-defined progression of job advancement based upon seniority, and well-defined rules with respect to demarcation of job tasks. In contrast, primary independent workers are represented by administrative and clerical workers. Both groups are non-unionized, and are located mainly at MacMillan Bloedel's head office in Vancouver. A number of administrative workers, however, are found at plant sites.

Apart from one case there has been a general decline in employment at all corporate plant and office locations (Table 7.2). Perhaps most striking is the decline in employment within the head office. This decline occurred, first, because of MacMillan Bloedel's

Table 7.2 Employment changes in selected facilities of MacMillan Bloedel in British Columbia

Employment location	Product	Employment 1980	1988	Net change 1978–88
Vancouver	head office	1200	487	–713
Chemainus	lumber	682	161	–521
Vancouver	lumber	740	277	–463
Vancouver	plywood	400	0	–400
Vancouver	particleboard	91	48	– 43
Port Alberni	plywood	450	447	– 3
Port Alberni	lumber (two mills)	1600	919	–681
Port Alberni	pulp, paper	1522	1387	–135
Powell River	pulp, paper, lumber	2335	2074	–261
Harmac	pulp/lumber	1399	1453	53
New Westminster	corrugated containers	161	—	—
Burnaby	paper bags	94	—	—
New Westminster	fine paper	222	—	—

take-over by Noranda which resulted in a transfer of jobs to Toronto; second, by the sale of a substantial part of its paper-packaging business in Canada and Europe; and, third, to reduce costs. While we cannot be precise about the relative importance of these various mechanisms the Vancouver head-office job loss was absolute and across the board. This is also reflected, as we shall see later, in declining employment levels of other administrative workers located at various plant-level sites. In fact, in proportional terms it has been the administrative workers that have suffered most from recession and restructuring. That this segment has been worse hit clearly counters the conventional view that primary independent labour markets enjoy the greatest employment stability. The strong decline of administrative workers is perhaps even more unusual given their predominantly male orientation (Grass and Hayter 1989). Admittedly our survey does not break down administrative workers into more specialized groups, but the evidence we do have indicates that even 'privileged' segments were vulnerable. For example, in-house R&D workers experienced lay-offs (Hayter 1988).

The case of the production workers is less easy to generalize. At the level of the individual manufacturing plant, employment change, overwhelmingly job loss, has proceeded at different rates within different contexts. As noted, MacMillan Bloedel sold con trolling equity positions, primarily to obtain cash, in its three major converting operations in the province. Employment in these facilities, that serve the local market, was maintained or expanded, but these jobs are now on the payroll of other firms. In the case of wood processing, massive job losses have occurred within the context of plant closure, as was the case of Vancouver plywood mill, or more generally within the context of modernization schemes as was the case at Chemainus and Port Alberni. MacMillan Bloedel has also invested considerably in new technology at its three pulp and paper mills in British Columbia; in two cases employment levels between 1980 and 1988 dropped, and in the other case employment increased slightly.

More broadly, what we see in both the primary independent and primary subordinate labour market segments is what we should not see. There were permanent job losses at both production and control levels within the corporation. Primary subordinate workers are not being re-hired as the economy recovers, as in the past, nor are the jobs of primary independent workers invulnerable. Such findings thereby undermine traditional views about the stability of the primary labour market. Furthermore, the spatial divisions of labour argument also does not hold either. Primary workers have not been replaced by secondary ones. Changes have all been *in situ*.

For this reason we now examine in detail the employment implications of particular *in situ* strategies implemented by MacMillan Bloedel, and also show how such strategies defined the specific pattern of labour vulnerability within the existing labour market segment. This is done by focusing on two plant-level case studies, the Chemainus and Port Alberni Pacific sawmills, that are both located on Vancouver Island.

The anatomy of employment change: the case of two sawmills

As noted, the employment impacts of the recession on the forest product industries were more severe in the coastal regions of British Columbia compared to interior regions as a result of different histories of development and situations (Grass and Hayter 1989). In particular, the larger established coastal plants, utilizing traditional technologies, have experienced the greatest degree of job loss. In addition, coastal mills have faced greater pressures as a result of rising wood costs, environmental concerns, aboriginal land claims, tougher labour relations, and the sometimes competing needs of fishing and tourism. Both the Chemainus and Port Alberni Pacific sawmills are large, export-oriented facilities. The Chemainus mill was an example of a long-established mill based on the so-called, traditional and rather wasteful 'large-log' technology. Indeed, sawmilling on the Chemainus site can be traced back to 1862. The Port Alberni Pacific sawmill is of more recent vintage and was originally built in the 1940s. Not surprisingly, recent employment changes at Chemainus have been particularly profound.

Chemainus

The Chemainus sawmill employed 600 workers in December 1981 (Figure 7.1). In 1982, however, it was shut down, only to be reopened two years later but employing just 140 workers. In the interim the mill was overhauled, with $22m. spent on computerized sawmill technology.

By 1980 it was known that the plant was obsolete. Wood and labour costs were high, the technology antiquated, and the commodity produced was specialized and of low value. At first the firm's solution was to use low-cost partial technology replacement. This did not succeed, however, and as a result the plant was finally closed with severance pay awarded on the basis of seniority. Not surprisingly, the community and union reacted strongly to the closure decision and formal representations were made concerning the reopening of the mill, or the establishment of new operations. Apart from the obvious implications for individual livelihood and community health, these pleas recognized that the mill's tide-water location is clearly excellent in terms of access to high quality resources, markets, skilled labour, and available infrastructure. It is also pertinent to note that the company owned the land on which the mill stood.

In the event, in a little over two years following closure, the company completely rebuilt the entire plant with new equipment and entirely new configurations. The new machinery consisted of numerically-controlled machine tools which enabled greater flexibility in producing higher-value products and in serving more diverse markets. In particular, the plant shifted its emphasis from construction-grade lumber in limited size to high-grade lumber of various dimensions to be ultimately converted to doors, window-frames, and edgings. In this sense, the new technology exemplified at least one of the characteristics of the so-called new post-Fordist regime, that of flexible machinery. It should also be noted that the new mill obtained a much higher yield of lumber from the raw log input compared to the old mill.

The *in situ* strategy pursued by MacMillan Bloedel at Chemainus is clearly one dominated by technological change, one that implied here a massive employment reduction in production (primary subordinate) workers. Associated with this strategy was also a

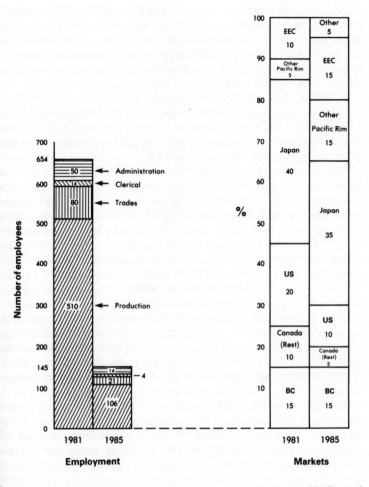

Figure 7.1 Employment and market change at a coastal sawmill, Chemainus, 1981–5

Source: Fieldwork, 1986.

redefinition of some of the core characteristics of that primary subordinate labour market segment. For along with the technological change came a breakdown in both the demarcation of tasks and the very idea of job advancement based upon seniority, both hallmarks of labour practices within a Fordist regime. For in the refurbished Chemainus mill workers were required to learn the manual' so that they would be able to undertake any task on the

159

plant floor. Furthermore, this was enforced by both written tests given by the company, as well as incentive schemes such as competitions among workers with respect to their abilities to master certain tasks in the milling process, for example, grading of wood. Once again, these changed management–labour relations accord with the characteristics of post-Fordism. In this case, the need for a 'functionally flexible' work-force (Morris 1988) is predicated upon a new corporate policy of flexible specialization. Workers must be able to operate at any point in the production process to enable the level and type of output produced by each mill to be easily changed (be more flexible).

That labour agreed to such 'functionally flexibility' was a result of the stick of closure that MacMillan Bloedel wielded over the Chemainus local of the IWA. Whether or not the firm had always planned to rebuild the mill is unknown to us. It is reasonable to argue, however, that the firm certainly gained a bargaining advantage with its unionized work-force by closing down the plant. In this regard, the timing of the firm's announcement to rebuild is instructive: a clause written within its contract with the IWA stated that if a plant closed and reopened within two years the laid-off workers have to be re-hired according to seniority. Knowing that the firm had no longer any obligation to meet this clause, and that the number of workers hired would be significantly lower than before, the union approached management and requested that the seniority of laid-off workers be respected in the firm's hiring policy. In brief, the firm agreed to do its best to meet the union request on the condition that the union accepted changed work conditions, notably the principle of team working, and greater flexibility in job descriptions and allocation. This suggestion was accepted by the union and the firm responded by hiring about 66 per cent of its workers from among those laid off, including some, but not all, with seniority.

Port Alberni Pacific

Our second case study is the Port Alberni Pacific mill. Its employment profile is quite different from the one at Chemainus (Figure 7.2). Although total employment fell slightly over the same period, production workers increased absolutely, while both administrative and tradesworkers fell.

Although there was investment in new technology at Port Alberni Pacific ($10.5m.) the mill was not closed. Rather, the *in situ* strategy used to combat recession was principally a marketing one. New machinery was not primarily introduced to reduce the variable costs represented by production workers, but rather to extract more

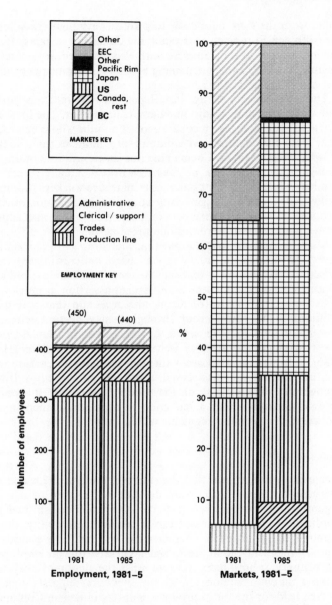

Figure 7.2 Employment and market change at a coastal sawmill, Port Alberni Pacific, 1981-5

Source: Fieldwork 1986

value from the fibre base so as to provide very high grade lumber for both the European, and especially Japanese markets. Indeed, the importance of the Japanese market is reflected in the fact that the mill now uses Japanese names to describe its principal products: *noya, neda, sujikai, shoji.*

The technological change introduced did require 'team-working' and a breakdown of traditional demarcation lines. The local IWA accepted such changes on condition that no jobs would be lost. It is clear from conversations with union representatives that the threat of what happened at Chemainus was sufficient to obtain compliance. As it turned out, production workers actually increased in number, while the major casualties were trades workers (traditional millwrights were no longer required given the new computerized technology) who were members of a different union, and administrative workers who were not unionized at all.

More broadly we would argue that that strategy of marketing as a way to cope with recession has been underestimated in the literature because of a tendency to emphasize only production relations. As a result, there is an implicit assertion in much of the work completed on restructuring and recession that a return to profitability can only occur through cost reduction within the production process. We argue, however, that in the case of the forest products industry, as well as in other sectors (see Hayter 1986), recovery can also occur through changing the nature of the product and the markets served. A marketing strategy will likely change the composition of the labour force, but it does not necessarily imply either a reduction of total employment nor the reduction of particular segments within it.

Conclusion

Increasingly it is argued that the slump of the late 1970s and early 1980s represented a cusp point dividing one system of industrial organization from another in North America; Fordism and post-Fordism. In terms of our concern of labour vulnerability, the pre-slump, Fordist era was characterized by high job security for primary independent workers, and cyclical swings in employment for primary subordinate workers with the depth of that swing dampening with seniority. All the evidence suggests that this pattern held for the forest products industry in British Columbia, a sector dominated by the primary labour market segments.

With the onset of prolonged recession in the 1980s, and the consequent effect on profits, firms began experimenting in terms of location, technology, and organization, thereby precipitating new spatial divisions of labour, and concomitant patterns of labour vulnerability across labour market segments. Although we do not want to deny such changes, the focus on them by industrial geographers has led to the neglect of those sectors, such as the resource industries, that neither create new spatial divisions of labour (change *in situ*) nor switch between labour market segments (change is internal to a segment). In this sense, we think that it is ironic that although many industrial geographers are calling for a theoretical sensitivity to the particularities of place, there is no corresponding call to take into account the particularities of individual industrial sectors. It is as if one theory explains all. This, however, may be changing with the emergence of a more recent literature on post-Fordism, emphasizing a new regime of flexible production. For as a number of researchers have already documented, the spatial implication of such a change is no change (Holmes 1987; Schoenberger 1987; Storper and Christopherson 1987). As a result, research on this new regime is concerned with examining the same issues that we examined here: *in situ* strategies of change and the consequent effect on the internal dynamics of labour market segments (on the latter, see Morris 1988). As such, rather than being theoretically peripheral, as it has hitherto, the resource sector is potentially an exemplar of the shape of things to come.

References

Cain, G. L. (1976) 'The challenge of dual and radical theories of the labor market to orthodox theory', *American Economic Review*, papers and proceedings.

Clark, G. L. (1981) 'The employment relation and spatial division of labor: a hypothesis', *Annals of the Association of American Geographers* 71: 412-24.

Clark, G. L. (1986) 'The crisis of the mid-west auto industry', in A. J. Scott and M. Storper (eds) *Production, Work, Territory*, Boston: Allen & Unwin: 127-48.

Cooke, P. (1983) 'Labor market discontinuity and spatial development', *Progress in Human Geography* 7: 543-65.

Danson, M. (1982) 'The industrial structure and labour market segmentation: urban and regional implications', *Regional Studies* 4: 255-66.

Doeringer, P. and Piore, M. (1971) *Internal Labour Markets and Manpower Analysis*, Lexington: D. C. Heath.

Farris, L. (1983) *The B.C. Forest Industry to 1990*, Vancouver, Canada: Employment and Immigration Commission.

Frederickson, C. and Lindmark, L. (1979) 'From firms to systems of firms: A case study of interregional dependence in a dynamic society', in

I. A. F. Hamilton and G. Linge (eds), *Spatial Analysis. Industry and the Industrial Environment*, volume 1, *Industrial Systems*, Chichester: John Wiley: 155-75.

Gordon, D. (1973) *Theories of Poverty and Underemployment*, Lexington: D. C. Heath.

Grass, E. and Hayter, R. (1989) 'Employment change during recession: the experience of forest product manufacturing plants in British Columbia 1981-1985', *Canadian Geographer* (forthcoming).

Hayter, R. (1976) 'Corporate strategies and industrial change in the Canadian forest product industries', *Geographical Review* 66: 209-28.

Hayter, R. (1985) 'The restructuring of traditional industries in a time of recession', *Tijdschrift voor Economische en Sociale Geografie* 72: 106-20.

Hayter, R. (1986) 'The export dynamics of firms in traditional industries during recession', *Environment and Planning A*, 18: 729-50.

Hayter, R. (1987) 'Innovation policy and mature industries. The forest product sector in British Columbia', in K. Chapman and C. Humphrys (eds), *Technical Change and Industrial Policy*, Oxford: Basil Blackwell: 215-32.

Hayter, R. (1988) *Technology Policy Perspectives and the Canadian Forest Products Industries*, Ottawa: Science Council of Canada.

Hayter, R. and Watts, H. D. (1983) 'The geography of enterprise', *Progress in Human Geography* 7: 157-81.

Holmes, J. (1987) 'Technical change and the restructuring of the North American automobile industry', in K. Chapman and G. Humphrys (eds) *Technical Change and Industrial Policy*, Oxford: Basil Blackwell: 121-56.

Kerr, C. (1954) 'The Balkanization of labor markets', in E. Bakke (ed.) *Labor Mobility and Economic Opportunity*, Cambridge Mass.: MIT Press: 92-110.

Krumme, G. (1971) 'The interregional corporation and the region', *Tijdschrift voor Economische en Sociale Geografie* 61: 318-33.

Loveridge, R. and Mok, A. (1979) 'Theoretical approaches to segmented labour markets', *International Journal of Social Economics* 7: 376-411.

MacKay, D. (1982) *Empire of Wood*, Vancouver: Douglas & McIntyre.

Massey, D. (1984) *Spatial Divisions of Labour*, London: Macmillan.

Massey, D. (1989) 'Reflections on the debate: thoughts on feminism, Marxism and theory', *Environment and Planning A*, 21: 692-7.

Massey, D. and Meegan, R. (1982) *The Anatomy of Job Loss*, London: Methuen.

Morris, J. (1988) 'New technologies, flexible work practices, and regional socio-political differentiation: some observations from the UK', *Society and Space* 6: 301-20.

Norcliffe, G. (1987) 'Regional unemployment in Canada in the 1981-4 recession', *The Canadian Geographer* 31: 150-9.

Rozen, M. (1985) 'Maximizing behaviour: reconciling neoclassical and X-efficiency approaches', *Journal of Economic Issues* 19: 661-85.

Schoenberger, E. (1987) 'Technological and organizational change in automobile production: spatial implications', *Regional Studies* 21: 199–214.

Schwindt, R. (1976) *The Existence of Corporate Power: A Case Study of MacMillan Bloedel Ltd*, Ottawa: Ministry of Supply and Services.

Steed, G. P. F. (1968) 'The changing milieu of a firm', *Annals of the Association of American Geographers* 58: 506–25.

Storper, M. and Christopherson, S. (1987) 'Flexible specialization and regional industrial agglomerations: the case of the US motion picture industry', *Annals of the Association of American Geographers* 77: 104–17.

Townsend, A. (1983) *The Impact of Recession*, London: Methuen.

Webber, M. (1988) 'The dynamics of capital accumulation and technical change in Canadian manufacturing industries, 1952–81', unpublished manuscript, Department of Geography, University of Melbourne, Parkville, Victoria.

Webber, M. (1989) 'Profits, capital flows, and the spatial division of labor', *Environment and Planning A*, 21: 689–91.

Chapter eight

Nissan Motor Company
Stages of international growth, locational profile, and subcontracting in the Tokyo region

Atsuhiko Takeuchi

Introduction

Since the 1960s, the automobile industry has sustained the development of Japan's industries. Recently, the high technology industry centred on micro-electronics has developed remarkably (Murata and Takeuchi 1987). However, the automobile industry is playing an increasingly important role as a leading industry. In 1985, the number of workers in the automobile industry accounted for 7 per cent of all industries, 2 per cent higher than ten years ago. In 1987, the facility investment of the automobile industry amounted to 25 per cent of all industries.

Presently, Japan, together with North America and Europe, is one of the world's three major automobile production and sales centres (Dicken 1986). Nissan, one of the two largest automobile manufacturers in Japan and the fourth largest automobile maker (1986) in the world, has an approximately 20 per cent share of Japan's automobile production, with Toyota at about 30 per cent. Toyota has its base in one industrial city in the Nagoya region, whereas Nissan's development is based on the technological complex of various machine industries in the Tokyo region. Nissan also has production bases in northern Kyushu and in northern Kanto (Outer Tokyo). Besides Nissan and Toyota, there are many automobile manufacturers in Japan, including Honda, Mazda, Mitsubishi, Isuzu, Subaru, Hino, Daihatsu, and Suzuki. All have generated characteristic regional developments (Takeuchi 1980).

The object of this article is to clarify Nissan's stages of development in the context of the growth of Japan's automobile industry, whereby Nissan is compared with Toyota and other automobile manufacturers. Particular attention is given to Nissan's locational pattern and regional subcontracting system.

Nissan's development prior to the Second World War

The incipient Japanese automobile industry

Nissan's production started in Osaka but soon moved to Tokyo. In analysing Nissan's development, the concentration of automobile production technology in the Tokyo region, which is the base of Nissan's development, cannot be ignored (Takeuchi 1973).

[Japan has a comparatively long history of automobile production. At the end of the nineteenth century, the Japanese, fascinated by the car, produced automobiles for themselves by copying European models with the techniques used in riksha construction and ironworking. Apparently, forty-three different makes were manufactured by thirteen firms in Tokyo.]

In 1907, unit production was carried out on the basis of one model. However, the technical level was low, and all the manufacturers went bankrupt. Nevertheless, even with the disappearance of these enterprises, the industry and technology spawned by the fascination for the automobile remained alive and spilled over into the next generation.

In 1911, Kaishinsha, a spin-off of coal-mining machinery technology in northern Kyushu, began Japan's first full-scale automobile production at a small factory in southern Tokyo while also engaged in the repair of imported automobiles. This automobile was called DAT (an acronym using the initials of the company's sponsors, Den, Aoyama and Takeuchi) and formed the origin of Japan's automobile industry. Since that period was the golden age of the Ford Model T, the DAT did not sell well. Kaishinsha soon ran into difficulties. Around that time, another company manufactured three-wheeled trucks, and later four-wheeled trucks, in Osaka, Japan's commercial centre. As these three- and four-wheeled trucks were for commercial use, they quickly became popular. This company merged with Kaishinsha, which was on the brink of collapse, and formed the DAT Company. However, this new company also ran into difficulties.

[After the First World War, the Japanese government assessed the role to be played by the automobile industry in the future and announced a policy of assisting in the production of military vehicles. Accordingly, Gasuden, a section of Ishikawajima, a shipbuilding company that provided automobile parts to the army, became an automobile manufacturer. Gasuden succeeded in producing vehicles independently by disassembling used trucks.]

After the Kanto earthquake of 1923, Japan became aware of the utility of the automobile, and the demand increased rapidly. The US automobile industry anticipated this increasing demand, and in

1924, Ford Motor Company established a subsidiary in Yokoham (Tokyo region) and General Motors did likewise in Osaka. Bo Ford and GM attained an approximate annual production 10,000 units, thereby overpowering the three domestic automobi manufacturers (approximately 500 in total) and divided the Jap nese market in two.

However, the impact that Ford and GM had on their respecti locations differed. GM had nothing to do with the industri development of Osaka, while Ford had a great impact on th development of the machinery industries in the Tokyo regio Machine manufacturers made efforts to raise their technical level t be able to supply parts to Ford and GM. Their share was low at th beginning but was gradually increased. Most of the companies th once supplied parts to Ford are now major subcontractors Nissan.

The presence of Ford played a great role in raising the level production in the machinery industry in the Tokyo region. Th formed the basis on which Nissan came into being. After th production was restricted by the Japanese government just befo and during the Second World War, GM vacated its factory. B Japan Ford maintained its legal presence and its land, and the merged with Mazda after the war.

Nissan's development

Nissan was established in 1933, having purchased the rights to DA production and the DAT factory when that company was in management crisis. Nissan is a joint corporation of the Tobata Imono Company, which controlled plants manufacturing electric machinery, special steel, paints, and other items, and the Niho Sangyo Company, a basic chemical concern which also controlle Hitachi. At Nissan's inception, it had a factory in Osaka. Th production of the Datsun automobile was started by DAT in 193 After the take-over, Nissan established a new factory in Yokoham and moved the production of Datsun there in 1935.

In 1936 Nissan purchased a conveyor system from the Graham Page Corporation in the USA and started mass production of new model of Datsun, thereby making great strides in th Yokohama–Tokyo area.

The Datsun is a mainstay of Nissan's production history. Afte obtaining the rights to produce the DAT, Nissan developed a ne small car. Originally, this small passenger car was to be called th 'Son of DAT'. However, as the word 'son' means loss in th Japanese language, the car was named 'Datsun'. The Datsu accounted for 80 per cent of all Japanese-made small cars. Datsun has become a synonym for 'small car'. The Datsun was exported to Australia as early as 1933. However, after the Second World War, the name Datsun had the connotation of a low-class, low-quality car.

At the same time, the Toyota textile machine company in the Nagoya region, which had also been making preparations for automobile production, started manufacturing cars in 1935. Toyota's automobile division became an independent corporation in 1937.

With the Second World War imminent, the Japanese government adopted the policy of developing the machinery industries by extending aid to the electrical machinery, optical machinery and other weak industries, all of which were concentrated in the Tokyo region. This influenced the development of the machine industries in the post-war era.

In 1936, a law was enacted to assist automobile production, which was a particularly weak sector. This law was intended to prevent foreign enterprises from gaining control of Japanese industries and to encourage and aid new or ailing Japanese enterprises.

Nissan and Toyota were the first to benefit from this law. The following year, Ishikawajima, Gasden, DAT, and other small companies merged to form one corporation, the present Isuzu Company. The Gasden division later separated from the group to form an independent corporation, Hino Motors, because Gasden produced only military vehicles.

As stated, Nissan was established on the basis of the machine industry complex that had existed in the Tokyo region since the nineteenth century. The region had many parts manufacturers that had supplied products to Ford, and Hitachi also belonged to the same capital group. Therefore, it was unnecessary for Nissan to secure new parts manufacturers.

The same can be said about Isuzu and Hino, which were also located in Tokyo. On the other hand, in 1938, Toyota built a large automobile company town which is now Toyota City (Takeuchi 1971a). In that year, Volkswagen also built an automobile industrial complex in Wolfsburg, Germany. As Toyota was located in the Nagoya region, which, unlike the Tokyo area, lacked a technical base, Toyota had to establish parts manufacturers there. These new parts manufacturers achieved a rapid growth in the 1970s and supported Toyota's great leap forward.

In 1943, Nissan, which concentrated its production in Tokyo, constructed a military vehicle plant in Yoshiwara, Shizuoka Prefecture, for national defence purposes. During the Second

World War, the government prohibited production of passenge
cars, with certain exceptions, and production was dedicatec
virtually 100 per cent to military vehicles.

Development in the period of rapid economic growth

The impetus for economic growth

To appreciate the remarkable development of Japan's automobile
industry after 1960, the difficult period prior to 1960 cannot be
overlooked. After the Second World War, the occupation force
only permitted Japan to manufacture trucks, but the ensuing
production was almost negligible.

Because of a disruptive labour dispute, Japan's automobile
industry, including Nissan, was on the verge of collapse. The
automobile industry was revitalized through defence contracts
resulting from the Korean War. At that time, however, Nissan was
much slower than Toyota in settling the labour dispute, and the gap
in growth dynamics between the two companies is attributable to
this fact.

The production of automobiles for the Korean War posed many
problems for Japan's car industry. Previously, the manufacturers
had been protected by the government. For defence contracts
however, both quality and pricing were closely monitored by the
occupation forces. This was the Japanese manufacturers' first
experience in the international market, and it led to the rationalization of Japan's production.

At that time, most Japanese automobile manufacturers
especially Isuzu and Toyota, emphasized the production of large
trucks and buses. In small cars, the Japanese manufacturers formed
(technical) joint ventures with European corporations. Isuzu produced the Hillman, and Hino produced the Renault, while both
failed to develop their own cars further.

Toyota, in contrast, took initiatives to develop small cars. In
1957, Toyota succeeded in developing its Crown at an international
level, and since then, Toyota has been a leader in the small-car
market.

Basically, Nissan's strategy emphasized the production of large
trucks and buses. However, Nissan also built Datsun; in 1952,
Nissan formed a joint venture with Austin (UK) in an endeavour to
introduce advanced technology while laying the ground for
domestic production. On the basis of the accumulated technology,
Nissan developed the Bluebird as demand for small cars increased
on both the domestic and the international market. The market for
Japanese cars was thus divided among Nissan and Toyota.

Expansion of demand and rationalization of production

Japan's automobile production increased rapidly from the latter half of the 1950s onward. However, Japan's automobile production in 1958 was approximately 188,000 units, far lower than the five million of the USA and the combined output of more than one million of West Germany, Britain, and France. What is more noteworthy, passenger cars accounted for only 25 per cent of the total Japanese automobile production. However, it should be noted that 287,000 three-wheeled commercial vehicles were produced by Mazda, Daihatsu, Mitsubishi, and other manufacturers. In this situation, in 1957, Nissan started exporting to the United States. It is noteworthy that the cars exported by Nissan were all built from domestic-made parts, which is a substantially different situation from the exports to the NICs in the 1980s, where materials and parts from other countries were used in exported cars.

Rapid increase in production

The 1960s was a period of rapid economic growth, and automobile production in Japan, including Nissan's, increased rapidly at that time. The pace has been sustained by increased exports and motorization in Japan. While the importation of cars was liberalized in 1965, exports increased, and full-scale export to the USA got underway in the 1970s.

This increase in exports was generated by lowering costs and improving quality. This was accomplished by three measures. The first was the rationalization of the assembly plants; in 1956, to supplement the existing conveyor system, a new type of transport was introduced. The second was the specialization of plants. And the third was the rationalization of parts production. A stringent selection of parts manufacturers and firm subcontracting agreements allowed each part to be produced in the right quantity at high quality; in addition, the 'just-in-time' system of supplying parts was introduced.

Mergers and new establishments

Enterprises merged to raise their productivity. A typical example is the merger of Prince and Nissan in 1966. The owner of Prince, who was also the president of one of the biggest tyre manufacturers, sold Prince to Nissan solely to increase sales of his tyres.

Previously an aerospace industry, Prince brought in high-level technologies in engines and other products. Like Nissan, Prince

171

also had its headquarters in Tokyo. Prince's development ability and processing technology were high, and in the post-war years, the company had developed a luxury passenger car ahead of Nissan. Nissan's most popular automobiles, including the Skyline and Gloria, were developed by Prince.

However, Nissan's take-over of Prince also had a negative side. It generated antagonism within the company and many disgruntled engineers defected to Honda and Mazda. Until recently, Nissan's development was carried out in an independent organization. Former Prince employees are still discontented with their treatment, especially since many of Nissan's top products have been developed by former Prince engineers. At about the same time as its take-over of Prince, Nissan also merged with Aich machinery company, based in Nagoya in the central part of Japan.

Since its inception, Nissan had its headquarters in the Tokyo region (Figure 8.1). Elsewhere, Nissan had a plant only in Yoshiwara, Shizuoka Prefecture. As its production increased, Nissan built two large plants: in Yokosuka (Nissan's first plant exclusively for the manufacture of passenger cars) in 1962, and in Zama in 1965. Nissan also established a factory exclusively for parts and a distribution centre in the Tokyo region. The shortage of labour did not seriously affect a big company, even in Tokyo region. In 1968, Nissan built its Tochigi plant in northern Kanto, set up a test course, and established a complex of parts plants in the vicinity. In 1974, as a base for its exports to Asia, Nissan built a plant in northern Kyushu, an area with a high labour potential.

On the other hand, Toyota also strengthened its production system, mainly in the Nagoya region. At the same time, Toyota merged with Hino (Tokyo) and Daihatsu (Osaka). Suzuki, Subaru, Daihatsu, Mazda, Honda, and other motorcycle and light automobile manufacturers participated in automobile production from the mid-1950s to the mid-1960s. As described above, Japan's automobile industry achieved rapid growth through severe competition among many enterprises.

Internationalization and the regional system of production

The oil crisis had serious repercussions for Japan's economy. However, it also raised the demand for small cars throughout the world. Japan, which had an excellent technology for the production of small cars, thus sharply increased its automobile exports. In 1985, Japan had the world's highest level of automobile production and export. However, as Japan's share of the world's automobile markets increased, trade protectionism was heightened globally.

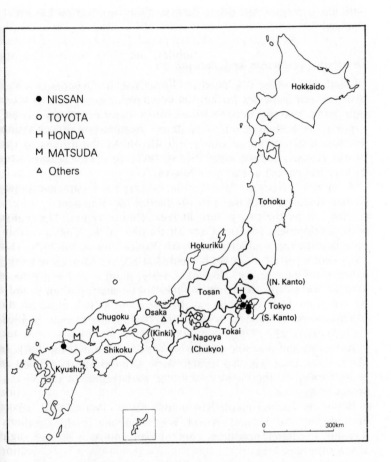

Figure 8.1   Distribution of automobile manufacturers, 1988
Source: Data by the Association of Motor Industry

Japan's automobile exports then slowed, partially because of self-restraint imposed in 1981 regarding export to the USA, which had received 40 per cent of all Japanese exports.

Since 1985, export conditions have worsened, due in part to the sharp rise in the value of the yen. As a result, the automobile companies have switched their international management strategies from the export of finished cars to the sale of knock-down units and to production overseas. In response to the change in the inter-

173

national strategies, the domestic systems of production have also changed.

Domestic production and distribution

Nissan's head office is located in Ginza, Tokyo. The company has two research institutes for automobile development, nine production plants, two parts distribution centres, two piers exclusively for exports, as well as training facilities. Automotive research and development are carried out independently by the groups of the former Nissan and the former Prince. This is one of the reasons why Toyota has gained a lead over Nissan.

At present, Nissan's fundamental research is conducted at the central research institute, and production development is jointly carried out by the two groups at the technical centre. The plants with development functions are all located in the Tokyo region, especially in the southern area with Yokohama as the hub. The parts centre for all of Japan is located at Sagamihara, close to the expressway interchange. Nissan's Tochigi plant is in the northern area of Kanto, on the fringe of the Tokyo metropolitan region. Nissan plans to have a base in this location, as it is close to the headquarters of Subaru, with which Nissan has formed a joint venture (Takeuchi 1978).

As design and machine processing are carried out at the Tochigi plant, a test course is also located there. An industrial complex is being formed in the vicinity, with the parts plants of the Nissan group as its core.

Beside its Tochigi plant, Nissan also has a plant at Yoshiwara, built during the Second World War, and one in the north at Kyushu. The latter, producing cars for export to Asia, has access to a rich supply of labour.

In addition to automotive research, Nissan is also engaged in aerospace research and development, and launched its first rocket in 1965. Nissan's research and development has spin-offs in textile machinery, forklifts, and other industrial applications, all in the Tokyo region.

Like Nissan, the other automotive firms disperse their functions over various locations. Whereas Nissan has its base in Tokyo, Toyota is based in the Nagoya region. Toyota plans to unite its Tokyo establishment (Hino) and its Osaka plant (Daihatsu), which are connected by expressways, into one entity. Toyota established a new research institute in inner Tokyo in 1988 as the R&D centre of the future.

Honda has its production centres in Tokyo and Nagoya and its research institute in Tochigi. Mazda has a production centre in Hiroshima and in 1988 the firm built a large research institute in Yokohama. Hino has its base in Tokyo; Daihatsu in Osaka; Suzuki in Shizuoka; Subaru, which belongs to the same capital group, in Ohta (northern Kanto) and in Tokyo (R&D and engines); and Mitsubishi in Nagoya, Tokyo, and Okayama.

Nissan's domestic sales network system is divided into five groups according to the type of car. It has 247 sales companies, 3,769 dealerships, 12,900 service depots and approximately 75,000 salesmen to carry out nationwide sales activities. Nissan's sales system is smaller than Toyota's employing a sales force of some 30,000 less than Toyota. One reason for Nissan's decreased domestic share is the antagonism between groups of former Nissan and former Prince employees in the sales activities.

Subcontracting

One of Nissan's greatest assets is its group of subcontractors consisting of automobile manufacturers (Dicken 1986). Fifty per cent of Nissan's production depends upon these subcontractors. A co-operative association called 'Takara-kai' is formed by 105 well-known subcontractors. Additionally, Nissan contracts twice as many smaller firms. The distribution of the subcontractors affiliated with Takara-kai is shown in Table 8.1. Approximately 70 per cent of the head offices of these companies are located in the Tokyo region. This situation is almost the same as the distribution of the 1960s. Approximately half the plants of these subcontractors are located in Tokyo. However, many are dispersed throughout northern Kanto, Tokai (Shizuoka), and northern Kyushu. These plants were built after the 1960s to provide for 'just-in-time' delivery (Takeuchi 1971b cf. the *kanban* system which was pioneered by Toyota, cf. Holmes 1986).

Most of the parts for the Nissan plants in the Tokyo region are supplied by the subcontractors in the Tokyo region, with the remainder supplied by subcontractors in Tokai and northern Kanto. Tokai is located between Tokyo, where Nissan is based, and Nagoya, where Toyota has its base. Tokai is a region which supplies parts throughout the country.

Forty-five per cent of the parts used by Nissan's Tochigi plant are derived from subcontractors in Tokyo, although there are two industrial parks for parts manufacturers near the Tochigi plant. Only 15 per cent of the parts are supplied from northern Kanto and Tokai.

At the outset, there were no plants in the Kyushu region with adequate technical levels to supply parts to Nissan, so Nissan

Table 8.1 Distribution of main subcontractors, 1987

	Head office	Factories
Tohoku	0	10
North Kanto	11	44
Tokyo (South Kanto)	75	131
Tokai	10	31
Nagoya (Chukyo)	1	15
Tosan	3	7
Osaka (Kinki)	4	10
North Kyushyu	1	21
Others	0	8
Total	105	259

Source: Data by Nissan Motor Company

established a few subcontractors in Kyushu. However, for the Kyushu plant, only 7 per cent of the parts are supplied from Kyushu while more is derived from Tokyo (45 per cent), northern Kanto (15 per cent) and Tokai (13 per cent). More parts are supplied to the Yoshiwara plant, a factory dedicated to parts production, from Tokyo than from Shizuoka. Apparently, delivery from subcontractors located far from the main Nissan plants is not economical. The cost of parts supplied is 5 per cent higher than those delivered to Toyota.

As automobile manufacturers promoted the rationalization of their parts manufacturers to reduce their own costs, many subcontractors dropped out because of stringent credit restrictions. Instead, they became sub-subcontractors. The parts manufacturers which grew into big enterprises as a result of rationalization were required by Nissan to expand their sales to Isuzu, Subaru, and other automobile makers or other industrial fields, to reduce the costs of parts by introducing mass production. Parts from subcontractors affiliated with Takara-kai are supplied to Nissan. Only 25 per cent of the Takara-kai members supply more than 70 per cent of their parts to Nissan, and it appears that parts manufacturers are now outgrowing their subcontracting role. However, these companies are unable to become independent, because they are controlled by Nissan in both the financial and sales aspects.

Subcontractors of Nissan and Toyota are supplying an increasing proportion of their parts to other companies. The profit margin of the parts manufacturers is severely restricted by Nissan. Since the sharp rise in the value of the yen, they are forced by Nissan to reduce their costs. Under these circumstances, the parts manufacturers continue their development efforts. If they are defeated in competition, the companies will most certainly collapse. Under this competitive system, most of Nissan's subcontractors are located in the Tokyo region. The same is true of the smaller subcontractors who do not belong to the Takara-kai.

Subcontracting plants are distributed throughout the southern area of the Tokyo region with the Nissan plant as the hub. The most densely concentrated area of machinery plants is the inner zone (southern Tokyo) of the southern area (Figure 8.2), where 65 per cent of Nissan's sub-subcontractors are concentrated. In southern Tokyo, a variety of machine industries in certain sectors are concentrated. In this zone, an increasing number of small, but high-level research institutes have been recently established to combine microelectronics with machine processing. Tokyo's machinery industries have formed a strong technological complex by combining the plants and research institutes of southern Tokyo (Murata and Takeuchi 1987), the systems houses of central Tokyo, and various enterprises, as well as their R&D. Nissan's rocketry development has also been achieved through combination with this technological complex. When user needs are diversified, and technical renovation is promoted, the position of Nissan is strong, with its R&D, subcontractors, and affiliated enterprises in this zone. Nissan, which was surpassed by Toyota in mass production, is now planning roll-back operations in its strategy to develop high-quality cars.

Management style

Toyota is called a 'family' because most of its managerial staff have moved up through automobile production, and its management is well organized with the founder's family at the centre. On the other hand, there have been long-standing problems in Nissan's management system, which is old and rife with discord. The cold treatment of employees who came from the former Prince, interference by union leaders in company management, and other problems have been criticized by the economists. These are at the root of Nissan's mistakes in many important policies and the reason why Nissan has been surpassed by Toyota.

In order to achieve new development, Nissan must improve its tactics for recruiting engineers. At present, Nissan only employs recent graduates from specific universities; graduates of the numerous other universities are not allowed to take the employment examination of Nissan. Although Nissan is now making efforts to

177

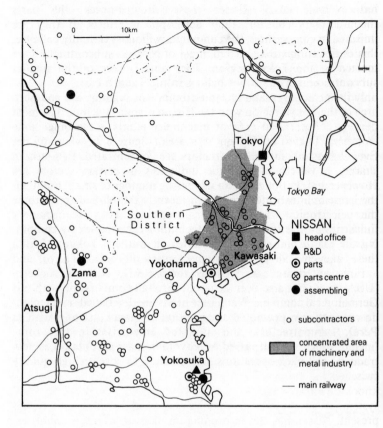

Figure 8.2 Nissan and its subcontractors in Tokyo region, 1987
Source: Data by Nissan Motor Company

improve its recruitment policy, it is still a closed system. Employees coming from other companies are always 'second-string' players. No matter how eagerly they work, they are just *ninja* under the elite group of *samurai*.

Toyota, which always treats employees from other companies warmly, and Honda, which employs people of various characters, are vigorous firms. In contrast, Nissan's closed employment system reduces the vitality within the company. Nissan cars are popular among young people, but the company is not. As a result, Nissan has a chronic lack of talented employees, even though they are in the best position to recruit superior engineers. Nissan now plans to improve its management and employment tactics, but movement in this direction is slow and unimaginative. The improvement of its management and employment style is imperative for Nissan to survive as one of the two biggest automobile manufacturers, since only then can the company capitalize on its advantageous position.

Strengthened international system

Even since 1980, Japan's automobile exports have increased sharply. In 1984, Nissan built a shipping pier exclusively for export. However, trade frictions have gradually become more severe. Also, the increase in export has slowed because of the rise in the value of the yen since 1985. Nissan presently exports 1,174 thousand finished cars and 294 thousand knock-down units to 150 countries. Nissan has 24 knock-down-based companies in 21 countries. Of these, 9 are Nissan subsidiaries and others are joint ventures.

Finished Nissan cars are exported mainly to North America (USA 46.6, Canada 4.3 per cent) and Europe (UK 9.2, West Germany 7.6, and the Netherlands 3.3 per cent). Nissan knock-down units are exported to Latin America (including Mexico and Peru), South East Asia (including Taiwan and Thailand), Europe (including Spain, UK, and Greece), and Oceania (Table 8.2). As trade frictions intensify, Japan's automobile manufacturers have switched the emphasis in their overseas production systems from knock-down to finished units. As a result, their international system of automobile production has changed substantially. At present, Nissan has eleven production bases in overseas countries. Six of these have been established since 1980. Nissan's overseas production has increased more than 10 per cent every year, reaching 422 thousand units in 1987.

Nissan established NMMC Inc. in the USA (in Tennessee) in 1980 and started production in 1983. Its monthly production is 250,000 cars, with 60 per cent of the parts used being made in the USA. Nissan established an R&D specialist company in the USA (in Michigan) in 1983 to increase its development capacity. Most Japanese automobile manufacturers have made inroads into the USA. In the future, as the core of car production in North America, a new system, which is connected with selected parts manufacturers of other Japanese groups mutually, will be introduced.

In Europe, NMUK was first established in north-east England in 1984 (at Tyne and Wear) in accordance with the British government's policy of attracting industry into peripheral areas of the

Table 8.2 Export of Nissan cars, 1987

	Finished cars	KD Set
South East Asia	42,363	79,720
North America	598,479	—
South and Central America	25,259	87,705
Oceania	20,622	35,834
Africa	33,916	22,637
Europe	401,177	68,280
Others	53,025	—
Total	1,174,841	294,176

Source: Data by Nissan Motor Company

country (Dicken 1987). The company started production in 1986. At present, 60 per cent of its parts are procured in Britain, but the government demands that the company must derive more than 80 per cent of its parts from within the country by 1991. In the meantime a major problem for NMUK is how to maintain the quality of its products.

In Spain, Greece, and Portugal, Nissan has established joint ventures with domestic enterprises in these countries. In 1983, Nissan established a company in the Netherlands to supply parts to Europe. In Mexico, Nissan started production in 1966. In Australia, Nissan established NMCA Inc. in 1986 by taking over a factory of VW Inc. . NMCA engines are exported to Japan.

The trend of change in the international system can be summarized as follows:

1 to increase overseas production bases in the USA, UK, and other countries, and to strengthen development capacity;
2 to send excellent subcontracting parts makers to overseas countries as a result of the growing capacity for self-supply of parts in various countries;
3 to strengthen a system for mutual use of the subcontractors of other manufacturers (USA);
4 to strengthen mutual connections between Nissan's production bases in other countries;
5 to strengthen joint ventures with overseas enterprises, as exemplified by the joint venture with Ford in the United States.

In the future, Nissan will, with a few production bases as a centre, establish a large system for international division of labour throughout the world, including the NICs, where Nissan has many joint venture companies.

Conclusion

Since the 1960s, the automobile industry has been the leader of Japanese industry. Its status will remain unchallenged in the future. Nissan, one of the two biggest manufacturers, has thrived for many years by building up firm subcontracting systems on the basis of the concentration of the machine industry in Tokyo. This is also true of Toshiba, NEC, Hitachi, Sony, and other companies. A mammoth technological complex has been formed through the combination of their R&D and various enterprises of a very high technical level. The importance of a technological complex has increased during the recent period of the location of this complex in the technological innovation. Furthermore, Tokyo region corresponds to its function as the national centre of information networks and marketing systems.

Nissan has a fossilized management system, harbours great antagonisms within the company, and lags behind Toyota in development. Yet Nissan is able to maintain its position because it is located in the industrial complex of the Tokyo region, the greatest hub of the national industrial system (Takeuchi 1983). At present, Nissan is making efforts to improve its management system.

Nissan has also succeeded in developing a new high-quality car. The demands placed on automobiles are diversifying. The international systems for the division of labour are becoming stronger. In this context, the conditions of Nissan's location, with the Tokyo region as its base, will become increasingly advantageous in the future.

References

Dicken, P. (1966) *Global Shift. Industrial Change in a Turbulent World*, London: Harper & Row.

Dicken, P. (1987) 'Japanese penetration of the European automobile industry: the arrival of Nissan in the United Kingom', *Tijdschrift voor Economische en Sociale Geografie* 78: 94–107.

Holmes, J. (1986) 'The organisation and locational structure of production subcontracting', in A. Scott and M. Storper (eds) *Production, Work and Territory*, London: Allen & Unwin, 80–106.

Murata, K. and Takeuchi, A. (1987) 'Regional division of labour in Japanese machinery industry and R&D', in F. E. I. Hamilton (ed.) *Industrial Change in Advanced Countries*, London: Croom Helm.

Atsuhiko Takeuchi

Takeuchi, A. (1971a) 'The automobile industry in Toyota City', *Tohoku-Chiri*, 4-10, 193-203 (J).
Takeuchi, A. (1971b) 'The areal structure of the automobile industry in Japan', *Geographical Review of Japan*, 44-7, 479-97 (J).
Takeuchi, A. (1973) *The Machinery Industry in Japan*, Tokyo: Taimeido (J).
Takeuchi, A. (1978) *A Theoretical Study on Regional Industrial Systems*, Tokyo: Taimeido (J).
Takeuchi, A. (1980) 'Motor vehicle', in K. Murata (ed.) *An Industrial Geography of Japan*, London: Bell & Hymann.
Takeuchi, A. (1983) 'Two elements supporting the high position of Tokyo Metropolitan Region in the national system of machinery industry', *Geographical Reports of Tokyo Metropolitan University*, 22: 129-38.

Chapter nine

Volvo
The organization of work:
a determinant of the future location
of manufacturing enterprises

Claes Alvstam and Kajsa Ellegard

The context of Volvo

The Volvo Group

The Volvo Group (AB Volvo) is Sweden's largest industrial corporation and ranks among the world's thirty biggest non-US manufacturing companies.[1] Volvo is one of the few European vehicle makers that have succeeded in keeping their profits at a satisfactory level during the 1980s.

One of the overall business strategies of the Volvo Group has been diversification, both within and outside the vehicle sector. The most important business areas other than motor vehicles are food production and oil trading. However, as is shown in Table 9.1, vehicle production in general and passenger car production in particular is still the heart of the group, as regards both sales and profit generation. As for diversification, Volvo differs from the second largest Swedish automotive manufacturer, the SAAB-Scania Group, which has concentrated on the vehicle sector.

However, as recently as the late 1970s, considerable concern was expressed about the future results of the car sector of Volvo. At that time truck production was the profit-generating business area. It was generally assumed, in Sweden as well as abroad, that Volvo's annual production capacity of 200–300 thousand units was far too small in a world output of thirty-two million cars (1978). The extremely high costs and length of time involved in designing a new model, and the subsequent economies of scale in passenger car manufacturing, implied an 'ideal' size for a European manufacturer of at least one million units annually.

At that time, however, instead of waiting for a larger European manufacturer to take over its operations, Volvo took the risky decision to increase its investment costs in order to develop a model – 700 series – in a more expensive segment, competing with Mercedes–Benz and BMW, rather than in the medium-size range. It is doubtful whether this decision could have been taken without the

Table 9.1 Sales of Volvo Group and return of capital by operating sector, 1985–7 (%)

	Sales			Return of capital		
	1985	*1986*	*1987*	*1985*	*1986*	*1987*
Cars (Volvo Car Corporation)	39	43	42	> 25	> 25	> 25
Trucks (Volvo Truck Corporation)	18	19	19	13	13	24
Buses (Volvo Bus Corporation)	2	2	2	8	12	23
Engines (Penta)	3	3	3	> 25	14	18
Aerospace (Flygmotor)	2	2	2	18	17	14
Trading and Energy (STC)	25	16	17	Neg	2	0
Food (The Provendor Group)	6	6	10	10	0	8
Others	5	5	5	—	—	—
Group total	100	100	100	20	18	20

Source: AB Volvo, annual reports

relatively better results in other sectors within the group during the same period. In this respect the diversification strategy has proved to be successful.

At the same time the different business areas were separated into independent corporations – Volvo Car Corporation (VCC), Volvo Truck Corporation, etc. which are 100 per cent owned subsidiaries of the parent company, AB Volvo.

The offensive measure of developing a new and more prestigious model in what looked like a declining total car market turned out very well indeed. The introduction of the 700 series in 1982 coincided with the dramatic increase in automobile sales in the United States, which was the result of the combination of a soaring US dollar and a plummeting Swedish krona. Between 1978 and 1985 the share of the North American market in Volvo's total car sales rose from 20 to 46 per cent, while the Swedish share declined from 24 to 14 per cent.

An important feature to keep in mind while analysing Swedish manufacturing companies, as compared with European, Japanese, and American competitors, is the extremely high dependence on foreign markets. A share of 80–90 per cent of foreign sales in the total turnover is not unusual in Swedish industry. The foreign share of 85 per cent in passenger car sales (average 1985–7) is not even the most extreme case within the Volvo Group itself. The share is 93 per cent in truck production and 90 per cent within the sector of marine and industrial engines. The share of Volvo cars within the Swedish market is 20–25 per cent, while it is only 1 per cent in the United States, which is in fact the most important single market. It is a particular challenge for a small automobile producer to depend that much on markets where their share is of such an inconspicuous size. On the other hand, the small share reduces critical monitoring on Volvo by protectionists. The Japanese competitors are in a different situation.

The spatial structure of Volvo Car Corporation

While most of Volvo's sales are abroad, production takes place mainly in Sweden. Around 75 per cent of the Volvo Group's total employment, varying between 62,000 and 76,000 people during the last ten years, is found in Sweden. About 50 per cent of the total number of cars and 30 per cent of the trucks are assembled at home. The number of cars produced has increased from 250,000 in 1978 to 420,000 in 1987 (Figure 9.1)[2].

The main Volvo plant at Torslanda, 15 kilometres west of Gothenburg was opened in 1964. It has retained its dominant position. It is Volvo's only complete car factory in Sweden, consisting of a body shop, a paint shop, and a final assembly shop. Already in 1963 Volvo decided to locate another complete factory in Ghent in Belgium in order to get a foothold inside the European Community. During the capacity expansion period in the early 1980s, the Ghent plant increased its production from 45,000 to 90,000 units annually (Figure 9.1).

Another early step towards operation within the European Community was the purchase of a majority stake in Dutch DAF in 1973 and the joint operation in the production of the 300 and 400 series in the plant in Born, the Netherlands. In the early 1970s another domestic assembly plant was built in Kalmar in southeastern Sweden. This plant was based on new principles for work organization, and has kept up a constant volume of about 40,000 units annually. Engines for all motor vehicle sectors are assembled in a plant in Skövde, 150 km north-east of Gothenburg, while the production of transmissions takes place in Köping, a further 200 km towards the north-east (Figure 9.2).

Volvo's emphasis on North America resulted in 1973 in a decision to build a plant in the US. A site was selected in Chesapeake, Virginia, and a building was completed. However, in

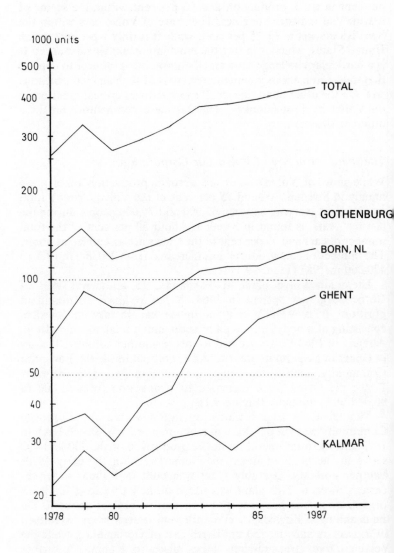

Figure 9.1 Annual production (units) in the main Volvo plants and total production, 1978–87
Source: Volvo annual reports

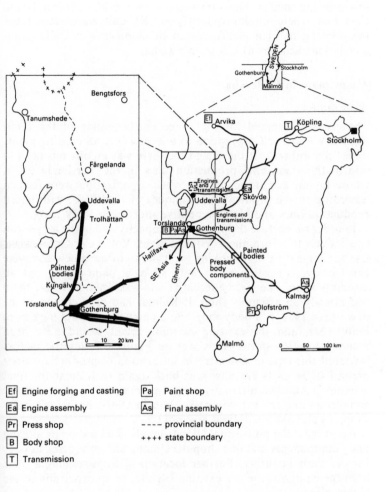

Ef	Engine forging and casting	Pa	Paint shop
Ea	Engine assembly	As	Final assembly
Pr	Press shop	- - - -	provincial boundary
B	Body shop	++++	state boundary
T	Transmission		

Figure 9.2 Main elements in the Volvo car production system

the declining market, the equipment of this plant was postponed in 1977, and the factory is still on ice. The facility has been used by Volvo's US import organization ever since.

Today the majority of cars for North American customers are shipped in completely built-up versions from Gothenburg. A small portion, for the Canadian market, about 10,000 cars annually, are assembled in Halifax, Nova Scotia. Another 10,000 cars are assembled in smaller plants throughout the world, mainly in South East Asia, where prohibitive tariffs on CBU units have necessitated the opening of such plants, served by shipments of CKD (completely knocked down) kits from Sweden.

A new plant in Uddevalla

Alternatives

The growing demand for cars since the beginning of the 1980s pushed Volvo Car Corporation to a level where all existing plants were fully utilized. At the same time there was an obvious need to reform the traditional production lines in the Torslanda plant, whose layout and principles for work organization were formed according to the production techniques of the 1960s, with paced production lines and highly repetitive short-cycle work tasks.

In order to increase the production capacity and in the longer run successively to reform the Torslanda plant, Volvo Car Corporation had for some time been looking for a site to locate a new complete car factory, consisting of a body shop, a paint shop, and an assembly shop. The main alternative site was Kalmar, where there was already an assembly shop. If Kalmar had been chosen as the new site in 1984/5, a body shop and a paint shop would have been built there, and the existing assembly plant would have been manned for two shifts. As is seen in Figure 9.2, logistic factors favoured this type of downstream integration of production, since pressed body parts are now sent back again to Kalmar for final assembly. Another alternative was an integration upstream, by complementing the existing press shop in Olofström with a body shop, a paint shop and final assembly.

Apart from the press shop, Olofström also had a shop producing body components and one shop developing and producing devices for car manufacturing. Further location alternatives might have been the equipment of the existing US site, or an expansion of the Ghent plant.

Background

Volvo did not opt for any of these alternatives, which would have been natural according to general location theory, as well as the current theory of the spatial behaviour of manufacturing enterprises. Instead, Volvo chose to make a 'greenfield' investment in Uddevalla, 80 km north of Gothenburg. By investigating the circumstances around this unconventional decision, we intend to draw attention to a few features in the geography of enterprises, which in our view have not been sufficiently noticed in earlier studies. These factors are:

• development of new ideas for work organization at the shop level, and their spatial effects on the macro structure of production;
• the interplay between the single enterprise and various actors, representing public interests at different geographical levels, and different sectoral issues, mainly environmental protection, local labour markets and regional development policies.

Several authors, notably Törnqvist (1970), Dicken (1976), Marshall (1982), and Clarke (1985) have paid attention to production organization as one explanatory factor behind the spatial structure of multi-plant enterprises. In their attempts to integrate concepts derived from organization theory within a spatial model of the internal structure of corporations, these studies have been the most useful starting-points for us. However, they all use an explicit macro approach, taking as their point of departure the structure of the business organization as such.

Our approach is to trace the macro structure as formulated at the board-room level back to micro-organizational features which have to do with the constraints of the organization of work at the shop floor. Our aim is thus to show how the company's intention to develop new ideas of work organization was one of the crucial factors behind the decision to select an entirely new site, rather than expanding the capacity at an existing site. One underlying assumption in generalizing from our case is that such considerations will become more important in the future, in Sweden as well as elsewhere.

Though the factor of work organization plays an important role in our study, it is evident that the details in the company's initial decision to locate a plant in Uddevalla underwent substantial transformations during the time from the public announcement in January 1985 to the planned completion of the project in August 1989. As a matter of fact, at least one of the key elements in Volvo's analysis of the locational advantages of Uddevalla in relation to other alternatives, namely, building a complete car factory there, was never realized. Instead, a final assembly plant only, dependent on painted bodies from Torslanda, has been built. The process in between where a number of public actors representing different sectoral and regional interests took a very active part in the decision-making, may be unique for countries, like Sweden, where the public sector is strong. That kind of situation may not allow the process to be generalized world-wide. Here reference can be made to Watts (1987:211–21). But there is a growing tendency among various interest groups in the community to take an active part in the locational game. It may be a matter of not only attracting but also refusing new plants. Earlier research may have concentrated too much on the role of the government and its instruments or lack of instruments to reach certain targets in its regional policy. In this respect, it may be correct to conclude that measures aimed at regional economic development have had little general impact on industrial geography. But if the spatial behaviour of enterprises is scrutinized in detail, e.g. as regards size, choice of technology, and layout, it may be possible to show that the interplay between the single enterprise and different public actors, among them the government, has been crucial in the final decision. This is clearly the case in our study.

In the process of elucidating the roles of various actors in the locational game, a growing number of studies focus on the management of the spatial impacts of industrial change. Linge (1988) points at the growing conflict between what is happening at various spatial levels. He notes that, ironically, this conflict partly arises because of a greater willingness on the part of the actors involved to effect changes in more collaborative and less confrontationist ways. He notes further that the implications for change are very considerable. In effect, the success of the top-down political response to change is creating an even greater need for bottom-up strategies at a more human and local level in order to carry through a change. Inspired by these statements, we wish to show how locational considerations, within a global strategy for a transnational multi-plant enterprise, initiated a process of changing the forms of work organization at the local shop level in a small Swedish town.

The role of actors on different levels

As late as the beginning of the 1970s, Sweden was the second largest shipbuilding nation in the world. Most of its huge shipyards were found along the west coast, where Gothenburg is the chief town.[3] When shipbuilding was struck by the severe crisis that set in after 1975, the government increased its role and took over the ownership of all existing yards, and subsequently also the responsibility for providing new jobs for the former shipbuilding workers. In Gothenburg, where decisions to close down three of the four yards were taken between 1976 and 1978, the expansion within the engineering sector in general, and Volvo in particular, saved the local labour market from disaster. In Uddevalla, however, a town of only 45,000 inhabitants, the shipyard accounted for more than 50 per cent of the total manufacturing employment. There were very few alternative jobs in other sectors. Thus the decision in December 1984 to close down the shipyard, with its 2,200 employees, was expected to cause considerable damage to the regional economy. The government had already taken a more active part in Uddevalla than in the other shipyards, since it had acquired a 50 per cent ownership in 1963, going up to 100 per cent in 1971.

Shortly after announcing the closing-down of the Uddevalla shipyard, the Ministry of Industry presented an extensive 'package plan' worth more than 1,000m. Swedish kronor. The plan included various special development measures, aiming, in the long term, at reforming the existing traditional structure of industry and service in the Uddevalla region, and in the short term, at finding alternative opportunities for the former shipyard workers. In addition, funds were raised to construct another 20 km of motor highway south of Uddevalla, in order to provide better connections with the Gothenburg region.

On the same day as the government's action plan was presented, Volvo announced its intention to build a complete car factory in the Uddevalla region, creating 1,000 new jobs. The former shipyard workers were a good recruitment source for the planned body shop, since the job was similar to the one they were used to: welding and the handling of steel sheets. The large scale of the plans presented by Volvo seems to have caught the government by surprise. It is a fair guess that the public resources allocated to Uddevalla would have become smaller in size if the government had known about Volvo's intentions in advance.

In any case Volvo's initiative turned out very favourably for the company. In the negotiations that were taken up with the ministry later on, Volvo was first of all permitted to take advantage of the opportunity to finance its investments in Uddevalla and in some other factories in Sweden by having a maximum of 12,500m. kronor released from its own special investment fund. Second, by obtaining ownership of the former shipyard and its land area, Volvo could use the accumulated losses of the shipyard to reduce its own taxes during the next financial year. Third, Volvo was granted a special locational support of up to 240m. kronor.[4] These favourable financing opportunities, together with the reduced time-distance between Gothenburg and Uddevalla estimated to result from the completion of the motor highway, were decisive for the choice of Uddevalla instead of Kalmar. In May 1985, the Volvo board took the decision to locate the plant in Uddevalla, and in the

following month the company received from the government
permission to locate a complete car factory with a maximum
capacity of 40,000 assembled units and 5,000 bodies for external
assembly, all in one shift.

There was, however, one additional problem. In Sweden, a
manufacturing company has to apply for permission to emit into
the environment a stated maximum amount of pollutants. That
permission was to be considered separately from the general
permission to locate the plant. Now, a paint shop is liable to cause
environmental pollution by emissions into the air. Hence, in June
1985 Volvo applied for permission to emit 1,700 tons of solvents
annually. The company did not get an answer right away. One of
the bodies to which the application was submitted for consideration, the government of the Province of Gothenburg and Bohus,
to which both Gothenburg and Uddevalla belong (Figure 9.2), did
not support the proposal, and public opinion against the planned
emissions was strongly expressed in several quarters, both locally in
Uddevalla and nationally. The province is in fact one of the parts of
Sweden that is hardest struck by acid rain.

In September 1985 Volvo handed in an application proposing a
reduced emission of 1,400 tons. As a definite stand had not been
taken by the relevant authority as late as January 1986, Volvo
decided to stop the projection of the body shop and the paint shop.
However, land was to be reserved for these two shops, which were
meant to be built later on. An additional factor was probably
important for the company's decision not to build a complete car
factory, namely, that the costs for the paint-shop were becoming
prohibitive. However, Volvo never adduced this as one of their
reasons for reducing the size of the plant.

Thus, after January 1986, the Uddevalla factory was planned to
become an assembly plant only, but still employing about 1,000
people. The level of employment could not be changed, as the
special grants and resources made available from the government
were based on the original figure. However, a body-shop and a
paint-shop are highly automated and technically more advanced,
and do not require so much manpower. Therefore, the total loss of
possible jobs was not so great in spite of the fact that the investment
was substantially reduced in size.

Finally, in March 1987 Volvo obtained permission to emit a
maximum of 470 tons of solvents in Uddevalla. The assembly plant
was to get painted bodies delivered by truck from the Torslanda
paint shop. As the environmental protection requirements are
higher on new facilities than on existing ones, the provincial
government had to accept a greater volume of emissions from the

paint shop in Torslanda in order to avoid emissions in Uddevalla. In addition, Volvo had to enter into a debate on their decision to send the bodies from Gothenburg to Uddevalla by road and not by rail, despite the existing railway tracks from door to door. In this case, however, Volvo persisted in its original transport solution. As can be seen from Figure 9.2, the Uddevalla location has few advantages from a logistical point of view, relative to other alternatives. The assembled units in Uddevalla will consist of the 740 model, meant mainly for the Scandinavian market.

Accordingly some fundamental elements of the initial decision had changed in the planning process. But as the financial support given by the government was still considerable, Volvo had no intention of reducing the number of employees or of withdrawing from the entire project. Moreover, the competition for good automobile workers became even stronger during the project period, as the other car producer in Sweden, SAAB, expanded its capacity in Trollhättan, only 30 km from Uddevalla (Figure 9.2), employing 9,000 workers in 1987 as compared with 5,000 in 1981.[5]

Volvo did not believe it was possible for an existing plant to accommodate the original plan of combining the need for an increased production capacity with the opportunity to introduce new ideas of work organization. Then, in 1987, it became even more important than in 1984 to realize the plan envisioned in the initial phase of the project, namely, to create a factory in Uddevalla based on radically new production techniques and a new form of work organization. The vision of tomorrow's automotive industry was coming to justify the whole project. By scrutinizing in detail how these new ideas were introduced in the Uddevalla project, we wish to point out that research in the geography of enterprise should attach more importance to the problem of competition for skilled labour. The competitive edge in tomorrow's car industry may in fact be the successful implementation of attractive conditions for workers on the shop floor.

Organization of work in the Uddevalla plant

Problems to solve

One reason for Volvo's decision to locate a plant in Uddevalla was the need to increase production capacity. But there were other factors too. One is the high rate of labour turnover in traditionally organized factories based on the technique of paced production lines. Another problem is the great number of injuries caused by organic attrition occurring in factories with repetitive work tasks.

Third, the youth cohorts in Sweden (aged 15–24) during the next decades will decrease considerably, and there will be competition among the employers to get hold of the youngsters.

A fourth problem is that the level of education of the Swedish work-force has increased to such an extent that the would-be recruits do not feel satisfied with the kind of work tasks that the automobile industry traditionally offers. People at work want to be able to use their problem-solving capacities as well as their hands. The short-cycle work tasks on traditional assembly lines do not allow that.

The fifth problem is related to values and norms. In today's Sweden industrial jobs have low status. People prefer work in the service sector and of course especially in the more glamorous jobs. The higher level of education makes people prefer white-collar jobs to blue-collar jobs. On the whole, at present no jobs exist in manufacturing industry where the work tasks are made from a mix of tasks taken from the shop-floor level as well as from the administrative office level. Jobs have been formed with the underlying assumption of Taylor's scientific management theory that one kind of people, the well educated leaders and technicians, should do all the thinking and problem-solving, while the poorly educated shop-floor workers should do just the simple manual work.

A special project group within Volvo tried to tackle these problems. The parties met at the beginning of the projecting phase to discuss their visions and ideas about what they wanted the new factory to look like. The project group agreed, in general, on the following goals.

1 The higher level of education among the would-be recruits should be used primarily as a positive factor in planning the plant. The work tasks should be formed in such a way that assembly work could be combined with administrative tasks of different kinds. The higher level of education in the working population would also make it possible to assign former specialist functions to the people assembling the cars. Examples might be some of the quality control and some maintenance. In such a way the work task of each individual could become a mix of different kinds of work (white- and blue-collar). Work tasks should be long-cycle and carry more responsibility. This was to be something quite different from the traditional short-cycle assembly line jobs.

2 The shrinking cohorts of young people should be met by a conscious policy to make the jobs so attractive in the ergonomic sense that the people employed could stay for a long time

without experiencing organic attrition. Further, the goal was to be reached by employing at least 40 per cent women. In industry, by tradition, not many women are employed because of the physically demanding work and the simple fact that a woman's hand is (normally) too small to grip the standardized tools in the shop. The project group therefore had to consider changing the tools too.

3 The high degree of organic attrition among the workers was to be mitigated by some special measures in the area of ergonomics (tools, devices, etc.), by lengthening the work task cycle time, and by mixing different kinds of jobs. The less repetitive work tasks, the less organic attrition was the philosophy.

4 The high degree of labour turnover should be countered by a mixed, extended, and thereby more satisfying work content, as described above. The idea was that people should take pride in the fact that they were working for Volvo.

5 The problem of creating a value system oriented towards downgrading service jobs and towards upgrading industrial jobs could be met, in the long run only, by putting the visions into effect. The project group hoped to show empirically that by abandoning the tedious assembly-line jobs in favour of creating mixed, extended tasks, the jobs would in fact be experienced as more attractive, and at the same time the productivity would rise.

There were some minor ideas too:

- working groups in 'small factories within the factory' (see below);
- few administrative staff;
- complete product made by each working group ('whole cars, whole jobs').

One wish that emanated from the company, intent on keeping the resources for its realization under control, was that the process of projecting the Uddevalla factory should result in real progress towards better relations between the company and the unions, especially in terms of extended co-operation between the unions and the management. That is why the union representatives were engaged from the very beginning, on a full-time basis and with special resources at their disposal, so that active co-operation could become meaningful. Because of the full-time engagement in the project, it was not possible for the unions simply to appoint their representatives from the cadre of people working at the union offices. The union representatives were instead taken from the level next to the shop floor, namely 'shop-floor representatives'. This was a new situation and it was important for the development of the project.

Critical points

Projecting the Volvo factory in Uddevalla has been a process of constant development. All alternative solutions were discussed in relation to the vision outlined in the first phase of the project. It is obvious now, in hindsight, that the forces that were in favour of the more radical alternatives have ended up by winning each separate 'race'. The result is an unusual assembly plant. It consists of six separate 'factories within the factory', so-called product shops (Figure 9.3). The product shops are more independent of each other than are traditional departments along an assembly line. There is one leader in each product shop and there are eight working groups (with about ten people) in each product shop. Hence, traditional white-collar work tasks formerly done by the foremen must necessarily be delegated to individuals within the working groups.

Competence growth

There is at least one pre-condition for the successful realization of the basic innovation in the Uddevalla plant: the idea of extended, long-cycle work tasks, resulting in a completed product, a complete car for each work group. The pre-condition is increased competence in the labour force. Each worker has to be able to master all, or nearly all, the different individual tasks needed to produce a car. In more conventional plants, the competence of course exists in the labour force as a whole. But it is divided among many persons, each of them knowing just his or her own individual work task. Those small pieces of fragmented competence can be learned by anyone – even instrumentally – provided he or she is not required to learn anything else than just that little task. Hence, in a conventional automobile plant the whole job of assembling a car is divided into small subtasks of about two minutes each, arranged in such a manner that they should in theory fit exactly into each other.

The individual subtasks of a particular worker may be related to different parts of the car: for example one subtask may be to put some clips in place on the windscreen cleaner; another subtask could be to put some electric cables in the right position, and so on.

Such extremely fragmented work tasks hardly help the worker understand how his own work contributes to the production of the car as a whole. By the same token, he is given little opportunity to suggest improvements in the production process. In the conven-

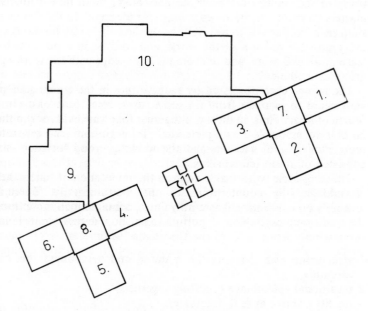

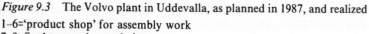

Figure 9.3 The Volvo plant in Uddevalla, as planned in 1987, and realized
1–6='product shop' for assembly work
7–9=final test and completion
  10=material store
  11=administration

tional system, therefore, such improvements are not expected from the individual workers but from the department of production techniques, from the maintenance department, and from the foremen. In the new system, with extended, long-cycle work tasks a great deal of these various competences have to be distributed among, and expected from, the individual workers.

To raise the level of competence of the individual workers Volvo decided to start a 'training shop' in Uddevalla. The training shop got under way in April 1986, two years before the start of the production in the new factory. The aim was to make the employees learn how to assemble cars in a functional way. This was something new to Volvo, and to large-scale automobile industry as a whole. The educational model used is that of the old craft trades, where the learner is successively introduced to the various competences and tricks of the trade, learning as he goes along, until he eventually masters them all – he becomes a 'master tradesman'. In the training shop each worker was to be given the opportunity to try his hand at every possible portion of the work, and thus be in a position to learn more and more, and to share his knowledge with the working group as a whole.

The competence possessed by each worker in the training shop was meant to increase from (in some cases) zero to at least one-fourth of a car. Thus, in theory, altogether four 'car builders' should be able to assemble a complete car.[6] To begin with, however, a more modest goal was set, and the working group for each car consisted of about ten workers.

The long-cycle work tasks, built on the foundation of functional assemblage (the counterpoint to the instrumentally founded assembly on conventional assembly lines), contain much more than the traditional assemblage = putting together. The new contents in the assembly work tasks of the Uddevalla factory are:

1 structuring and checking the material and components before assembly;
2 traditional assemblage (=putting together);
3 quality control and, if necessary;
4 adjustments.

The workers are therefore able to control their own workday in a way that differs radically from the usual situation in the automobile industry.

But the work of the working groups was not only meant to contain ordinary blue-collar tasks. The groups were also to attempt tasks formerly assigned to the administrative level. As there are no traditional foremen in the new factory, the groups have to be able to do some of the planning and follow-up of their own work during the day, the week, and for some questions even longer time periods. For example, the groups must, through some of their members, be involved in such things as recruitment, budgeting, and production technique. Different group members may specialize in different tasks, but still be engaged in the assembly tasks.

In the beginning there were about fifteen workers in the training shop. Some ten months later there were about sixty people, and in 1988, just before the start of the first one of the in total six smaller 'factories within the factory', there were about 300 people. About 45 per cent of that work-force were women, compared to the 40 per cent which was set as the goal.

The learning in the training shop was always directly related to a production situation. The idea was that a human being is not satisfied if, when he has done a work task resulting in a product, someone else picks his product to pieces for instruction purposes, in order for the process to be repeated again and again. The product itself comes to be seen as of no value, and the 'destructive' procedure becomes pedagogically self-defeating. In Uddevalla's training shop, on the contrary, the employees were to assemble real cars. They were training in a production-like situation. During the first two years of its existence the people in the training shop assembled nearly 2,000 cars.

The training shop will be continued at least until all the people making up the working groups in the 'small factories in the factory' are employed. The experience gained from the training shop is that the 'functional' way of building cars in working groups seems to be a step in a positive direction, given the circumstances in Sweden today and in the next few decades.

The training shop has also played another, no less important, role in the creation of the new factory in Uddevalla: it has served as a shop for 'testing' new techniques and new ways to organize the product flow. As the principles for functionally oriented assemblage were being successively developed, there arose a need to test them. Before a decision was taken to build the whole factory (or at least the first of the six 'factories in the factory') according to the new technical and organizational principles, those principles had to prove their worth empirically in the training shop.

Alternative production techniques

Traditionally the product flow in an automobile assembly plant is described in terms of the layout. A layout is a map showing just where in the halls each work task in the production flow can be done. Thus the static spatial description of the flow is used to show a process. To use a static instrument to show a dynamic process is possible only when that process is divided into separate stations where each worker performs separate work tasks. Specialization and division of labour are necessary if this method of representing the organization of a process is to be used successfully.

The assembly plant in Uddevalla has undergone a very thorough change from the way it was first projected. This process of gradual development has been encouraged by the top level of the Volvo Group and by the union representatives in the project. Some future-oriented technicians within the project group and from the Chalmers Institute of Technology in Gothenburg were looking for alternatives from the very start of the project in 1985. But at first those forces were not able to put their ideas into effect.

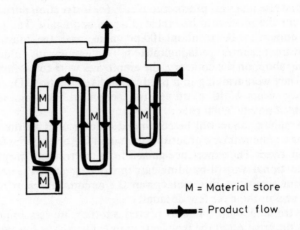

M = Material store

➡ = Product flow

Figure 9.4 The first plan for the product flow in the Uddevalla plant from 1985. The work tasks for each assembler were calculated to have a duration of about two minutes, and about 700 assemblers would have performed their work tasks every day. This plan was abandoned.

The alternative techniques took as their point of departure the shortcomings of the conventional production line system, in which several models of what is basically the same car have to be accommodated. In such cases it is often impossible to fill up exactly all the short-cycle (1–2 minutes) work tasks. This of course implies a loss of productivity. Long-cycle work tasks should substantially reduce such losses.

The first suggestion from the project group was a factory that was very much like the Chalmers assembly plant, started in 1974 (Figure 9.4). The car was moving through the factory on a transfer line, stopping at each station for a while. It more or less looked as if the car was moving in a store of parts. In that first sketch, about 700 people would each have done their own little piece of work on each particular car before completion. The product flow could very well have been described by a static layout. This was not as big a step forward as both the top level of Volvo Group and the unions had hoped for, and thus they abandoned the idea and asked for a better alternative.

The second sketch of the factory was one further step forward towards the vision outlined in the beginning of the project. That sketch ended up in eight organizational units, so-called 'product shops' in each of which one-eighth of a car was completed. In the 'product shops' there was a relatively high degree of parallel work to be done. In that way about 100 people would have been working on each car before it was completed.

One prerequisite for this way of assembling cars is that the components and material are sent to the assembly site in specific batches, in good order and at the right time. Thus the car is not moving through a store of piled up parts. A logistic solution involving an information system based on computer techniques has been the responsibility of a subproject within the Volvo Uddevalla project group. This way of handling the material for the specific cars is the basis for the following development as well.

The third step in this development process advanced the idea of 'whole cars, whole jobs', with small organizational units responsible for these 'whole units'. The decision was to keep the 'product shops' geographically separated from each other. The idea was to assemble complete cars in each product shop (compared to one-eighth of a car in the former sketch). In this way there were still about 100 people producing the whole car together. But they were now able to see the completion of the car, since they worked in the same organizational unit and in the same room.

It was from this sketch of the 'product shop' that the idea of the 'training shop' was formed. Each person was meant to be able to build at least one-fourth of a car. The training shop was divided into four different work groups, and each of these was responsible for learning their one-fourth of the car. Thus the car was moved from the first group, assembling the first of the four functional parts of the car, over to the second group and so on until all the four groups had done their work and the whole car was completed.

Two further ways of laying out the production flow were worked out in theory, and in a theoretical analysis were found to be better than their predecessors.

The final solution (up to now) was a layout where the working group itself assembled the whole car completely on their own. This means that not more than ten people are now involved in the assembly of one complete car. The car was to be moved only once, and thus the static spatial dimension to describe the product flow in a layout is not adequate any more, though it is used until a better one is found. But it is clear that the new way of organizing the production really demands a combined time–space layout, in order to give the same information as the purely spatial layouts of the traditional production lines (Figure 9.5).

The last two ideas for the layout of the product shops were tried

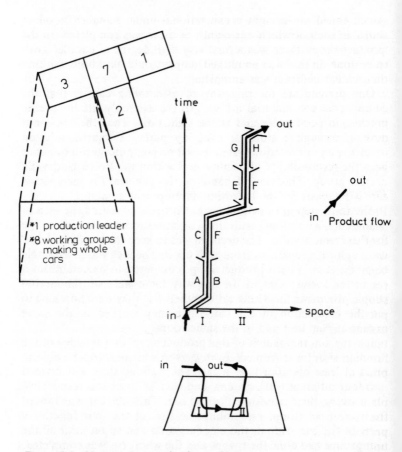

Figure 9.5 New work organization at Volvo

Above: In each 'product shop' there is a 'product leader' and eight separate working teams (groups). Each team (about ten people in each) produces entire cars. There are eight parallel product flows in each 'product shop'. This means that about ten people are needed for different types of administrative and assembly tasks for the complete mounting of one single car, and the duration of each work task is about two hours, and can be extended to the assembly of a whole car.

Below: A time-space illustration of the principles for assemblage in one working team. A map of the part of the shop where the team works shows the two stations where all assembly is done (I and II). A–H are the work tasks in the example, performed in the time–space by eight different people in the team. Not more than two people work on the car at the same time in the example.

202

out empirically in the training shop before the decision was taken to develop them any further. It is just the last one of those two ideas that is to be realized in the first three of the total of six product shops making up the heart of the Uddevalla factory. In this solution there will be working groups who have work tasks considerably extended when compared to traditional jobs in assembly plants. The work tasks also give a higher degree of responsibility to the group and implicate needs for ongoing education and personal development in the group.

Conclusions

Projecting a factory: a continuous process

Projecting the factory in Uddevalla has been a process of constant change. It has not been easy to grasp all the subtle phases of the development. Most probably, the process of constant development would never have become this lively if on the one hand, there had been different goals set up by the company and the unions, respectively, and on the other hand, if there had been no training shop in the Uddevalla factory. The training shop showed that it was possible for 'ordinary people', men and women, to learn the work of assembling at least one fourth of a car, provided the jobs were taught in a functional way and by people who were themselves familiar with functional assemblage. Instrumental teaching would probably not have attained the same results.

One thing of importance is that in the discussion as to where the plant should be located, the alternative of extending the capacity of the factory in Gothenburg was never considered. The reason is probably that the labour force in Gothenburg was used to looking upon Volvo as a traditional assembly line plant. In Uddevalla there were no such preconceptions. Still, Uddevalla is within the wider Gothenburg region, and this is clearly a positive location factor, the more so since Volvo has many factories (producing components for the cars) in this region.

In Uddevalla the closure of the shipyard created opportunities for getting hold of a competent work-force. Shipyard workers in Uddevalla had a good reputation. In 1986 about 75 per cent of the blue-collar workers recruited by Volvo were fomer shipyard workers, and in the considerably increased work-force of 1988 they still comprised about 20 per cent. It is too early to say anything about the long-term results of upgrading the automobile assembly workers' work tasks. There is obviously a need for creating new kinds of industrial jobs, a mix of former white-collar and blue-collar tasks. Up till now it seems as if the ways of achieving this have been centred on the former blue-collar workers. It will be interesting to see if enough effort will be made to create attractive jobs for the white-collar workers as well. This seems to be necessary, especially if some of their tasks are to be carried out on the shop floor.

It is obvious that the Volvo Uddevalla project has taken at least one step forward in the direction of co-operation between Volvo and the unions.

First, the representatives from the unions were for the first time treated as full members of a project staff, with equivalent resources. Their experience had never before been acknowledged as containing such a high value as here.

Second – and this should be seen as further support for the first point – the union representatives were taken from the level of production in existing factories, not from the central union cadres of the company. These people had their shop floor feeling very clearly in mind.

Third, the coinciding interests of the Volvo management and the unions were important for the decision not to accept the first, rather traditional layout for the new factory. Without the support from the top level, the unions would once again have become just obstructive no-men, and no further steps would have been taken in the co-operation between the parties.

Fourth, for the first time the representatives from the blue-collar union felt that it was possible to make suggestions which were really listened to. This in itself was worth the hard work done discussing alternative solutions to problems.

A factory project: implications for spatial theory

What conclusions regarding the spatial behaviour of enterprises can be generalized from the Uddevalla case?

The first concerns the intricate interplay between various actors at different spatial levels. While the national level, represented, say, by the Ministry of Industry, still has a main role in the initiation phase of a new project aiming at regional restructuring etc., its ability to manage details in the implementation process has diminished. Particularly as regards the expected environmental effects of a location, and the competition for qualified labour, other actors at various levels seem to have grown in strategic importance. Accordingly, the time period from decision to realization is likely to grow considerably. There will be less opportunity to plan in detail such things as size, capacity, choice of technology and integration or fragmentation between the separate units in a multi-plant enterprise. The issue of environmental control will certainly be of crucial importance in the future in this interplay of actors.

Second, and even more important to the spatial behaviour of enterprises, the Uddevalla plant has chosen a method of work organization that is likely to be a forerunner in car production in the 1990s. The most obvious impact of this type of work organization is that the average scale of output in a car assembly plant will decrease considerably if this system becomes widely adopted. There will be a dispersed pattern of smaller plants rather than a concentration in larger facilities.

Third, the qualitative improvement of the product due to better utilization of human resources may very well balance the supposed economic advantages of large-scale production units. Large-scale production units are difficult to combine with a more customer-oriented production, since the economy in large-scale production arises from the identity of the products. When different products have to be mixed on the same assembly line there will be substantial productivity losses. Thus, increased demands for flexibility, involving changes of models and personal equipment in cars, will favour smaller rather than larger car plants.

Fourth, capacity expansion at an existing plant may also be a disadvantage in that the idea of a radically new type of work organization is more difficult to realize in an environment dominated by traditional thinking.

Fifth, and last, the automotive industry has historically been a forerunner in introducing new production techniques and work organization. Therefore, the lessons of the Uddevalla case may be valid for a large variety of enterprises within the whole manufacturing sector.

Notes

1 The sales in 1987 amounted to 92,500 million Swedish kronor ($US14,600m.). The net income during the same year was 4,600 million kronor ($US730m.) (*Fortune*, 1 August 1988).
2 About 120,000 of the total 420,000 cars were produced by Volvo Car B.V., the Netherlands, where Volvo owns a minority share. Volvo Car B.V. is a complete car factory producing cars in the 300 and 400 series. Since 1981 Volvo has owned 30 per cent of the Volvo Car B.V.
3 Of a total number of 38,000 employees in 1975, 18,000 were in the province of Gothenburg and Bohus, of whom 14,000 were in Gothenburg and 3,000 in Uddevalla.
4 However, Volvo could never get more than 15 per cent of the total sum of investment. If the investment was reduced compared to the plan, the locational support would also be reduced.

5 Already in 1983, when the first reduction of jobs at the Uddevalla shipyard took place, the resultant crisis began to make itself felt. In the 1980s, SAAB had been approached by the provincial government, who suggested they should increase their capacity by locating a new plant in Uddevalla. SAAB apparently refused this informal offer. In December 1985, facing the need to make a new location decision, SAAB announced plans to build a new car factory at a former shipyard in Malmö in southern Sweden. This solution of the expansion problem was chosen by SAAB in order to obtain the same favourable financial support as the Ministry of Industry had granted to Volvo in the case of Uddevalla. In view of the precedent created by Volvo, the ministry accepted SAAB's conditions. But when implementing the project, SAAB had to face the same discussions regarding expected environmental effects as Volvo did in Uddevalla.

6 A 'car builder' is a new concept that will make the traditional concept 'operator' obsolete. An 'operator' is just supposed to handle his/her instrumentally learned tasks. A 'car builder' is supposed to understand why he/she is doing what he/she does, and how. His/her training has to be functionally oriented.

References

Clark, I. M. (1985) *The Spatial Organisation of Multinational Corporations*, London and Sydney: Croom Helm.

Dicken, P. (1976) 'The multiplant business enterprise and geographical space; some issues on the study of external control and regional development', *Regional Studies* 10: 401–12.

Fortune Magazine, 1 August 1988.

Linge, G. J. R. (1988) 'Managing the Spatial Impacts of Industrial Change', Introductory speech to the meeting of the IGU Commission on Industrial Change, Rutherglen, Launceston, Tasmania, August.

Marshall, J. N. (1982) 'Organisational theory and industrial location', *Environment and Planning*, Series A, 14: 1667–83.

Törnqvist, G. (1970) *Contact Systems and Regional Development*, Lund Studies in Geography, Series B, No 35, University of Lund, Sweden.

Volvo, annual reports.

Watts, H. D. (1987) *Industrial Geography*, Harlow: Longman.

Chapter ten

Daewoo
Corporate growth
and spatial organization

Sam Ock Park

Introduction

The growing economic importance of large business organizations
has been a global trend during the present century. The spread of
such organizations has contributed to the emergence of a distinctive
geography of enterprise, as 'the geography of modern society is
increasingly determined not by the actions of isolated individuals,
but by the strategies of large organizations' (Chapman and Walker
1987:22). This geography of enterprise, or the enterprise approach,
which was pioneered by McNee (1958, 1960) and followed by a
number of others (see e.g. Krumme 1969; Hayter and Watts 1983),
focuses on the spatial ramifications of decision-making within large
firms. The geography of enterprise has been defined in a recent
reappraisal as 'the study of the influence of the policies and
structure of multiproduct, multiplant enterprises on changes in
industrial location and on processes of regional economic development' (Hayter and Watts 1983:157). This definition emphasizes the
importance of the large enterprise as an agent of spatial change.

An individual firm may itself be part of a larger organizational
structure which constitutes an enterprise, and the enterprise
approach emphasizes the role of such enterprises as, what McNee
(1960) termed, 'area- or space-organizing institutions'. Even in
developing countries, especially in the newly industrialized countries (NICs), the role of large enterprises in leading the nation's
industrial growth and shaping its dynamics has been growing
during the last two decades (Linge 1984; Park 1986).

Despite a considerable number of studies based on the enterprise
approach, no clear framework within which large enterprises can be
studied has yet been generated. Numerous empirical studies focus
on the role of the large enterprises of NICs as agents of spatial
change. Yet the findings from the studies of developed countries
cannot be directly applied to the case of the NICs.

More than one hundred 'groups' or 'chaebols' (conglomerates) have been established in Korea during the last two decades. Among them, the Daewoo Group, the fourth largest conglomerate in Korea, has experienced a rapid growth in a relatively short period of time. As such, Daewoo can be regarded as a model of a rapidly expanding and restructuring enterprise in the context of Korea's rapid industrialization. The organizational and spatial structure of the Daewoo Group has changed tremendously through mergers and restructuring during the last two decades.

The present study analyses the growth and spatial organization of Daewoo from the standpoint of the enterprise approach. The major research questions addressed in this study are as follows: What are the major strategies and methods of corporate growth of Daewoo? How are the strategies and the methods related to (changes in) the spatial structure of operating units of the corporate system? What are the locational strategies and patterns of spatial linkages? The present study is descriptive in nature and empirical in content, drawing upon published information, unpublished corporate material, and interviews performed both inside and outside of the Daewoo Group.

The Daewoo Group: organization

The Daewoo Group, which started as a small textile company in 1967, now encompasses 27 member companies, 17 subsidiaries in 14 countries, and more than 60 sales organizations (branch offices) in more than 40 countries. Daewoo ranked fourth in Korea and thirty-fifth in Fortune's International Big 500 (outside the US) by total sales in 1987. According to Averitt's (1968) notion of the dual economy, Daewoo is a core firm, a large business organization representing the nucleus of the Korean economy.

Chapman and Walker (1987:101) identified four organizational structures based on stages in the development of the large industrial enterprise: functional, multidivisional, holding company, and area/product structures. In this framework, the organizational structure of Daewoo is essentially a holding company, though it is also multidivisional. At present, Daewoo is organized in nine divisions: trading and construction, machinery, electric and electronics, telecommunications, automotive and automotive parts and components, shipbuilding, chemicals, finance, and leisure (Table 10.1). Therefore, the organizational structure of Daewoo can be regarded as a combination of multidivisional and holding company structures (Figure 10.1).

The complexity of its organizational structure resulted from

Table 10.1   Divisions and companies of Daewoo Group

Division	Company	Business field & products
Trading and construction	Daewoo Corporation	— Trading: export, import, international finance, resource development — Construction: plants, architectural and civil works
	Keangnam Enterprises Ltd	— Plants, architectural and civil works
	Daewoo Engineering Co.	— Construction, consulting, licensing, feasibility studies
Machinery	Daewoo Heavy Industries Ltd	— Diesel engines, rolling stock, construction equipment, industrial vehicles, machine tooling, aerospace
	Daewoo Precision Industries Ltd (machinery)	— Precision machines, defence products, musical instruments
	Daewoo–Sikorsky	— Helicopters
Electric and electronics	Daewoo Electronics Co., Ltd	— TVs, VCRs, PCs, audio products, home appliances
	Orion Electric Co., Ltd	— TV tubes, monitors, VCR heads
	Daewoo Electronic Components Co., Ltd	— TV turner, capacitor
	Daewoo Carrier Corp.	— Air conditioners, rotary compressors
	Daewoo Electric Motor Industries Ltd	— Motors for electric products
Telecommunications	Daewoo Telecom Co., Ltd	— Telecom switching system, PCs, fibre optics, O/A machines, semiconductors
Automotive and automotive parts and components	Daewoo Motor Co., Ltd	— Passenger cars, buses, trucks, specialty vehicles
	Daewoo Precision Industries Ltd	— Auto parts and components
	Daewoo Automotive Components Ltd	— Cranking motors, alternators, ignition distributors, ignition coils
	DHMS Industries Ltd	— Steering gears, axles, brakes, radiators
	Koram Plastics Co., Ltd	— Polyurethane bumpers
Shipbuilding	Daewoo Shipbuilding & Heavy Machinery Ltd	— Ships, offshore structures
	Shina Shipbuilding Co., Ltd	— Medium-sized vessels, yachts, ship repair
	Daewoo Engineered Products Ltd	— Prefabricated pipes for power plants, pipe hangers and support
Chemicals	Korea Steel Chemical Co., Ltd	— Coal tar derivatives, carbon black products, agrochemicals
	Pungkuk Oil Co., Ltd	— Coal tar derivatives, benzol
Finance	Daewoo Securities Co., Ltd	— Securities brokerage, underwriting dealer operation
	Daewoo Research Institute	— Economic analysis & survey
	Daewoo Investment & Finance Corporation	— Operation of short-term Cp, dealer operation in money markets
	Daewoo Capital Management Co., Ltd	— Investment consulting
Hotels	Dongwoo Development Co.	— Seoul Hilton International
	Sorak Development Co.	— Sorak Hotel

Source: Materials from Daewoo Planning and Co-ordination Division

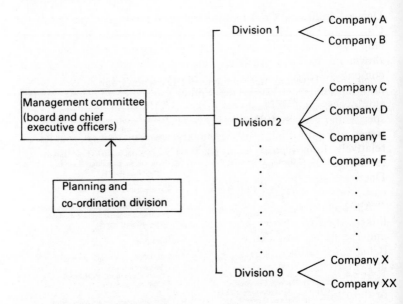

Figure 10.1 Organizational structure of Daewoo

rapid diversification by means of external growth. Each division is run exclusively by one chief executive officer who holds the power and responsibility within his own division. Although companies within each of these divisions are fairly independent, the leading company in each division operates like a parent company and has strong linkages in material, technology, and information with other companies of the division.

The management committee is the supreme decision-making authority of Daewoo. The committee consists of fifteen members who represent the major business fields of Daewoo. The committee meetings are held once a week and make final decisions on:

1 budgets and annual projects;
2 new investments in important projects and facilities;
3 take-overs, mergers, and dissolution of firms;
4 capital increase and stock matters;
5 major manpower and recruiting matters;
6 other issues considered important by the chairman.

Daewoo: growth strategies and methods

The Daewoo Group originated from a small trading company,

Daewoo Industrial Co. Ltd, established in 1967. Daewoo Industrial Co., launched with a paid-in capital of US$9,000 and five employees, became a seedbed of the Daewoo Group, which has shown a remarkable growth during the last twenty years. The small company, with annual sales of $US0.6m. in 1967, has grown into a multinational enterprise with annual sales of $US15bn., 108,000 employees, and annual exports of $US5.1bn. in 1988. The spectacular growth of Daewoo in a relatively short period of time is traced in Figure 10.2. Most of the large enterprises in Korea have a relatively long history compared to Daewoo, since they were established before the 1950s. Because of its remarkable growth, Daewoo's strategies and methods of growth provide an interesting case study of industrial dynamics in Korea.

Although strategies and methods of growth are inextricably linked, the former are concerned with the direction of expansion and the latter with the mechanism by which growth is achieved (Chapman and Walker 1987). In Figure 10.3 two methods of growth are differentiated. In the first, growth is achieved internally and reflected in the expansion of existing production facilities and/ or the establishment of new ones; in the second, growth is achieved by acquiring the assets of other firms. Integration implies that 'corporate development follows a sequence which represents a "natural" extension of the enterprise's existing activities', while diversification means that the enterprise diversifies its activities 'as a result of involvement in a progressively wider range of apparently unrelated sectors of the economy' (Chapman and Walker 1987:85).

During the last twenty years, Daewoo has promoted different methods and strategies in its subsequent phases of growth. The trend of growth in employment, total sales, and exports exhibits four phases:

1 early development;
2 take-off of heavy industry and chemicals;
3 restructuring;
4 global structure, with development of technology-intensive industry.

Each phase is characterized by distinct strategies and methods of growth.

Early development phase (1967 to 1972)

Daewoo Industrial Co. was launched in 1967 in order to export textile products. Until 1972, the company depended completely upon foreign sales. As a result, the total sales volume of the

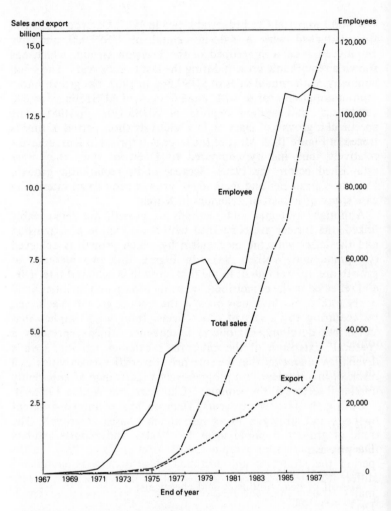

Figure 10.2 The growth of Daewoo

company was equal to its export value. At this stage the company acquired several plants and expanded existing plants in order to meet the increased demand for textile products on foreign markets. Horizontal integration in the textile industry was the main growth strategy and the method of growth was mainly internal until 1971. The strategy of horizontal integration in Daewoo's early development phase supports findings from other countries in the developed

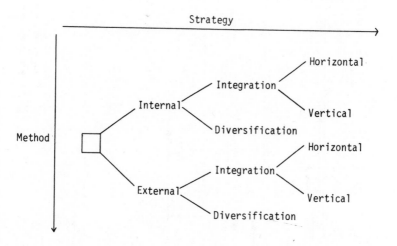

Figure 10.3   Methods and strategies of corporate growth
Source: Chapman and Walker 1987:86

world that horizontal integration appears to be the principal objective of initial business growth (Lloyd and Dicken 1977; Chapman and Walker 1987). It is interesting that the initial development of Daewoo may have benefited from governmental export promotion policies.

Take-off phase (1973 to 1979)

Daewoo experienced a rapid growth from 1973 to 1979. In this period the strategies and methods of growth were completely different from those of the previous phase. Diversification was the major strategy and the method of growth was mainly external. Decisive merger/acquisition and diversification strategy were first implemented in 1973. In that year Daewoo Industrial Co. acquired seven firms in the textiles, machinery, construction, and finance sectors. In 1978, five more firms were acquired, all of which were in the heavy industrial and chemical sectors. This intensive merger/ acquisition activity reflected Daewoo's explicit growth strategy in this phase. Some of the acquisitions were, however, related to governmental pressure and its support for insolvent firms in the heavy industrial and chemical sectors. Daewoo's heavy automotive and shipbuilding branches originated from acquisitions of such insolvent firms. By successful management and governmental

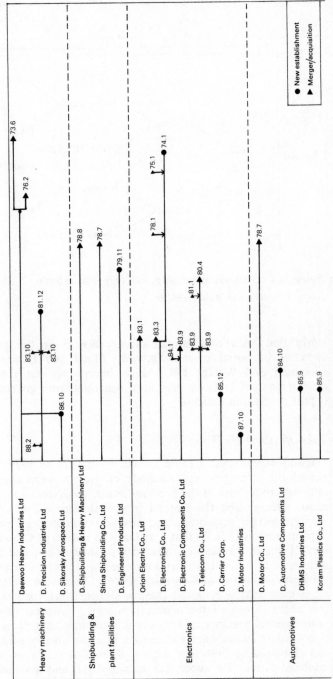

Heavy machinery	Daewoo Heavy Industries Ltd
	D. Precision Industries Ltd
	D. Sikorsky Aerospace Ltd
Shipbuilding & plant facilities	D. Shipbuilding & Heavy Machinery Ltd
	Shina Shipbuilding Co., Ltd
	D. Engineered Products Ltd
Electronics	Orion Electric Co., Ltd
	D. Electronics Co., Ltd
	D. Electronic Components Co., Ltd
	D. Telecom Co., Ltd
	D. Carrier Corp.
	D. Motor Industries
Automotives	D. Motor Co., Ltd
	D. Automotive Components Ltd
	DHMS Industries Ltd
	Koram Plastics Co., Ltd

● New establishment
▲ Merger/acquisition

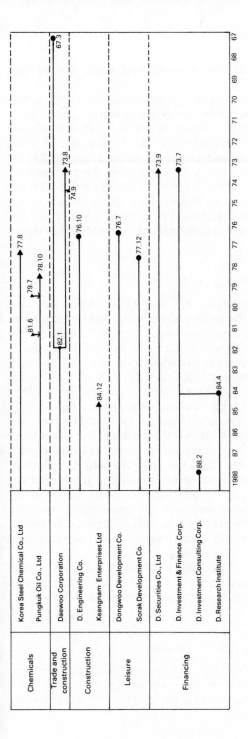

Figure 10.4 Expansion of Daewoo

support, all the insolvent firms acquired by Daewoo have become profitmaking.

In general, Daewoo diversified its economic activities by embracing the sectors of construction, finance, machinery, shipbuilding, automotives, and chemical industry in addition to the textile and leather industries. The foundations of the development of heavy industry and the chemical sector were laid in the second half of the 1970s; this diversification surely benefited from the government's industrial policies of the 1970s. The trends in major acquisition and diversification are shown in Figure 10.4. Some of the firms, acquired in this phase, especially in the textiles sector, do not appear in Figure 10.4 because they were shed by the Daewoo Group in the 1980s.

Restructuring phase (1980 to 1982)

In the early 1980s, Daewoo's external environments were not favourable because of the impact of the world-wide oil crisis and turmoil on the domestic political scene. In order to ride out the world-wide recession, Daewoo emphasized the rationalization of management, which entailed curtailing expenses and fostering office automation (Daewoo Planning Co-ordination Division 1984). In 1980, for the first time, Daewoo recorded an absolute decrease in both annual total sales and employment (Figure 10.2). The parent companies, Daewoo Industrial Co. and Daewoo Construction Co. merged into 'Daewoo Corporation' in 1982 in order to enhance the international competitiveness and to rationalize the management further. The launching of 'Daewoo Corporation' provided the momentum for the second take-off in growth and was even regarded as the second foundation of Daewoo. Total employment of Daewoo fluctuated greatly in this restructuring phase but total sales began to increase again in 1981 (Figure 10.2). Export values increased continuously in this phase even though there was a slight change in the rate of growth.

The trend of restructuring from a dominant structure of light industry to heavy industry is shown in Table 10.2. The export value of heavy industry and the chemical sector outweighed that of light industry in this phase.

Global structural phase (1983 to present)

Since the establishment of 'Daewoo Corporation' the enterprise has promoted diversification with expansion to high technology at the group level, while vertical integration has been emphasized at the

Table 10.2 Exports by product (Daewoo)

Unit: % Product	1976	1978	1980	1982	1985*	1986**	1987**
Heavy and Chemical Industrial Products	9.1	30.0	46.6	57.1	73.0+	70.0+	71.0+
Steel & Metal Pro- ducts	2.8	15.2	25.3	15.4	13	18	13.5
Chemicals	1.3	4.8	7.0	3.4	6	8	6.6
Electric and Electronic products	3.8	5.4	4.6	3.9	6	15	23.6
Machinery	0.9	1.8	3.7	2.4	7	4	3.8
Vehicles	0.1	2.2	2.4	2.1	(X1)	7	18.0
Ships	—	0.1	1.5	38.0	41	18	5.5
Other	0.2	0.6	2.3	1.8	(X2)	(X1)	(X1)
Light Industrial Products	90.9	70.0	53.4	42.9	15+	20+	19+
Garments & Textiles	73.4	44.7	31.6	28.0	15	20	19.0
Others	17.5	25.3	21.8	14.9	(X3)	(X2)	(X2)
Total	100.0	100.0	100.0	100.0	100.0	100.0	100.0
(Export value in $USm.)	(319)	(727)	(1,415)	(2,002)	(3,009)	(2,756)	(3,281)

Source: News from Daewoo, 1985, 1986, 1987; unpublished material from Daewoo

Notes: * The sum of (X1), (X2) and (X3) is 12%.
  ** The sum of (X1) and (X2) is 10%.

division level. Furthermore, Daewoo has expanded its international network, not only in the trading but also in the construction and manufacturing sectors. Since its restructuring phase, Daewoo has endeavoured to lay a firm foundation 'for coping more flexibly and effectively with rapidly changing international situations, for maximizing scope, and for internationalizing structure' (Daewoo Corporation 1983:2).

The most distinct characteristic of the methods of growth is the establishment of new firms and plants instead of merger/acquisition, which was formerly a common method of growth. In 1983, there was a considerable amount of merger activity, and since that time, seven new firms have been established (Figure 10.4). Most of the newly established firms have backward linkages to previously existing companies, reflecting a vertical integration within each division of Daewoo. The vertical integration is especially obvious in the electronics and automotive divisions.

A structural shift from heavy industries such as shipbuilding to technology-intensive industries such as electronics has been prominent since 1986. The export value of ships amounted to 41 per cent of the total annual exports in 1985, but the figure fell to only 5 per cent in 1987. On the other hand, the share of exports of the electric and electronics products in the total export volume of Daewoo increased from 6 per cent to 24 per cent in the same short period (Table 10.2).

In order to enhance national and international competitiveness, the establishment of R&D centres has been emphasized during the 1980s. Out of fifteen Daewoo R&D centres, four were established in 1982 and ten more have been established since then (Table 10.3). In recent years, Daewoo has reorganized its structure to a multi-divisional form in order to improve efficiency. Quite clearly, Daewoo has continuously promoted managerial innovations since its re-establishment as 'Daewoo Corporation'.

Furthermore, manufacturing activities have been expanded to foreign countries since 1986. Ten overseas subsidiaries were established before 1980, but they were all in the trading sector. Most of the overseas subsidiaries in the manufacturing sector of Daewoo were established in 1986 and 1988 (Table 10.4). A joint venture plant was also planned in France. Actually, Daewoo has advanced steadily into a global structure since the mid-1980s as it introduced managerial innovations and improvements in technology. Shifts from light industry to heavy industry and the chemical sector, and then to the high technology sector, have been the major structural changes since the foundation of Daewoo.

Since 1984, more than seven firms have been dissolved by Daewoo, most of which were in the light industrial sector, especially textiles and leather products. Because of this dissolution, some fluctuations in employment growth have occurred even though total sales and exports have continuously increased since 1985. Overall, diversification has been the major strategy of growth, but vertical integration within each division of Daewoo has been emphasized in recent years. This has produced a nested hierarchical structure in which diversification is sought after at the group level (higher order) and vertical integration is pursued at the division level (lower order). This nested hierarchy in the growth strategy suggests that Bannock's (1971) three-stage sequence in the evolution of large enterprises, in which horizontal integration is followed by vertical integration and vertical integration is followed by diversification, does not apply to the case of Daewoo.

Table 10.3 R&D Centres in Daewoo, 1988

Name of R&D	Year of establishment	Location	Researchers (% total employees)	% R&D expenditure to total sales
Daewoo Heavy Industries Central R&D Institute	1978	Capital region (Inchon)	663 (7.3)	3.7
Daewoo Electronics Ltd R&D Centre	1982	Capital region (Inchon)	1,450 (8.1)	4.5
Daewoo Telecom R&D Centre	1982	Capital region (Inchon)	647 (18.9)	5.1
KOSCO R&D Centre	1982	Capital region (Kyonggi)	73 (9.8)	7.8
Daewoo Shipbuilding & Heavy Machinery Technical Centre	1982	SE Region (Kyongnam)	97 (0.7)	0.2
Daewoo Construction Research Institute	1983	Capital region (Seoul)	57 (—)	0.2
Daewoo Engineering & Construction Institute	1983	Capital region (Seoul)	35 (4.5)	1.7
Daewoo Motor Technical Centre	1983	Capital region (Inchon)	1,196 (8.6)	3.6
Daewoo Precision Industries Technical Centre	1983	SE region (Kyongnam)	192 (5.5)	6.5
Daewoo Electronic Components R&D Centre	1984	Capital region (Kyonggi) (Kyonggi)	75 (5.3) (5.3)	6.1
R&D Laboratory of Orion Electric Ltd	1985	SE region (Kyongbuk)	84 (2.5)	1.2
Daewoo Automotive Components Technical Centre	1985	SE region (Kyongbuk)	150 (16.6)	—
Daewoo HMS Industries Technical Centre	1986	SE region (Kyongbuk)	30 (2.0)	—
Daewoo Carrier R&D Centre	1986	SE region (Kwangju)	0 (9.0)	—
Daewoo Electric Motor Industries R&D Centre	1987	Capital region (Seoul)	32 (—)	—

Source: Materials from Daewoo Planning and Co-ordination Division

Spatial organization and linkages

Locational dynamics of production units

Industries cannot exist without locations and, accordingly, corporate growth has spatial ramifications. Specific strategies of corporate growth may have particular spatial manifestations, and the choice of strategy may have an impact on the spatial growth of firms

Table 10.4 Overseas subsidiaries

Subsidiary	Location	Year of establishment	Activities
Daewoo UK Ltd	London	1971	Trading
Daewoo International (America) Corp.	New Jersey	1973	Trading
Daewoo Electronics Corp. of America	New Jersey	1973	Trading
Daewoo Canada Ltd	Toronto	1973	Trading
Daewoo Handels GmbH	Frankfurt	1973	Trading
Daewoo Hong Kong Ltd	Hong Kong	1974	Trading
Daewoo International (Panama) SA	Panama	1975	Trading
Daewoo France SARL	Paris	1976	Trading
Daewoo Malaysia SDN. BHD	Kuala Lumpur	1977	Trading
Daewoo Japan Ltd	Tokyo	1978	Trading
International Tyre Manufacturing & Distribution Co., Ltd	Port Sudan	1980	Tyre manufacturing and distribution
Daewoo Nigeria Ltd	Lagos	1980	Trading and construction
The Sudanese Korean Construction & Contracting Co., Ltd	Khartoum	1980	Construction
Universal Refining NV	Antwerp	1986	Oil refining
Cordata Technologies, Inc.	California	1986	PC manufacturing
ZyMOS Corporation	California	1986	Semiconductor design and manufacturing
A joint venture company	China	1988	Refrigerator manufacturing

Source: Materials from Daewoo Planning and Co-ordination Division

(Watts 1980). Even when growth is achieved externally, decisions on expansion implicitly involve a spatial search for merger/ acquisition candidates (Green and Cromley 1984).

Nineteen companies of Daewoo can be regarded as manufacturing firms, and these operate thirty-four plants. Seoul is the overall control centre of Daewoo and the spatial division of labour is considerable. All the company headquarters which have spatially dispersed plant(s) are located in Seoul, and companies with headquarters elsewhere have their administrative offices in Seoul.

The locational dynamics of the manufacturing plants of Daewoo over time are displayed in Figure 10.5. Until 1972, the operational space of Daewoo was limited to the city of Pusan, the second largest city and the biggest port in Korea. From 1973 to 1982, the operational space extended from Pusan to the south-eastern coastal industrial area and the Seoul-Inchon industrial area. Expansion of the operating space in these two areas is clearly related to the strategy to diversify beyond the light industrial sector. Hence, diversification to include shipbuilding spread Daewoo into the south-eastern coastal region, while diversification to include the automobile industry, spread it towards the two largest cities (Seoul and Pusan) in preference to market-oriented locations. Expansion of the operating space in the Seoul–Inchon area was also influenced by the diversification to include machinery manufacturing.

Even though the method of growth was mainly external, the locational decision-making was limited to two regions: one is the area surrounding the original centre of operation; the other is the area surrounding the centre of control. This locational pattern centred on Seoul and Pusan is apparently consistent with the bipolar concentration of industrial activities during the developmental phase of heavy industry and the chemical sector in Korea (Park and Wheeler 1983; Park 1988).

Since 1983, a diversification strategy to include technology-intensive sectors and internal growth has been emphasized. Accordingly, different locational patterns have evolved. The strategies and methods of growth implemented since the firm was restructured are manifested in space, and the operational space has been expanded to include peripheral areas. Even the R&D centres established in recent years are mostly located in areas far from Seoul and Pusan (Table 10.3). Within the broader operational space three clusters of industrial activity have been established: the Seoul–Inchon area; Kumi City, and Kwangju City. These three clusters are the outcomes of the diversification to include the electric and electronic sector. Merger/acquisition activities are mostly limited to two areas (Seoul–Inchon area and Kumi industrial zone) where electronics industries are concentrated, but new plant locations are mainly selected in the areas far from the group headquarters. Locational decisions on the areas far from the control centre were apparently affected by governmental industrial dispersal policy. The locational decisions regarding Kwangju City were also related to labour availability and the strategy of increasing the market share of Daewoo in domestic electronics. New locational decisions have been limited mainly to industrial zones, however, suggesting that availability of industrial land was regarded as an important factor in new location decisions. New plant location in the Seoul

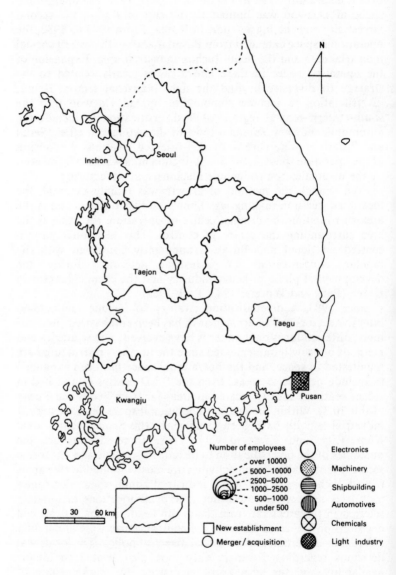

Figure 10.5a) Locational pattern and dynamics of manufacturing plants of Daewoo, 1967–72

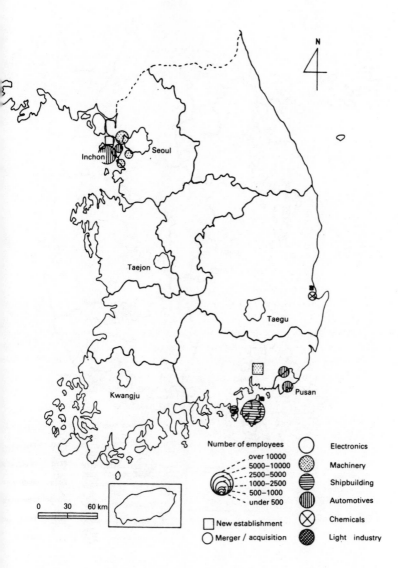

Figure 10.5b) Locational pattern and dynamics of manufacturing plants of Daewoo, 1972–83

223

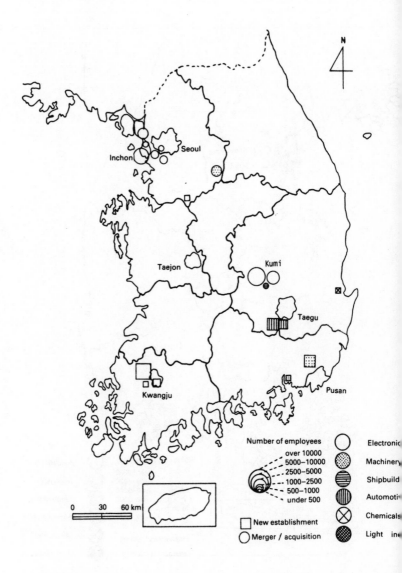

Figure 10.5c) Locational pattern and dynamics of manufacturing plants of Daewoo, 1983–8

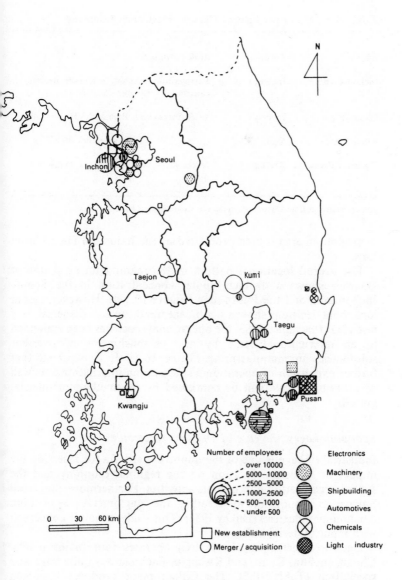

Figure 10.5d) Locational pattern and dynamics of manufacturing plants
of Daewoo, total 1967–88

Table 10.5 Major products of Daewoo Electronics Company

Plants	Location	Major products
Inchon Plant	Inchon City	Refrigerators, washing machines, heaters, electric fans, vacuum cleaners, etc.
Chuan Plant	Inchon City	VCR decks (both Beta and VHS), cylinders
Kumi Plant	Kumi City	Colour TVs, VCRs, monitors, PCs.
Kwangju Plant	Kwangju City	Microwave ovens, gas ranges, audio products

Source: Materials from Daewoo Planning and Co-ordination Division

metropolitan area is even prohibited by the Industrial Distribution Law.

The overall locational pattern of the manufacturing plants of Daewoo shows a distinct bipolar concentration in the Seoul–Inchon area and the Pusan area (Figure 10.5-d). However, recent locational decisions show a significant trend towards dispersal. It is also clear that, since 1983, the operational space has been expanded to an international scale by new establishments of overseas subsidiaries in manufacturing (Table 10.4). It is expected that further expansion of operational space on an international as well as a national scale will be continued by the method of internal growth.

Spatial linkages: the case of Daewoo Electronics Co.

Industrial linkage is one of the important criteria for assessing the impact of industrial location on the regional economy and the spatial organization of economic activities. Furthermore, industrial linkage is important in creating the agglomeration of high technology industries (Oakey 1984). This study is mainly concerned with input material linkages.

Daewoo Electronics Co. (DEC) operates four major plants: Chuan, Inchon, Kumi, and Kwangju. Each plant is quite large and specialized (Table 10.5). The Chuan plant produces high-tech products. All the products of this plant are supplied to the Kumi plant as productive inputs. Except for the linkage between the Chuan and Kumi plants, there is no material linkage among the plants of DEC.

In general, the technology-intensive industries are concentrated

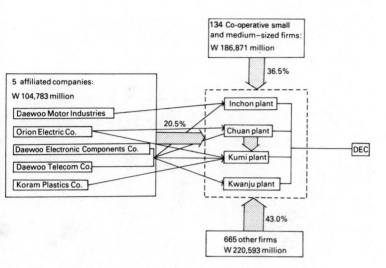

Figure 10.6 Backward linkages of DEC plants, 1988

in the capital region. More than 70 per cent of the plants in the electric and electronics sector are concentrated there, especially within 30 km of the city of Seoul (Park 1987). However, plants of DEC as well as other plants of the electric and electronics division of Daewoo, are relatively dispersed from the capital region. As the product life cycle concept suggests, the production per worker is higher in the plants of DEC located in the capital region than in plants located elsewhere (Hansen 1988; Suarez-Villa 1984).

Four plants of DEC purchased 20.5 per cent of their total input materials (parts and components) from five companies of Daewoo, 36.5 per cent from 134 co-operative small and medium-sized firms, and 43 per cent from 665 other firms (Figure 10.6). Even though the percentage of intra-organizational material linkages is lower than that of interorganizational linkages, the average amount of annual material linkage per company in the group is about $US30m. This is much higher than that of the co-operative small and medium-sized firms (about $US2m.) or the other non-group firms (about $US0.5m.).

The spatial linkages of DEC are mapped in Figure 10.7. This figure shows only the location of the plants which supplied a large amount of materials (more than $US1m.) in 1988. Two clusters of firms which have backward linkages to plants of DEC are located in the Seoul–Inchon area and Kumi City, where the large-scale

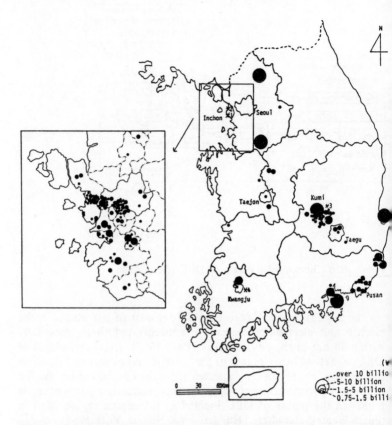

Figure 10.7 Major firms which supply parts and components to DEC, 1988

Kumi electronics industrial estate has been developed. Firms in these two areas supply more than 75 per cent of the total input materials. Plants in the south-eastern coastal region supply about 14 per cent and plants in the rest of the country supply less than 5 per cent. Even DEC's Kwangju plant has only limited local linkages in purchasing input materials and a high level of spatial linkages to the Seoul–Inchon area (Figure 10.8). The limited local linkages of the Kwangju plant reveal that branch plants in developing areas have only a limited impact on the local economy, as has been suggested in other studies (Watts 1981). The limited local linkages also indicate that localization economies have yet not been realized

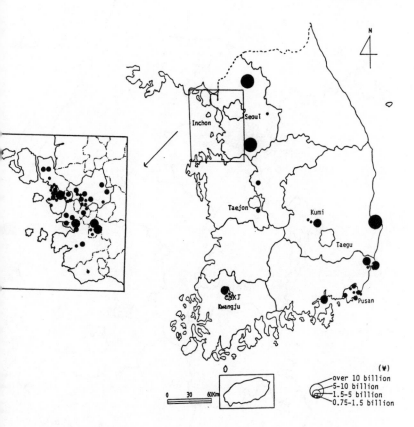

Figure 10.8 Major firms which supply parts and components to Kwangju
plant of DEC, 1988

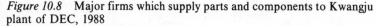

in the electronics industry in Kwangju.

The clusters of plants with backward linkages to DEC plants are
clearly seen in the location of small and medium-sized firms which
supply input materials. DEC selected co-operative small and
medium-sized firms which are capable of supplying qualified input
materials on time. The co-operative small and medium-sized firms
have priority in supplying parts and components to DEC plants.
More than 81 per cent of the co-operative firms are in the capital
region and about 12 per cent are in the Kumi industrial estate
(Figure 10.9). About 70 per cent of the co-operative firms are
concentrated in the Seoul–Inchon area.

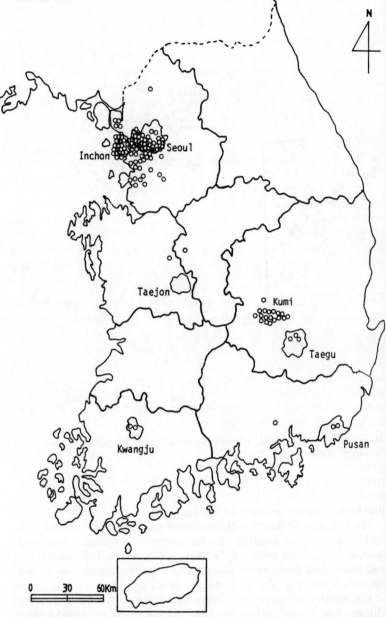

Figure 10.9 Co-operative small and medium-sized firms which supply input materials to DEC, 1988

The concentration of co-operative small and medium-sized firms may be related to vertical disintegration. Important parts and components for DEC plants, which require high technology, are mainly supplied by group companies according to the strategy of vertical integration within the electric and electronics division. However, DEC purchases ordinary parts and components from subcontractors when internal transaction costs are higher than the cost of subcontracting. In general, subcontracting is preferred when the optimum scale is very small. Furthermore, subcontracting can be an effective means of holding down wage and fringe benefits (Scott 1983).

Vertical disintegration in the electronics industry provides agglomeration economies in the Seoul–Inchon area. Because of the agglomeration economies in this area, even the Kwangju plant should have strong spatial linkages to the Seoul–Inchon area. Kumi City is specialized in the electronics industry and is now evolving as another agglomeration centre for that sector.

Conclusions

This study focused on the corporate growth of Daewoo and the spatial ramifications of its strategies and methods of growth. Horizontal integration was the major strategy in the initial development phase of Daewoo, but diversification at the group level has been the major growth strategy since it reached a certain threshold. Under the diversification strategy, Daewoo shifted its leading industrial sector from light industries to heavy industries, and then to high-tech industries. Since 1983, however, as part of the diversification trend at the group level, vertical integration at the division level has been established, representing a hierarchical structure in the strategies of growth. The dynamic trend in the strategies of growth of Daewoo suggests that there are a number of possible routes for corporate growth and the three-stage model of Bannock is not appropriate in the case of Daewoo.

Merger/acquisition was the major method of growth espoused by Daewoo, especially under the diversification strategy. However, internal growth by means of the establishment of new companies and plants is emphasized when vertical integration is pursued at the division level.

The operational space of Daewoo has been expanded over time. Under the external method of growth with diversification strategies, a distance decay effect existed in merger/acquisition activities from the control centre (Seoul) as well as from the original plant location (Pusan), representing spatial impacts of the method of external growth. This spatial behaviour in the merger/acquisition activities suggests that existing industrial agglomeration economies are important for external growth.

On the other hand, dispersal of production units to other areas, especially to peripheral areas, has been the major trend of the internal strategy. However, the dispersal of newly established manufacturing plants has not progressed to all regions, but only to selected industrial estates located in or near regional cities such as Kwangju and Taegu. The dispersal of production units is to a certain degree related to the governmental industrial dispersal policy for balanced regional development, to labour availability in the peripheral areas, and to labour dispersal in the core region. New locational decisions in the peripheral area can also be regarded as part of the leadership role of large enterprises. The impact of this dispersal on the regional economy is, however, relatively limited because of a lack of local backward linkages. The formation of external economies with vertical disintegration and strong local linkages in the peripheral areas is a necessary pre-condition for making the new locational decisions of enterprise a seedbed for regional development.

The case of Daewoo suggests that strategies and methods of growth have impacts on the spatial organization of an enterprise. Therefore a carefully wrought regional industrial policy should accompany the decision to disperse the production units of enterprises. Future growth of Daewoo towards a global structure will presumably represent diversification at the group level on a global scale on the one hand, and vertical integration at the division level on the other hand. The progress of the global structure of Daewoo will further promote a spatial division of labour at both a global and a national scale.

Acknowledgement

This study was supported by a non-directed Research Fund, MOE.

References

Averitt, R. T. (1968) *The Dual Economy*, New York: W. W. Norton.
Bannock, G. (1971) *The Juggernauts: the Age of the Big Corporation*, Harmondsworth: Penguin.
Chapman, K. and Walker, D. (1987) *Industrial Location*, Oxford: Basil Blackwell.
Daewoo Corporation (1983) *Daewoo*, Seoul.
Daewoo Planning Co-ordination Division (1984) *Growth History of Daewoo Divisions*, Seoul (in Korean).

Dicken, P. (1986) *Global Shift: Industrial Change in a Turbulent World*, London: Harper & Row.

Green, M. B. and Cromley, P. G. (1984) 'Merger and acquisition fields for large United States cities 1955–1970', *Regional Studies* 18: 291–301.

Hansen, N. (1988) 'Regional consequences of structural changes in the national and international division of labor', *International Regional Science Review* 11: 121–36.

Hayter, R. and Watts, H. D. (1983) 'The geography of enterprise: a reappraisal', *Progress in Human Geography* 7: 157–81.

Krumme, G. (1969) 'Towards a geography of enterprise', *Economic Geography* 45: 30–40.

Linge, G. J. R. (1984) 'Developing-Country multinationals', *Pacific Viewpoint* 25: 173–95.

Lloyd, P. E. and Dicken, P. (1977) *Location in Space*, New York: Harper & Row.

McNee, R. B. (1958) 'Functional geography of the firm, with an illustrative case study from the petroleum industry', *Economic Geography* 34: 321–37.

McNee, R. B. (1960) 'Towards a more humanistic economic geography: the geography of enterprise', *Tijdschrift voor Economische en Sociale Geografie* 5: 201–6.

Oakey, R. (1984) *High Technology Small Firms*, New York: St Martin's Press.

Park, S. O. (1986) 'Regional changes in the industrial system of a newly industrializing country: the case of Korea', in F. E. I. Hamilton (ed.) *Industrialization in Developing and Peripheral Regions*, London: Croom Helm, 311–34.

Park, S. O. (1987) 'Recent development and linkage of high technology industries in the Seoul Metropolitan Area', *Korean Journal of Regional Science* 3: 21–36.

Park, S. O. (1988) 'The role of government in managing industrial change in the Republic of Korea', paper presented at the IGU Commission on Industrial Change Meeting at Rutherglen, 20–26 August, Australia.

Park, S. O. and Wheeler, J. O. (1983) 'Industrial location policies and manufacturing employment change: the case of Republic of Korea', *Regional Development Dialogue* 4: 45–64.

Scott, A. J. (1983) 'Industrial organization and the logic of intra-metropolitan location: I Theoretical considerations', *Economic Geography* 53: 233–50.

Suarez-Villa, L. (1984) 'The manufacturing process cycle and the industrialization of the United States–Mexico Borderlands', *Annals of Regional Science* 18: 1–23.

Watts, H. D. (1980) *The Large Industrial Enterprise*, London: Croom Helm.

Watts, H. D. (1981) *The Branch Plant Economy: A Study of External Control*, London: Longman.

Chapter eleven

The geography of enterprise
Elements of a research agenda

Peter Dicken

Introduction

The term 'epilogue' implies an air of finality or a summary, either of the contributions to this book or, more broadly, of past research in the field. This brief chapter is neither of these. Rather, it is an attempt to look forward, albeit with some necessary references to the past. I want to pose two related questions. First, does the 'geography of enterprise' have a future? Second, if it does, what form might it take? It is very much a personal, Anglo-American, perspective from one who has been actively involved in this area of research for more than twenty years. It is not, however, personal in the manner of Robert McNee's (1986) paper but, then, I would not claim to have been a pioneer in this field as McNee undoubtedly is. The term 'geography of enterprise' was effectively introduced into the literature by McNee in 1960.

Although McNee (1960:205) stated quite explicitly that the concepts of a geography of enterprise should be applied 'to the study of firms both large and small' his own work, and that of most others who have followed in his path, has concentrated over-whelmingly on the very large corporate enterprise. For example, although Krumme (1969) incorporated the single plant firm into his classificatory chart of the processes of spatial behaviour of firms the impression was clearly that of a large firm focus. Most explicitly Hayter and Watts (1983:157) in their review paper, defined a geography of enterprise as 'the study of the influence of the policies and structures of multiproduct, multiplant enterprises on changes in industrial location and on processes of regional economic development'.

To all intents and purposes, therefore, the geography of enterprise has been a geography of the very large firm. It has also been, for the most part, an essentially empirical endeavour. In one sense this has been a source of strength. Too often, abstract theorizing bears little relationship to empirical reality. But in another, perhaps more important sense this lack of a strong theoretical basis poses a major problem for future work. McNee (1986:348), observed that 'theoretical incoherence and methodological disunity follow as the night the day from a continued pragmatic approach. Perhaps enough "facts" have been discovered. Perhaps it is time to step back, stressing theoretical coherence and consistency to a higher degree'. Although I do not agree that 'enough "facts" have been discovered', particularly given the volatility of the subject matter with which we are concerned, I do agree with McNee's general assertion and with that made by Michael Taylor (1980:151) some years earlier that 'the geography of enterprise requires a theory of enterprise'.

The first of the two questions posed at the beginning of this chapter, 'does the geography of enterprise have a future?' can be answered in the affirmative, therefore, only in so far as that future is founded upon a robust theoretical, as well as empirical base. Walker (1988) alludes to a 'requiem for corporate geography' but without revealing the full score. In fact, the chapters of this volume testify to the vitality of this body of research. We now have a much richer empirical knowledge of how firms behave and how their investment decisions modify geographical space whilst, at the same time, moving away from an isolationist focus on the 'location decision' *per se*. However, many of the points made by Walker in his stimulating, though essentially classificatory, paper are well taken and are clearly relevant for the future of a geography of enterprise if such a term really captures the essence of our research. It will do so only if we move away from a total preoccupation with the large corporate enterprise, emphasize research in enterprises of all types and sizes and, especially, the complex interrelationships between them. At the same time, we must situate firms within their overall structural context.

Before commenting on some of the specific issues which I personally feel we must address in future research, there is an important general point to be made. This relates to the need to draw together what are, too often, separate bodies of literature and approach. Within geographical research in this area two quite distinct strands have evolved, both of them, initially, as reactions to the restrictive assumptions of neo-classical economic/location theory. One strand, which effectively became the 'geography of enterprise' following McNee, took the form of attempts to incorporate a more realistic set of behavioural assumptions into the modelling of the locational decisions of firms (Pred 1967; Dicken 1971). An initial focus on locational behaviour at the microscale became transformed during the 1970s into a focus on the organizational structure of firms and their strategies. Examples of this genre were those of Rees (1974), Lloyd and Dicken (1977), Watts (1980). Some writers emphasized, in particular, the need to explore the environment within which firms operate. The early work of Steed (1971) in this vein was subsequently followed by the more formal development of a structural contingency approach by McDermott and Taylor (1982).

With the primary exception of McDermott and Taylor's espousal of structural contingency theory the conceptual basis of much of this research was rather tentative and fragmented. In contrast, the other strand which developed in reaction to the perceived inadequacy of neo-classical theory was more confidently based in the apparent certainties of Marxist theory. Although part of a more general Marxist movement within geography as a whole, the work most directly relevant to our present discussion was produced by such writers as Massey (1977, 1984), Storper and Walker (1983) and Walker and Storper (1981). Whereas the 'geography of enterprise' school concentrated on the individual firm and on particular aspects of managerial behaviour, the 'Marxist' school concentrated on the economic system as a whole and, especially, on the conflict between capital and labour. The tendency seemed to be to regard the firm as a responder to external changes in the capitalist system. This early rejection of the firm as a legitimate focus of attention has been modified subsequently, not least by such as Sayer (1985) and other writers in a 'realist' mode. Conversely, the conventional geographers of enterprise have become far more aware of the need to place their firms into their broader structural context. As Le Heron observes in his contribution to this book, there is a need for 'a blending of structural knowledge with the finer details of individual company experience'.

But, although there has been some convergence from both directions, the fact remains that the two strands of research continue to be relatively separate. Very often there is little overlap in the bodies of literature which are drawn upon or even in the journals to which papers are sent. There is a real need to encourage and facilitate cross-fertilization between different approaches. Of course, such a plea immediately raises the spectre of the dreaded eclecticism (Fincher 1983). Clearly, there are dangers in combining different approaches. Equally, however, there are dangers in adopting an overly dogmatic and ideologically pure approach. There are some good examples of less blinkered approaches in both traditions. Outside the examples provided in this book the work of Scott (1986) and Schoenberger (1986) are cases in point from a radical/

left perspective. Scott incorporates ideas from institutional economics, notably transactions costs analysis, based on the work of Coase (1937) and Williamson (1975). Schoenberger draws heavily upon the literature on competitive strategy in emphasizing the need to produce a more rounded explanation of spatial change. My plea, therefore, is for a much greater cross-fertilization between researchers in different traditions: for a geography of enterprise to be more firmly embedded within the broader structure of the production system as a whole and for students of the production system to pay more explicit attention to the enterprise. It is in this context that I agree strongly with Michael Taylor's assertion (1984:8) that 'the business enterprise is the basic unit of the economy, the point of production, the crucible within which both macro and micro-forces meet and are played out'.

The geography of enterprise: where to go?

The second question raised in the introduction to this chapter was: given that the geography of enterprise has a future, what form might that future take? In part, I have already answered this question. It must be a more broadly-based, more theoretically well-founded field of research. I cannot offer a fully worked-out theoretical framework; all I can do is to point to some specific areas with which I believe a 'geography of enterprise' (broadly defined as I have argued) should be concerned. The list is by no means exhaustive.

Conceptualizations

One very basic issue concerns the conceptualization of the firm or enterprise itself. It is one thing to assert that the 'business enterprise is the basic unit of the economy' or that it is a major means by which the division of labour is organized. But such statements beg the question of where the boundaries of the firm lie and how these boundaries change over time. A useful way into this problem which, at the same time, establishes the firm in its broader structural context, is to accept that the production and distribution of any commodity, product or service consists of a complex chain of interconnected activities of functions. Porter (1985) uses the term value chain; a roughly equivalent term in the European literature is the *filière*. The tendency in much of the geographical literature has been to focus on limited components of this chain (mostly production at the expense of marketing and distribution) and to devote little attention to the interconnections between functions other than in the mostly superficial 'linkage' studies.

We need to develop studies which investigate the different ways, both organizationally and spatially, in which the chain or *filière* may be structured and articulated. Organizationally, each element in the chain may be performed entirely within a single business firm (complete integration) or each may be performed by separate, specialist business firms (complete disintegration) or by a varying mixture of these two extremes. There is much debate at present about the extent to which the boundary between organizational integration and organizational disintegration is shifting. One approach to this question is to take the Coasian-inspired view that the determining factor is the relative cost of internalizing or externalizing transactions, that is, the regulatory mechanisms inside the firm or outside in the market. This is the approach adopted in some of the literature on transnational corporations by, for example, Buckley and Casson (1976) and by Rugman (1981) and also followed by Scott (1986) in the geographical literature. More recently, Cowling and Sugden (1987) have suggested that the Coasian-based argument is fundamentally misguided in that the critical issue is not so much whether transactions are internalized within the firm in terms of ownership relationships but rather that of who co-ordinates such transactions. Hence, they define a firm not in terms of equity holding but as 'the means of co-ordinating production from one centre of strategic decision-making' (Cowling and Sugden 1987:60). One benefit of adopting this perspective is that it permits a more satisfactory conceptualization of the relationship between firms and their suppliers and customers, including subcontracting relationships. In the latter case, the contracting or principal firm does not own the subcontractor but invariably has substantial control of part of its operations through the co-ordinating mechanism. It also helps to connect the firm into the broader set of power relationships within the production system, a particularly important component of the concept of a segmented economy (Taylor and Thrift 1983). Such an approach also helps us to situate firms of different sizes and types, both large multi-locational firms and small and medium-sized enterprises in their broader context. It helps, therefore, to break down the barrier between studies of large firms and of small firms which has tended to develop in the literature.

Spatial organization

We need, too, to adopt a more rigorous approach to the

multiplicity of ways in which the elements in the value chain or *filière* may be organized spatially. Some functions may need to be located in proximity to others in the value chain; others may be separated. Some elements may be geographically dispersed; others may be geographically concentrated. In aggregate terms, such spatial organization of individual business functions leads to the development of different spatial divisions of labour, to various forms of production hierarchy and geographical centres of control, to territorial production complexes, including those of small and medium-sized enterprises. Each of these developments has been the subject of substantial research in recent years. However, there has been a tendency to oversimplify and to create stereotypes of what are, in fact, highly complex and variegated spatio-organizational forms. We need to probe beyond the simplistic conceptualizations of the relationship between organizational hierarchies and spatial hierarchies and also beyond the over-generalized examples of small firm-based territorial production complexes to explore these organizational-spatial processes in a more rigorous and penetrating manner.

There has been an impressive development of research into subcontracting relationships and other forms of firm–supplier links by geographers in recent years (see, for example, Holmes 1986; Sayer 1986). But subcontracting is only a part of a much larger universe of collaborative arrangements between firms which cries out for investigation by geographers. So far in the geographical literature few have dealt explicitly with this question. Exceptions include Cooke (1988) and de Smidt's chapter in this volume. Yet it is such a significant phenomenon today that it must form part of any future research agenda. Collaborative ventures between firms within, and across national boundaries are not new in themselves. What is new is their current scale, their proliferation, their multilateral nature and the fact that they have become central to the strategic behaviour of many firms. More and more firms appear to be forming not just single alliances but networks of alliances; firms are increasingly polygamous rather than monogamous. 'Few firms have only a single alliance. Instead they form a series of alliances, each with partners that have their own web of collaborative arrangements. . . . Companies . . . are at the hub of what are often overlapping alliance networks which frequently include a number of fierce competitors' (*Business International* 1987:113–14).

Enterprise and strategy

A further priority for a future research agenda is to build links

between those researchers who focus upon the business enterprise
per se and those working in the 'labour process' tradition. This is
especially necessary in the current debate on the alleged transition
from Fordism to post- or neo-Fordism which is concerned with the
influence of both technological and organizational changes on the
labour process. So far, the two strands of research have proceeded
almost as if each did not exist, a situation which is clearly ludicrous.
However, some of the contributions in this volume indicate a shift
away from such isolationism, at least on the part of some geographers of enterprise. For example, Kelly and Keeble's analysis of
IBM in Europe refers to the Fordism-flexibility debate. More
fundamentally, the chapters by Alvstam and Ellegard, Fuchs and
Schamp and Barnes, Hayter, and Grass explicitly set their analyses
in a labour organization, labour process framework. As Fuchs and
Schamp rightly observe, there is strong justification for a 'geography of enterprise from the labour perspective'. Conversely, there
is also an argument for a geography of labour process from a more
rounded enterprise perspective than the one-dimensional approach
so often adopted which tends to reduce the variety of enterprise
strategies to a narrow stereotype of labour control. Again, what is
needed is much more cross-fertilization between different conceptual approaches.

The question of business strategy has been at the heart of most
work in the geography of enterprise tradition. Here, it might be
argued, there is a strong record of achievement and, to a degree,
this is true. Indeed, the theme of corporate strategy is woven
throughout all the chapters in this book, most clearly in the
chapters by de Smidt, Park, Takeuchi, and Wever. Most of the
work by geographers draws heavily, and reasonably so, on the
business and management literature for its conceptual foundation.
However, the flow of ideas has been uni-directional even though
there is no reason why geographers themselves should not make a
valuable contribution to the business and management fields. After
all, the geography of an enterprise is fundamental to its existing and
future operations. Every business enterprise is a creature of both its
geography and its history.

In the current literature on corporate and competitive strategies
at the international scale, a major issue is the necessity for firms to
resolve the tension between two apparently counterpoised forces.
One force is the pressure to integrate the firm's operations on a
global basis. The other, opposing force is the pressure to respond to
national or local differences; that is to tailor or customize activities
to fit such variations. Some writers have argued that it is possible to
categorize industries into two discrete types: global industries and

multi-domestic or nationally-responsive industries (Porter 1985; Doz 1986). Each has very different attributes. However, it is arguable as to whether entire industries can be so simply categorized. Even if they can it does not necessarily follow that all firms in a particular industry will follow the same strategy. For example, there are several possible variants on the global strategy theme. Some of the more recent work on international competitive strategy rejects this stark polarization between global and local strategic orientation, arguing for a more dynamic and sophisticated approach (see, for example, Bartlett and Ghoshal 1987; Hamel and Pralahad 1988). Geographers should be able to contribute to this debate, not least because as Johnston (1984:444) points out 'geography is about local variability in a general context'. Certainly we should be just as concerned with the influence of geographical variety (economic, political, social, and cultural) on corporate behaviour and strategy as with the influence of corporate behaviour and strategy on geographical space and geographical place.

Enterprise and politics

The political dimension is especially important (Dicken 1986) yet neither geographers of enterprise nor writers on such issues as the new international division of labour have taken it very seriously. We need to incorporate a clearer understanding of the state and, especially its relationships with business enterprises into our analyses. The 'state', of course, has many definitions and many functions. Here, I will confine my comments to just one aspect: the nation-state and its relationships with transnational corporations. Writing just twenty years ago, Charles Kindleberger (1969:207) asserted that 'the nation-state is just about through as an economic unit'. Like the reported death of Mark Twain, this has proved to be a considerable exaggeration. It is certainly true that an individual nation-state's degrees of economic freedom – its economic autonomy – is constrained both by the actions of global corporations and of other nation-states. But national governments, whether singly or collectively (in such bodies as the EEC), play a most important role in shaping the global industrial map and, indeed, in either encouraging or inhibiting the global integration or nationally-responsive strategies of business firms. National boundaries create significant differentials on the global economic surface. Political spaces are among the most important ways in which location-specific factors (of both supply and demand) are 'packaged'. Political boundaries create discontinuities of varying magnitude in the flows of economic activities. Governments can modify comparative advantage, both positively and negatively.

There is a particular need for careful empirical study of the relationships between business enterprises and nation-states. Each constitutes a critical component of the other's external environment. Each co-exists in a somewhat uneasy relationship with the other; a relationship which tends to fluctuate between conflict and co-operation. The business enterprise, and especially the global corporation, understandably seeks to maximize its freedom to place its value activities in the most advantageous locations for the corporation as a whole in its pursuit of profit. Equally understandably, an individual national government would prefer to have the entire value chain within its own boundaries or, at least, to capture the higher value-adding activities and those which have maximum spin-off effects. What determines the outcome of this interaction is the nature of the bargaining process and, especially, the relative bargaining power of the two sides. This seems to be a function of (a) the relative demand by each of the parties for resources controlled by the other (b) the constraints on each which affect the translation of potential bargaining power into control over outcomes; (c) the negotiating status of the participants. So far, there has been very little empirical work on the bargaining process between firms and nation-states or of work which tests the hypothesized 'obsolescing bargain' which has been identified in the natural resource-based industries (Kobrin 1987).

Epilogue

Readers will no doubt have their own additions to this short list of possible priorities in a research agenda for a geography of enterprise. I have no doubt that the geography of enterprise does have a future but it can only be one in which, although detailed empirical work must continue, the theoretical base is strengthened and developed. In my view this requires a far greater degree of interaction between the various strands of research from different traditions. But there is little point in developing a geography of enterprise which remains separate from wider considerations. We must demonstrate our ability and willingness to contribute to the broader field outside geography, particularly in business and management. In that regard, I would support Walker's assertion (1988:377) that 'one must treat geography as integral to the matter of organisation, rather than as an outcome of pre-existing organisational units that make location decisions'. The chapters in this book go some way in these directions but, without any doubt, there is still a long way to go. We are perhaps approaching the end of the beginning; we are certainly not at the beginning of the end.

References

Bartlett, C. A. and Ghoshal, S. (1987) 'Managing across borders: strategic requirements', *Sloan Management Review*, summer, 7–17.

Buckley, P. J. and Casson, M. (1976) *The Future of the Multinational Enterprise*, London: Macmillan.

Business International (1987) *Competitive Alliances: How to Succeed at Cross-Regional Collaboration*, New York: Business International.

Coase, R. (1937) 'The nature of the firm', *Economica* 4: 386–405.

Cooke, P. (1988) 'Flexible integration, scope economies, and strategic alliances: social and spatial mediations', *Environment and Planning D: Society and Space* 6: 281–300.

Cowling, K. and Sugden, R. (1987) 'Market exchange and the concept of a transnational corporation: analysing the nature of the firm', *British Review of Economic Issues* 9: 57–68.

Dicken, P. (1971) 'Some aspects of decision-making behaviour in business organisations', *Economic Geography* 47: 426–37.

Dicken, P. (1986) *Global Shift: Industrial Change in a Turbulent World* London: Paul Chapman Publishing.

Doz, Y. (1986) *Strategic Management in Multinational Corporations*, Oxford: Pergamon.

Fincher, R. (1983) 'The inconsistency of eclecticism', *Environment and Planning, A*, 15: 607–22.

Hamel, G. and Pralahad, C. K. (1988) Creating global strategic capability', in N. Hood and J. E. Vahlne (eds) *Strategies in Global Competition*, London: Croom Helm, Chapter 1.

Hayter, R. and Watts, H. D. (1983) 'The geography of enterprise: a reappraisal', *Progress in Human Geography* 7: 157–81.

Holmes, J. (1986) 'The organisation and locational structure of production subcontracting', in A. J. Scott and M. Storper (eds) *Production, Work and Territory: The Geographical Anatomy of Industrial Capitalism*, London: Allen & Unwin, Chapter 5.

Johnston, R. J. (1984) 'The world is our oyster', *Transactions of the Institute of British Geographers*, New Series 9: 443–59.

Kindleberger, C. P. (1969) *American Business Abroad*, New Haven: Yale University Press.

Kobrin, S. J. (1987) 'Testing the bargaining hypothesis in the manufacturing sector in developing countries', *International Organisation* 41: 609–38.

Krumme, G. (1969) 'Towards a geography of enterprise', *Economic Geography* 45: 30–40.

Lloyd, P. E. and Dicken, P. (1977) *Location in Space: A Theoretical Approach to Economic Geography*, London: Harper & Row, 2nd edition, Chapter 9.

McDermott, P. J. and Taylor, M. J. (1982) *Industrial Organisation and Location*, Cambridge: Cambridge University Press.

McNee, R. B. (1960) 'Towards a more humanistic economic geography: the geography of enterprise', *Tijdschrift voor Economische en Sociale Geografie* 51: 201–5.

McNee, R. B. (1986) 'One perspective on the enterprise perspective', in M. J. Taylor and N. J. Thrift (eds) *Multinationals and the Restructuring of the World Economy: The Geography of Multinationals*, Volume 2. London: Croom Helm, Chapter 12.

Massey, D. (1977) *Industrial Location Theory Reconsidered*, Milton Keynes: The Open University.

Massey, D. (1984) *Spatial Divisions of Labour*, London: Macmillan.

Porter, M. E. (1985) *Competitive Advantage: Creating and Sustaining Superior Performance*, New York: The Free Press.

Pred, A. R. (1967) 'Behaviour and Location', *Lund Studies in Geography*, *B27*, Lund.

Rees, J. (1974) 'Decision-making, the growth of the firm and the business environment', in F. E. I. Hamilton (ed.) *Spatial Perspectives on Industrial Organisation and Decision Making*, London: Wiley, 189–211.

Rugman, A. M. (1981) *Inside the Multinationals*, London: Croom Helm.

Sayer, A. (1985) 'Industry and space: a sympathetic critique of radical research', *Environment and Planning, D: Society and Space*, 3: 3–29.

Sayer, A. (1986) 'New developments in manufacturing: the just-in-time system', *Capital and Class*, 30: 43–72.

Schoenberger, E. (1986) 'Competition, competitive strategy and industrial change: the case of electronic components', *Economic Geography* 62: 321–33.

Scott, A. J. (1986) 'Industrial organisation and location: division of labour, the firm and spatial process', *Economic Geography* 62: 215–31.

Steed, G. P. F. (1971) 'Plant adaptation, firm environments and location analysis', *Professional Geographer*, 23: 324–8.

Storper, M. and Walker, R. (1983) 'The theory of labour and the theory of location', *International Journal Urban and Regional Research* 7: 1–41.

Taylor, M. J. (1980) 'Space and time in industrial linkage', *Area* 12: 150–2.

Taylor, M. J. (1984) 'Industrial geography and the business organisation', in M. J. Taylor (ed.) *The Geography of Australian Corporate Power*, Sydney: Croom Helm, Chapter 1.

Taylor, M. J. and Thrift, N. J. (1983) 'Business organisation, segmentation and location', *Regional Studies* 17: 445–65.

Walker, R. (1988) 'The geographical organisation of production systems', *Environment and Planning, D: Society and Space* 6: 377–408.

Walker, R. and Storper, M. (1981) 'Capital and industrial location', *Progress in Human Geography* 5: 473–509.

Watts, H. D. (1980) *The Large Industrial Enterprise: Some Spatial Perspectives*, London: Croom Helm.

Williamson, O. E. (1975) *Markets and Hierarchies*, New York: The Free Press.

Index